Joint Ventures

Joint Ventures

1st Edition

LINKLATERS & PAINES

with

Christopher Nightingale

Solicitor

LAW & TAX

© Linklaters & Paines and Hackwood Service Co and
Christopher Nightingale 1990
© Pearson Professional Limited 1995

ISBN 0 85121 318 9

First Edition 1990
Reprinted 1991
Reprinted 1992
Reprinted 1993
Reprinted 1996

Published by
Longman Law, Tax and Finance
Longman Group UK Ltd
21–27 Lamb's Conduit Street
London WC1N 3NJ

Associated offices
Australia, Hong Kong, Malaysia, Singapore, USA

A CIP catalogue record for this book is available from
the British Library

Printed and bound in Great Britain by
Antony Rowe Ltd, Chippenham, Wiltshire

Contents

Contents

Preface

The purpose of this book is to explain and illustrate in a practical manner, for the benefit of all those who deal with the subject, the variety of different legal arrangements within which business partners describe themselves as being in 'joint venture' under English law.

The term 'joint venture' originated in commercial rather than legal usage, and businessmen seem to find it easy to plan a project in terms of a joint venture, regardless of the legal basis of the relationship they wish to create, and often before that basis has been chosen.

Much has been written about joint ventures overseas, particularly in the United States where there is a much more standard approach to the concept. In the United Kingdom, however, lawyers and other professional advisers still have to play detective when instructed to act in connection with a joint venture and seek the legal material required from a multiplicity of sources dealing with broader areas of law. Part of the purpose of this book is, therefore, to try to draw together those principles of law which are particularly relevant to joint venture relationships in their various forms, but which are currently spread throughout the lawyer's library.

Handled well, joint ventures are demanding jobs for lawyers to deal with. Not only is an awareness of a broad range of legal issues relevant where a joint venture is under consideration, but the experienced adviser may be able to make a significant contribution to the success of the venture by influencing his client to choose the form of joint venture structure best suited to all the circumstances. It is a trite observation that joint ventures require for their success a continuing spirit of goodwill and co-operation among the participants throughout the life of the venture, and the human dimension of joint ventures is one which should not be ignored by professional advisers: will the individuals concerned be able to work together as a simple matter of personality and character? Do their respective organisations share a substantially similar corporate culture? What other interests do the organisations have which could create a conflict of interest with the joint venture? In what circumstances is it envisaged that the joint venture may come to an end? All these are matters which may influence the type of structure to which the joint venture is best suited.

Above all, it must be remembered that every joint venture is different and raises different issues. There is no 'joint venture formula' which can be applied in each case: the same investigation must go into every project. This book and the material in the appendices must be construed on that basis, and we would remind readers of that well-worn but important adage that precedents make good servants but bad masters.

Given the extensive range of the subject matter, which embraces all the various forms which economic or commercial co-operation between legally distinct bodies may assume, this book cannot claim to be a definitive study of all types of joint ventures. Instead, it discusses in a practical manner some examples of joint ventures and the related legal problems which may be encountered in relation to them, and considers the circumstances in which one kind of structure will be more appropriate than another. It also sets out some preliminary warnings concerning broader areas beyond the scope of this book and concludes with a checklist and a number of specimen documents, which it is hoped will be of practical assistance to those dealing with the subject.

In view of the practical bias of this book, we have tried consciously to ration ourselves in the detailed examination of cases to those areas where conflict between or uncertainty in the cases is, in our judgment, capable of affecting adversely the clarity of effect which every draftsman seeks. Readers will be aware that any joint venture may give rise to complex questions of employment, competition, patents, pensions, tax and other areas of law where it would be prudent to seek specialist advice. Some of the more common considerations in these areas are, however, dealt with in the text of this book, which therefore provides a useful starting point for those involved in setting up and establishing a new joint venture.

The overall emphasis of the book is on the practical approach. It is hoped that it will be useful not just to the lawyer but also to businessmen generally, and to financial and other business advisers. It is appreciated that, in addition to purely legal matters, these latter may wish to consider the broad commercial issues raised in the context of joint ventures in greater detail than is dealt with in these pages.

How to use this book

The format of this book has been designed so that it can be used in one of two ways. First, as a practical textbook and secondly, as a transaction-related manual.

For those who wish to use the book in the first manner, the text has been set out so that the chapters follow each other in what we hope is a logical manner through the practice and law of the subject. Used in this way the appendices form illustrative examples. For those who wish to use this book for the second purpose (as a manual for a particular transaction) the starting point will be the checklist in Appendix 1. Against the checklist are marked, where relevant, text sections and clause numbers. We hope this will help brief the transaction-related reader upon the relevance of any particular question, and direct him to potentially useful clauses.

We have described the agreements and other documents in the appendices as specimen documents, rather than precedents, since they do not contain the range of alternatives, plus drafting notes, which one would expect of lawyers' precedents suitable for pulling off the shelf and marking up. We hope, nevertheless, that lawyers will find the specimen documents useful, both as a framework and as containing particular useful clauses.

We also hope that any reader, whatever his purpose, will find what follows to be a clear and comprehensive introduction to the subject.

Acknowledgements

This book is, in its own way, a joint venture. Christopher Nightingale conceived the book, settled its basic format and did much of the early work on the text before he left England to pursue his career in Hong Kong.

Thereafter, the text was progressed by a team within Linklaters & Paines led by Adrian Montague and including Bill Allan, Tom Wethered, Raymond Jeffers, Stephen Cromie, Robin Whaite, Marshall Levine, Virginia Reed, Susan Hayes, Richard Kempner, Philip Heyes, Su-Mei Chew, Bill Todman and Richard Wheen. In the final stages, when clients' demands on Adrian Montague became too great, Richard Wheen took over the editorial responsibility for the book.

Finally, we must record our appreciation for the advice and encouragement we have received from our publishers, Longmans, notwithstanding that we have sorely tried their patience and understanding in our attempts to maintain an equitable balance between the pressures of their publishing schedule and the demands of our own clients.

Linklaters & Paines
CGE Nightingale
31 May 1990

Table of Cases

Table of Statutes

Abbreviations

In this book the following abbreviations are sometimes used:

CA 1985	Companies Act 1985
CA 1989	Companies Act 1989
FSA	Financial Services Act 1986
IA	Insolvency Act 1986
ICTA	Income and Corporation Taxes Act 1988
FTA	Fair Trading Act 1973
RTPA	Restrictive Trade Practices Act 1976
PA	Partnership Act 1980
SOGASA	Supply of Goods and Services Act 1982
UCTA	Unfair Contract Terms Act 1977

Chapter 1

General considerations

1.1 What is a joint venture?

When an English lawyer is instructed to form a joint venture there is no particular legal structure that springs to mind, as there would be if he were instructed, for example, to set up a company or partnership. His client may have a particular form of relationship in mind or may not realise that there is a choice to be made. One of the adviser's first tasks is therefore to establish the legal basis on which the parties intend to proceed, and to ensure that, in the process, the consequences of entering into one form of relationship or another are fully understood.

A 'joint venture' is not a term of art in English law, and the cases do not provide any satisfactory definition of what is meant by a joint venture. Although judges have frequently used the term 'joint venture', this has usually been in a broad commercial sense in a wide variety of contexts, in most cases simply to denote intentional co-operation, or as a loose term for partnerships (see for example *Dodd and Tanfield v Haddock (HM Inspector of Taxes)* (1963) 42 TC 229). The term has even been extended to decisions in criminal and family law cases—but the sentiment of Ashworth J was not unusual when he admitted in *Inglefield v Macey* (1967) 2 KIR 146:

> I use the phrase 'joint venture' not in the sense of suggesting that in this case there was anything in the way of a legal partnership between the plaintiff and the defendant, but merely to describe what perhaps some ordinary person might think of the relationship between the two.

In practice the search for a legal definition of the term serves little purpose, save to illustrate that generally the English courts have not yet found it necessary to create a new type of relationship for joint ventures, and to reassure the lawyer that, in general terms, he is still dealing with the familiar concepts of contract, partnership and company law.

The general difficulty of searching for an exhaustive definition was

1

confirmed recently by the Organisation for Economic Co-operation and Development (OECD) who in their publication *Competition Policy and Joint Ventures* (1987) said:

> The specialist literature gives many definitions . . . although none provides a truly definitive answer. They are based on one or other of the following criteria: comparison with mergers, common objective, decision-making procedures, legal, economic and financial structures. Each of these definitions is in fact open to criticism, because none covers all the characteristics of joint ventures, in particular all the different actors, objectives, types of organisation and contractual relationships.

The EEC acknowledges joint ventures for the purposes of Article 85 of the Treaty of Rome, and defines them as 'enterprises subject to joint control, by which two or more undertakings which are economically independent of each other can engage in a variety of activities, ranging from joint research and development projects, to joint buying, production and distribution' (Comp Rep EC 1983). Although this definition will undoubtedly be applied in the context of Article 85 of the Treaty of Rome (see 12.3), it remains to be seen whether it will be adopted by the English courts in the context of current English law practice.

Foreign courts are more familiar with the term. The US courts have defined a joint venture as an association of two or more natural or legal persons combining property and expertise to carry out a single business enterprise and having a joint proprietary interest, a joint right to control, and a sharing of profits and losses (*Mallis v Bankers Trust Co* (1983) 717 F2d 683).

English practice is less strict than that in the United States since it is common usage in England to describe as a 'joint venture' not merely associations between two or more natural or legal persons, but also ventures where a legally distinct entity is created (the joint venture company), and cases where the parties simply co-operate in pursuing a common business objective without forming any entity or association for the purposes of their collaboration (collaboration agreements).

It is not unreasonable to conclude that the search for an adequate definition of joint venture under English law and practice would be arduous, if not fruitless. In lieu of a satisfactory definition, a lawyer must perforce be content with description. If the structure cannot be defined, is it at least possible to identify its distinguishing characteristics? At first glance, at least, this appears to be a more promising approach to pursue, since experience suggests that joint ventures do tend to share certain common characteristics, for instance:

(a) Pursuit of a common commercial purpose: the common perception, reflected in the extract from the OECD publication cited above, is that joint ventures involve a common objective among all the participants. To a limited extent this view is correct insofar as all participants enter into a joint venture intending to make a commercial success of the enterprise which is to be conducted through the joint venture, and it is the commercial basis of the relationship which distinguishes it from, say, a club. On the other hand, it is important to differentiate between a common purpose and a mutual purpose. Mutuality of purpose (in the sense that the objectives of each participant are shared reciprocally by the others) is rarely achieved in joint ventures. This may be because, within the structure of the joint venture itself, one party is given a role which sets it apart from the others, as happens, for example, in the case of oil and gas joint ventures where one participant would typically be designated as the operator and, in that capacity, would be given power to conduct the joint operations on behalf and at the cost of all participants. More often, it may simply be because the joint venturers have in mind different benefits which they hope will accrue by virtue of their participation in the joint venture. For example, an industrial project in the Third World may be conducted through a joint venture company which includes among its participants not only the government of the state in which the project is to be built, but also the plant's technology supplier who will also provide technical assistance and management services during the operational phase, the contractors whose interest is to secure the contract to construct the project and, perhaps, the purchasers of its production who will be linked to the project for many years after the start of commercial production by means of their offtake contracts. In such cases it is not the mutuality of interest which is important but the fact that each party is making a different but necessary contribution to the whole. It is important in devising the joint venture arrangements to be aware of the different interests and objectives of the participants in order that any strain to the commercial relationships of the parties resulting from their individual rewards, or the different timescales over which each reward is likely to accrue, can be anticipated and accommodated in the structure eventually developed.

(b) Bargaining power: the position of a minority shareholder in an English company is hapless. Subject to the protection which the law offers in relation to various types of abuse of power by a majority shareholder (see Chapter 4), a minority shareholder is very much at the mercy of the majority and has no influence over decisions affecting, even profoundly affecting, the affairs of the company, if the decisions are taken in due form and in accordance with the company's articles of association. The essence of all arrangements involving joint ventures, whether incorporated or not, is a system of checks and balances designed to give to the minority an influence over the venture's affairs in excess of that which the law affords. Such enhanced protection of a minority participant can only be achieved if the participant concerned is of broadly similar bargaining power as the majority participants. The source of such bargaining power, notwithstanding the position of the participant as a holder of a minority interest, is likely to lie in the contribution which the minority participant is to make to the common goal. A compelling example of this lies in management buy-outs (which are discussed in Chapter 8). Transactions of this sort are not conventionally classed as joint ventures but, in fact, they employ many of the same techniques in devising the checks and balances to control the respective interests of management, the providers of equity capital and lenders. In many such cases, the management provides only a negligible contribution to the capital required for the buy-out, and yet the management buy-out arrangements may well give management a very substantial degree of at least day-to-day control over the company's affairs, a just reflection of the importance of management contribution to the venture.

(c) Sharing of risks and rewards: a further element which joint ventures tend to have in common is the sharing of risk and reward by the co-venturers. This does not necessarily result in a sharing of profit and loss, because the risk or reward which a venturer undertakes or receives may not necessarily be measured in terms of conventional profit or loss, and some joint ventures are organised as conduits rather than to be profitable on their own. This factor is, however, one which tends to distinguish the equity interests of joint venturers themselves from those of financiers.

Disappointingly, it is difficult to go much beyond this in identifying the common features of a joint venture. Certain of the factors conventionally identified as characteristic of joint ventures are revealed, on closer examination, to be disappointing or unreliable indicators. For example, three of the factors relied upon in the US definition of a joint venture are not by any means universally applicable in English practice:

(1) A single business enterprise: although there are many joint ventures established for the purposes of a single contract or project, probably the majority have as their intention the formation of a new

jointly owned enterprise intended to achieve consistent and continuing growth over an indeterminate future term.

(2) Joint right to control: in many joint venture companies, while a minority shareholder may be given a right to board representation and, perhaps, the right to veto certain specified transactions on the company's part, it is stretching matters thereby to attribute to him a right to control. At best his control will be the negative control of the holder of a veto power, but he will not have the right to influence the overall conduct of the company's affairs to the extent which the expression 'joint right to control' connotes.

(3) Sharing of profits and losses: many unincorporated associations which do not constitute partnerships at law (especially those commonly encountered in the construction industry) do not involve any mutual striking of profit and loss, and although the participants simply share gross receipts according to a pre-determined formula, they are nonetheless regarded as joint ventures in English practice.

Probably the truth of the matter is that, just as the term is incapable of definition, so too the joint venture defies consistent and comprehensive description, beyond noting that joint ventures tend to involve parties of more or less equivalent bargaining power and pre-suppose the pursuit of a common goal. To the pragmatic legal mind, the apparent imprecision of the concept may not be a matter of great concern. Although intellectually unsatisfying, it is sufficient for the lawyer to conclude that a joint venture is simply any transaction which requires the deployment of the range of what might be called 'legal engineering' techniques described in this book and which have as their objective the implementation of a system of checks and balances to control the rights and liabilities of each participant inter se and the conduct of their common business undertaking in its relations with third parties.

Looked at from this perspective, joint ventures will be seen as a truly generic term. Rather like a species of animal, the term cannot be adequately defined and description tends to mislead for want of truly uniform characteristics shared by the entire species, but experts are united in agreeing that they can recognise an example of the species when they see one.

1.2 When are joint venture techniques appropriate?

Abandoning preconceptions as to what is and is not a joint venture is a necessary condition to being able to identify at all clear-sightedly those situations where joint venture techniques may be relevant. Of course,

5

there are transactions which typify joint ventures (such as the examples from the oil and gas and construction industries which are referred to in Chapter 3), but these are indeed no more than examples of the species.

Just as a joint venture can as well be accommodated in a joint venture company as in an unincorporated association, so too it is wrong to suppose that joint ventures require the formation of a new corporate entity or association at all. The same 'legal engineering' techniques may apply equally to other types of transaction involving existing companies, even though the transactions may not conventionally be described as joint ventures. We have already referred to management buy-outs where a corporate disposal can involve joint venture techniques. The same techniques can also be applied in the case of acquisitions (of a type common in the financial services sector in recent years) where the purchaser leaves a minority interest in the issued share capital of the company in question in the hands of employee vendors subject to put-and-call options on terms related to the company's financial performance in future years and safeguards to protect the minority's interest in the company's performance until the options are exercised. Similarly, even mergers may call into use joint venture legal engineering on certain occasions.

Whatever the type of transaction calling for the use of joint venture techniques, there is no doubting their popularity. A study of joint ventures and their use has been carried out by the OECD and the results made available in their publication *Competition Policy and Joint Ventures* (1987). They took as their terms of reference:

> . . . the effects on market structure and competition, and the treatment under competition law, of joint ventures in which the operations of two or more firms are partially, but not fully, functionally integrated in order to carry out activities in one or more of the following areas:
>   (i) buying and selling operations;
>   (ii) natural resource exploration, development and/or production operations;
> (iii) research and development operations;
>   (iv) engineering and construction operations.

Generally, the report noted that joint ventures appeared to be an increasingly popular form of enterprise organisation. In Germany, joint ventures falling within merger control accounted for 25 per cent of total merger and acquisition activity during the period 1973 to 1982, whilst in Japan such ventures doubled between 1970 and 1982.

In other countries, however, including the United Kingdom, joint ventures appeared to be less significant than mergers. Research also indicated that international joint ventures represented a significant proportion of international operations, particularly amongst the largest enterprises.

The report was able to break joint ventures down into particular economic sectors of activities, of which it seems the following are most common:

(a) Research and development joint ventures

(b) Natural resource exploration and exploitation joint ventures

(c) Engineering and construction joint ventures

(d) Production/Manufacturing joint ventures

(e) Buying and selling joint ventures

(f) Services joint ventures.

1.3 Types of joint venture

The characteristics of joint ventures and the circumstances when use of joint venture techniques may be relevant have been considered above. It is now appropriate to turn to the question of the legal form which joint ventures may take, and to make use of the opportunity to define the terms which will be used in this book to describe different types of joint venture. In English law, joint ventures typically take one of three forms:

(1) a company whose share capital is held by the joint venturers (in this book referred to as an 'incorporated joint venture' or 'joint venture company');

(2) an unincorporated association which has the legal status of a partnership (a 'joint venture partnership'); and

(3) an unincorporated association which does not fall to be treated as a partnership (an 'unincorporated association').

1.4 Joint ventures distinguished from other relationships

Before proceeding to consider in detail the methods of structuring the different forms of joint venture, it will be helpful to distinguish joint ventures from other, often confusingly similar, relationships.

Collaboration agreement

Parties may wish to collaborate in pursuing a common business objective under a simple contractual arrangement without giving rise to any of the forms of joint venture referred to in 1.3 above. These arrangements are frequently encountered in relation to scientific research and development projects and carried out on the basis of collaboration agreements. The key distinction between the formation of a joint venture and a mere collaboration arrangement lies in the presence in the former, and the absence from the latter, of any common business undertaking: in collaboration agreements, although parties may pool the results of a research programme, they would not typically create any common enterprise to pursue a joint business objective, and this may also prevent them from being construed as partnerships within the Partnership Act 1890. Nonetheless, a collaboration agreement may lead to the establishment of a joint venture and could, perhaps unintentionally, result in the formation of a partnership, and such agreements are an important vehicle for research and development projects. Chapter 5 accordingly covers them in greater detail.

Contract for services

An objective analysis of a proposed joint venture, especially where only two parties are involved, may lead to the conclusion that, notwithstanding casual use of the label 'joint venture', the relationship is merely a contract for services.

A contract for services should set out the obligations and rights of the parties in clear terms and not provide for the sharing or pooling of those obligations or duties, thus avoiding the necessity of addressing complex issues of management, sharing of risk, ownership of property and division of profit and capital.

If these obligations and rights can be clearly identified and separated at the outset and the commercial objectives of the parties are clear and separate, then the complex (and often more expensive) joint venture relationship may well be found to serve little purpose.

Section 12(1) of the Supply of Goods and Services Act 1982 defines a contract for supply of services (not overhelpfully) as a contract under which a person ('the supplier') agrees to carry out a service. There is excluded from this definition contracts 'of service or apprenticeship' ie contracts of employment.

Good examples of contracts for services are distributorship or marketing agreements, where one party will be providing the services of manufacturer (as principal) and another of distributor of goods or services. In such cases, however, the requirement for regular mutual accounting and reporting, intellectual property licences and marketing policies on a long-term basis may so complicate the basic nature of the contract that the form is no longer clear.

When moving into a new sphere of operations, a business with confidence in its own products or services and in its market may prefer to seek a distributor or agent to market its goods or services on the basis of payment on commission, and guidelines and restrictions laid down by itself, rather than by inviting the distributor to participate in a joint venture relationship with a share of management and rewards. In distribution contracts the onus to perform and the market risk can be placed on the distributor without the principal necessarily sharing the responsibility of failure. Know-how, intellectual property and most other assets usually remain with the principal, who is therefore able to switch distributors if circumstances dictate, without the problems of having to consider whether dropping that distributor will bar him from the market or jeopardise the commercial objective altogether. In this type of relationship the principal is in a dominant position, which would not be the case in a joint venture.

If, however, the distributor's know-how, local knowledge or personality are vital to the penetration of the market, or to the establishment of the business, the principal may find it to his advantage to bind the distributor to him in a joint venture.

If there is a distribution network over a small area the complexities of joint venture techniques mean that simple contractual arrangements or franchises will normally be better. In such a case the contract clearly remains a contract for services.

What is important is that SOGASA provides that a contract remains a contract for the supply of services notwithstanding that it also deals with the transfer of goods (s 12(3)). It follows that the definition in s 12(1) above is not restricted to cases where the contract only deals with the supply of services, and that any contractual joint venture may be subject to the terms implied by the Act.

The ability to direct the distributor may be of overriding importance to the principal, especially where the principal feels that he is unsure of the distributor or is particularly sensitive to the method by which the commercial objective is achieved, but direction has its price, too, and may tend to diminish the distributor's ability to function as an independent contractor or the extent of its liability in the case of non-performance.

In most relationships created by contracts for services the obligations of each party are easy to define and separate, and although no doubt important, the particular identity of the contractor is not vital to the principal's ability to achieve his aim.

Where the particular identity of the contractor is vital, or the risk is to be shared, or agency is not economically feasible (eg where goods are too bulky or expensive to transport), or legally feasible (eg when a foreign partner is required by law), then the proper relationship may be that of joint venture.

A joint venture will often itself require to be provided with services, such as a distribution network or management services. Such contracts are discussed further in Chapter 10.

Syndicate

Syndicate agreements set out terms for the group ownership of an asset, sometimes with power of management of that asset delegated to one of the syndicate members or a manager, sometimes by trust but more often not. As these normally arise in relation to an investment asset, eg land, they are generally neither partnerships nor joint ventures, and should not attempt to go much further than to define each member's interests in the syndicate asset nor subsist after disposal of that asset.

Licence or franchise

Licensing and franchising are both methods used by businessmen to achieve some of the commercial objectives in respect of which joint venture techniques may also be appropriate. Although licensing, and to a greater extent franchising, both involve a continuous liaison between the parties, the licensor or franchisor has less opportunity to interfere with the running of the business and to benefit from business developments created by the licensee or franchisee.

For the licensor the arrangement offers a guaranteed return with little or no investment risk or start-up cost, which will be particularly important where the start-up cost and risk for the licensor is disproportionate to the benefit, where he is uncertain as to the market, or where he does not really wish to get involved in the day-to-day problems of the licensee's business or in the direct aspects of production or marketing. The licensor may also be able by this method to test a market without risk prior to setting up a joint venture or subsidiary.

For the franchisor, in addition to those factors relevant to a licensor, there may be other positive advantages in avoiding a joint venture. The franchisee will be benefiting from a whole business system and may be prepared to pay for it, and a franchisor will also be able to incorporate a franchisee in his overall business strategy to a greater extent than would be the case in a joint venture arrangement.

The cost of limiting the risk to the licensor or franchisor is the limitation of reward and control. Licence or franchise fees or royalities are usually fixed percentages or amounts and may give rise to VAT or tax complications. Furthermore, the reputation of the licensor or franchisor is in the hands of the licensee or franchisee, and the appointment of the licensee or franchisee may prevent the licensor from developing his own operation in the licensee's territory, where the success of the licensee may have indicated that a full joint venture or subsidiary would have been merited.

Club

Although the formation of a club will normally involve the association of persons with a common objective, that objective is not usually carried out on a commercial basis, and so clubs cannot be thought of as joint ventures in the commercial sense. Furthermore the particular nature or identity of a club member is not vital to the continued existence of the club, as is normally the case in a joint venture. Also, a club normally has an interest in obtaining as many members as possible, and making entry and exit from the club easy, while a joint venture will restrict the number of members and present a number of obstacles to departure. The difference between a club and other types of organisation was probably best summed up by Lord Linley in *Wise v Perpetual Trustee Company Ltd* [1903] AC 149 as follows:

> [Members'] clubs are associations of a peculiar nature. They are societies the members of which are perpetually changing. They are not partnerships; they are not associations for gain; and the feature which distinguishes them from other societies is that no member as such becomes liable to pay to the funds of the society or to anyone else any money beyond the subscriptions required by the rules of the club to be paid so long as he remains a member. It is upon this fundamental condition, not usually expressed but understood by everyone, that clubs are formed.

Direct participation

Before a businessman decides to proceed by way of joint venture he will no doubt have considered the alternative of forming a subsidiary with the other 'joint venturers' as minority shareholders. In most cases he will have decided that this is not feasible or in his best interest, often on the basis that the participation of his fellow venturers in the management or conduct of the joint venture is vital.

The distinction between a subsidiary and a joint venture can often be very slim, particularly where minority shareholder protection is weak. The difference will normally turn on control of the board of directors, although it does not follow that control by one party of the day-to-day management of a joint venture company prevents that company from being in joint venture.

Other

Other examples of relationships, mainly in the field of property development, which are in some ways similar to joint ventures are set out in Chapter 7.

Chapter 2

Handling the negotiations

2.1 Introduction

Having decided that the relationship between the parties is one of joint venture, or that joint venture techniques are appropriate to achieve the objectives of the parties, it will fall to the parties and their advisers to consider the means by which their objectives should be achieved.

This early stage is likely to be the only point at which the parties' attention will be exclusively focused upon the form or vehicle of the joint venture and problems created by the parties' relationship, rather than the project or business to be undertaken.

This chapter addresses some of the issues which are raised at this stage, such as whether the parties should prepare heads of agreement or exchange a confidentiality agreement, and which vehicle they should select.

2.2 Secrecy agreements

While negotiating a joint venture one or more of the parties may wish the existence of the negotiations to be kept confidential until a proper announcement regarding the proposed joint venture can be made. Furthermore he may wish to ensure that any other party to the negotiations to whom he supplies information will keep that information confidential. This will be particularly true where it is necessary to provide high technology information or sensitive business information to another party. The provider of the information will be anxious to ensure both that the information does not come into the hands of competitors, and also that the person to whom the information is disclosed will not use it for his own purposes unrelated to the joint venture.

Although there are general common law duties of confidentiality between co-venturers, it would appear that the remedies in such cases are restricted to rescission and an account of secret profits (*Uphoff v*

International Energy Trading Ltd (1989) *The Times*, 4 February) and accordingly the party supplying such information should obtain from the proposed recipient a confidentiality undertaking. This will often be included in the heads of agreement (see below) and if so it will be important to ensure that that part of the heads of agreement is legally binding.

The specific undertakings which should be sought will include some or all of the following (many of which will be reciprocal):

(a) to keep confidential the fact of the negotiations for the joint venture until the parties are ready to announce it;

(b) not to pass on to a third party any information or documents supplied, other than to those who need to know (financial or legal advisers, etc);

(c) to restrict disclosure within the recipient's organisation to a limited class of persons, or to named individuals;

(d) possibly to require any individual receiving the documents or information to have undertaken first to keep them confidential;

(e) to prohibit anyone receiving the information from using it for any purpose other than in connection with the joint venture;

(f) if the negotiations break down to return the original documents and any copies made, and to destroy any secondary information based on them (memoranda, minutes of meetings, etc).

A specimen secrecy agreement is contained in Appendix 5.

A party handing over documents should keep a copy of each document supplied and a note of any confidential information given otherwise than in documentary form. It may be desirable also to keep a list of those to whom information is disclosed; and it is not unheard of for a fee to be charged for disclosure (although it is important that such fee should not be mistaken for a licence fee or royalty).

2.3 Heads of agreement

Once an agreement in principle has been reached on the main terms (if not before) the lawyers should be instructed and one of them should take responsibility for drafting the joint venture agreement. It will inevitably take some time for the lawyers to produce a draft in a form suitable to be seen by their clients, let alone by other parties, and meanwhile the parties may wish to record in writing the main terms which have been agreed. These will be recorded in a document which will often be called (and is referred to below as) heads of agreement but which can equally be called a memorandum of understanding, heads of terms or anything else. This is normally a short letter or memorandum which seeks to encapsulate, generally in layman's terms, the fundamental objectives and understandings of the parties. Such a document may form the basis of the instructions to the lawyer; alternatively he may be requested to draft it.

The two principal questions which need to be addressed when drafting heads of agreement involve the scope of the document (ie how far it should go in identifying and covering the main features of the joint venture) and the extent to which the document should constitute a binding commitment between the parties.

It has already been stated in 2.2 above that if the heads of agreement are to include confidentiality undertakings, these should be expressed to be legally binding. Certain other clauses in the document may fall into the same category, for instance any agreement on reimbursement of expenses if the negotiations break down. (It may be noted in passing that it is notoriously difficult to draft the sort of clause which provides for the 'guilty' party in such an event to reimburse the expenses of the 'innocent' party, because defining what constitutes 'guilt' is well nigh impossible.)

It may be suggested that the heads of agreement as a whole be legally binding. There is, however, a problem with this. In order for a document to constitute a binding contract it needs to set out in sufficient detail all the important terms of the deal. (This is because under English law an agreement will be void for uncertainty if major terms are left unagreed.)

Accordingly, in order to have binding heads of agreement it would be necessary for all the main elements of the arrangement to be incorporated in the heads of agreement (and not left to be worked out later). This would in practice result in the heads of agreement taking almost as long to settle as the definitive agreement, particularly since any provision needed by one party for his own protection (eg warranties or restrictive covenants) will need to be set out in full, otherwise he will find himself a party to a binding contract but without that protection. It is generally much more satisfactory for the heads of agreement to be short and, with the exceptions we have noted, not legally binding. The longer it is, the more protracted the discussions on the heads of agreement are likely to be and, in the end, this may delay rather than speed up the execution of the joint venture agreement.

Even though the heads of agreement may, for the most part, be non-binding they can still play an important role. For instance, it often happens that in drafting the heads of agreement it will be realised that there are one or more important aspects of the joint venture which have not yet been settled, and these can be negotiated and agreed before it is too late. Also, when negotiating the definitive agreement reference will often be made to the heads of agreement and it will be difficult for a party to seek to change the deal at that stage lest he be accused of going back on his word. Furthermore, heads of agreement can include an outline timetable for negotiations which, even if not binding, can concentrate the minds of the negotiators.

2.4 Conditions precedent and consents

Often the setting up of a joint venture will require the approval of some third party or some clearance will need to be obtained. This may be because the business to be conducted by the joint venture needs some official licence, or because some step in setting up the joint venture specifically requires approval from some governmental authority or other third party.

The necessary consents etc will, unless obtained beforehand, need to be referred to in the contractual documents as conditions precedent to the obligations of the parties. It should be made clear who is responsible for applying for the various consents. Usually each party will accept responsibility for satisfying the conditions most closely under his control.

The types of approval or clearance which may be necessary will of course depend on the circumstances, but the following are some common examples.

FTA and EEC Treaty

The need for clearances and notification under the Fair Trading Act 1973 and the EEC Treaty are discussed in Chapter 12.

Government licences, clearances, etc

If the joint venture is to carry on business in a regulated industry, such as banking, insurance, financial services, TV or radio, or wine and spirit retailing, a licence to carry on the business may well be required under the Banking Act 1987, the Insurance Companies Act 1981, the Financial Services Act 1986, the Wireless Telegraphy Act 1967, the Licensing Act 1964 or other governing legislation.

In addition, certain steps to be taken in forming the joint venture may necessitate or make desirable certain additional consents or clearances. Examples would be tax clearances under s 88 of the Capital Gains Tax Act 1979 (capital gains tax rollover), s 707 of the Income and Corporation Taxes Act 1988 (transactions in securities) and s 776 of ICTA (artificial transactions in land).

Consents from third parties

If the joint venture is to use property leased to others (including any of the joint venturers) it will usually be necessary to obtain consent from the landlord to an assignment or sub-lease to the joint venture.

Similarly if the joint venture is taking over an existing business including contracts, then it will normally be necessary to obtain the consent of the other parties to those contracts in order for the contracts to be novated to the joint venture.

Finally, if the joint venture is to acquire a business or assets from one of the joint venturers, then the latter will need to check its own contracts, including especially bank loan agreements or loan stock trust deeds, to ensure that the transaction does not fall foul of contractual restrictions eg on disposal of assets.

The Stock Exchange

A joint venturer which is a company listed on The Stock Exchange, or dealt in on the Unlisted Securities Market, will need to comply with any Stock Exchange requirements which may apply to the setting up of the joint venture. In particular circumstances these could require a public announcement or even a circular to shareholders and, where the joint venture is with a director or large shareholder or is of a particular size, it may be necessary to seek shareholders' approval to the joint venture. The requirements are set out in the so-called Stock Exchange Yellow Book (Admission of Securities to Listing) or the Green Book (The Stock Exchange Unlisted Securities Market).

Other

In particular circumstances other consents or clearances may be required. If the joint venture is to operate overseas, then local advice will need to be taken as to foreign consents required; if an existing business is to be acquired by the joint venture, then under the Transfer of Undertakings (Protection of Employment) Regulations 1981 (SI No 1794) the employees of the business will automatically become employees of the joint venture but the vendor may be required to consult with trade union representatives in advance of the transfer; also if a business is transferred to the joint venture then any government grants made to the business may be repayable unless the Department of Trade and Industry otherwise agrees.

2.5 Choice of vehicle

In the simplest terms the choice of legal form within which to operate a joint venture is between an incorporated structure or an unincorporated structure. In practice the choice is normally between the formation of a limited company, creating a partnership joint venture by agreement, or establishing an unincorporated association by means of a contract between the parties. By virtue of the wide ambit of the PA it is most difficult for a joint venture to be created by a single contract between the parties without it becoming a partnership, and parties who wish to avoid a partnership will need either to form a company to carry on the joint venture or to ensure that their relationship does not result in 'a business being carried on in common with a view of profit' (see Chapter 3).

The selection of the joint venture vehicle will depend upon a variety of different factors; not only the legal implications but also the commercial objectives of the parties, the tax aspects, market usage, and professional or political pressure.

Although the lawyer's job is primarily to present the legal advantages and disadvantages of one vehicle over another, he should also recognise that other factors are important to his client, so that the legal structure as far as possible reflects the practical relationship between the parties.

Where many parties are involved administrative grounds alone may dictate the use of a company, as may s 716 of CA 1985, which prohibits most partnerships of over 20 persons.

Although the reporting and publicity requirements for a company may be greater this will probably not deter venturers who want regular and proper records to be kept, unless they wish to avoid publication of their results. An unincorporated joint venture is not required to deliver accounts to the Registrar of Companies nor (by virtue of CA 1985, s 254 introduced by CA 1989) is an unlimited company which does not have a limited company as its parent or subsidiary. With the abolition of companies capital duty, this is the main advantage of an unlimited company compared with a limited company.

The structure of articles of association and the shareholders' agreement provides a ready-made and familiar framework within which the parties can manage the venture, define their interests and allow for the arrival or departure of parties without upsetting the business generally.

A company, unlike an individual or partnership, can give security by means of a floating charge. This will be an important commercial consideration if outside funding is to be sought.

The most potent reason, however, why most joint ventures are incorporated is that the joint venturers thereby can have limited liability and reduce the element of risk common to most joint ventures, especially technology ventures. The benefit of limited liability may be considerably reduced, however, to the extent that the venturers are required to guarantee the obligations of the joint venture to bankers or others with whom the venture is doing business.

The statutory obligations for disclosure and administration contained in the Companies Acts, and the associated costs, will in some cases militate in favour of the partnership venture, and in general terms many venturers may see their enterprise as a partnership. On the other hand, a contractual joint venture may be attractive where the parties wish to pool the benefit of services provided, but to avoid actually setting up a separate and independent business.

Before advising on the appropriate vehicle for any joint venture, the legal basis of the relationship between the venturers themselves and of the relationship they intend to have with third parties should be clearly defined and the alternatives examined. Such relationships may be difficult to establish but at the very least should concentrate the parties' minds upon the real nature of the enterprise they are undertaking.

In considering the appropriate vehicle for a joint venture it will also be necessary to take into account the provisions of the Companies Acts relating to 'subsidiaries' and 'subsidiary undertakings'.

Subsidiary

In the past a company was a subsidiary of another if (inter alia) that other held more than half of its *equity share capital* (ie share capital other than normal preference share capital) or (being a member) controlled the *composition* of its board of directors. Thus it was formerly possible to arrange matters so that, by constructing artificial share rights and/or weighted voting rights of directors, a company would or would not be a subsidiary, both for accounting and non-accounting purposes. In practice, such structures were often used so as to avoid consolidation in the parent's accounts of the results and assets of the 'subsidiary'. The 1989 Act changed this, so that now a company is a subsidiary of another if (inter alia) that other holds a majority of the *voting rights* or (being a member) has the right to appoint or remove directors holding a majority of the *voting rights* at board meetings. It should be noted that only a body corporate can be a subsidiary, not for instance a partnership.

In the context of a joint venture, the main relevance of the definition of 'subsidiary', now that it is no longer relevant for accounting purposes, is likely to be in relation to restrictions in the articles of association, trust deeds, loan agreements and other contracts of the shareholder or its parent company, eg in relation to provisions limiting the borrowings of 'the company and its subsidiaries'.

Subsidiary undertaking

This is a new definition introduced by CA 1989, and takes the place of the definition of subsidiary for accounts purposes. It is much more widely drawn than the former definition of a subsidiary, and in certain respects its scope is very uncertain. Any company which is a 'subsidiary' of another following the 1989 Act will also be a 'subsidiary undertaking' of the other, but so will partnerships and unincorporated associations, when the 'parent undertaking' holds or controls a majority of the voting rights or exercises board control (or the equivalent). The term will also cover any undertaking where a company:

(a) has the right to exercise a 'dominant influence'; or

(b) holds a 'participating interest' (ie an interest held on a long-term basis to secure a contribution to its activities by the exercise of control or influence arising from or related to that interest, a 20 per cent interest being rebuttably presumed to be a participating interest) and either the company *in fact* exercises a 'dominant influence' over the undertaking or both are 'managed on a unified basis'.

The scope of these two concepts will no doubt prove as troublesome as their lack of precision.

Arising from these changes is the question whether it is any longer possible, as it formerly was, to have a 50/50 joint venture vehicle as a subsidiary undertaking of neither participant. The answer is that it is possible, but more care is needed than in the past. Each of the participants will have a participating interest, so it will be necessary to ensure that neither of the participants *in fact* exercises a dominant influence or manages the joint venture on a unified basis with it. While matters may be arranged initially so that this is the case, things inevitably change over time so that eventually it may become clear that one participant is in fact exercising a dominant influence over the joint venture.

Features of different forms of joint venture vehicle

Some of the principal differences between the different types of joint venture are set out in the table on pp 20–1 (Features of Different Vehicles). Some of these aspects are dealt with in greater detail in the following chapters.

Documentation	Unincorporated association by contract
Objects	Not generally stated as may not be mutual.
Capital	Must be expressed as contract terms. Subscription limited to contractor's fixed obligation but liability unlimited. Details not available to public.
Management	Not implied; must be expressed— one, two or three tier committee normally established.
Liability of venturers to third parties	Unlimited.
Liability for unauthorised acts of co-venturers	Potential liability to third party. Common law agency and 'good faith' principles apply.
Security for lender	As partnership. Property not 'partnership property' so charges may fall unevenly on assets of venturers.
Termination	Performánce of contract, effluxion of time, termination of agreement, frustration or otherwise by operation of law.
Protection for minority venturer	Contractual rights. Duties of good faith implied at common law.
Transfer of interest	Assignment of benefit of contract. (Note: burden retained unless agreed).
Ownership of property used for joint venture	Remains property of participant contributing unless otherwise agreed.
Duties of good faith	Implied by common law where joint venture or 'quasi partnership' situation arises.
Disclosure	No formal requirements (but beware competition law).

Partnership	Incorporated company
Generally mutual and stated but flexible. Operates as a restriction of authority of partners.	Fixed in memorandum of association. In general, limits activities to those stated.
Obligation to contribute initial capital in the partnership contract, thereafter liability for loss unlimited. Details not available to public.	Authorised and issued capital required by CA 1985. Details available for public inspection.
Implied by PA, s 24 if not expressed. Generally by committee.	Board of directors established in accordance with CA 1985 and articles of association.
Unlimited (unless limited partnership).	Limited to share capital (unless third party able to 'pierce the corporate veil' by common law or statute).
Potential liability to third party. Defaulting venturer liable to others on agency and *uberrimae fidei* principles.	Directors liable to company, company potentially liable to third party. No liability for shareholders unless corporate veil pierced.
Over specified joint venture assets only. Normally fixed charges or hire-purchase arrangements. Floating charges not available. Beware PA, s 3.	Over assets of company not members. May be fixed or floating. However guarantees may be required from members.
Dissolution under PA, effluxion of time, termination of agreement or application to court.	Winding up or insolvency of company, or (exceptionally) striking off.
Contractual rights. Duties of good faith and other terms implied by PA or common law.	Rights in memorandum or articles or shareholders agreement: CA 1985, s 459; Insolvency Act 1986, s 122
Assignee of partnership share only has right to receive profits. Full assignment only. Agreement of other parties to new partner or other arrangement in contract.	Sale of shares.
Becomes 'partnership property' owned by parties in common unless otherwise agreed.	Belongs to joint venture company.
Implied by law. Certain duties implied by PA.	Owed by directors to company but not by shareholders to company. May be owed by shareholders inter se as a result of common law implication.
No formal requirement for disclosure. Public notices in *London Gazette* required on retirement of partner or dissolution of partnership (but beware competition law).	Registration of memorandum, articles, accounts, annual return and major charges with Companies Registry for public inspection.

Chapter 3

Unincorporated joint ventures

3.1 Introduction

The distinction between unincorporated associations that constitute partnerships and those that do not is central to the structuring of joint ventures which do not take corporate form. In 3.2 the rules contained in PA for determining whether a partnership exists are considered, and 3.3 illustrates the application of those rules by reference to the usual forms of joint venture in the oil and gas and construction industries. The legal nature of unincorporated associations is considered in 3.4, and 3.5 contrasts the position of a partnership and an unincorporated association in relation to liability to third parties, termination and dissolution, rights to property, and the rights and duties of partners and members inter se.

3.2 Partnership Act 1890: does a partnership exist?

Question of law and fact

The question of whether a partnership exists is a mixed question of law and fact: *Spicer (Keith) Ltd v Mansell* [1970] 1 All ER 462. The intentions of the parties are not conclusive in determining whether their relations amount in law to a partnership, and if the statutory conditions for the creation of a partnership are fulfilled, the parties will be treated as being in the relation of partners to each other, even though they may assert an entirely contrary intention. Particular difficulties may sometimes arise in this connection in circumstances where parties intend to conduct a venture through the medium of a corporate entity formed for the purpose, but commence the business in common before their vehicle company has become available.

This was the case in *CH Pearce and Sons Ltd v Stonechester Ltd* (1983) *The Times*, 17 November, where the parties were working together in joint venture prior to incorporating a limited company and were held to have created a partnership, notwithstanding the absence of any formal documentation or understanding and an assertion by one of the parties that the relationship was merely contractual. In *Keith Spicer Ltd v Mansell* (above) the facts of a similar situation supported a different conclusion.

Just as the parties' intentions cannot prevent a partnership arising if the necessary conditions are fulfilled, so too the parties cannot override the application of the rules contained in PA by a declaration that they are not partners. In *Pawsey v Armstrong* (1881) 18 Ch D 698, Kay J observed that:

> there are certain legal relations which are entered into by agreeing to certain conditions, and when those conditions are agreed to, it is quite idle for people to superadd, or attempt to superadd, a stipulation that the necessary legal consequences of these conditions shall not follow from the arrangement. In this case, supposing it was proved to my satisfaction that there had been a stipulation that the two persons were not to be partners, I could not regard that as altering the legal relation which they have entered into by making this contract.

Kay J's remarks find support in *Adam v Newbigging* (1888) 13 AC 308, per Lord Halsbury LC at p 315 and, in *Fenston v Johnstone* (1940) 23 TC 29, a partnership was found to exist notwithstanding an express declaration that the agreement between the parties should not constitute a partnership.

Definition of partnership

Section 1 of PA defines partnership as 'the relation which subsists between persons carrying on a business in common with a view of profit'. Three conditions are therefore postulated, and there can be no partnership unless (a) there is a business being carried on (b) in common (c) with a view of profit.

'Business' is defined in PA, s 45 as including 'every trade, occupation or profession'. Occupation is to be construed eiusdem generis with other words, and therefore although persons may be occupied in doing something, they will not be partners unless the undertaking has some commercial characteristics. The business does not have to be a long-term one. People who work together for one single purpose or deal can still be partners (*Mann v D'Arcy* [1968] 2 All ER 172).

Indicia of partnership

Section 2 of PA lays down certain indicia of partnership to which regard is to be had in determining whether or not a partnership exists.

The tests laid down by s 2 are as follows:

(1) Co-ownership: co-ownership of any property does not, of itself, create a partnership as to anything so owned, whether or not the owners do or do not share any profits made by the use of such property. The qualification 'of itself' is important: although co-owners who merely share expenses of management and divide income according to their ownership shares are not partners, the use by co-owners of their joint property for the purposes of a business will cause them to be treated as partners in relation to the business, and may also cause them to be treated as partners as regards the property.

(2) Sharing gross returns: the sharing of gross returns does not, of itself, create a partnership, whether the persons sharing such returns have or have not a joint or common right or interest in any property from which or from the use of which the returns are derived. The receipt of a share of gross returns, as distinguished from the receipt of a share of the profits, is not even prima facie evidence of partnership. In *Burnard v Aaron and Sharpley* (1862) 31 LJCP 334 joint owners of a ship were held not to be partners where one of them took the exclusive management of the ship, bore all the expenses and paid a proportion of the gross receipts to the other co-owner.

(3) Sharing profits: the receipt by a person of a share of the profits of a business is prima facie evidence that he is a partner in the business, but the receipt of such a share or of a payment contingent on or varying with the profits of a business does not, of itself, make him a partner in the business. Particular examples referred to in s 2 of more remote interests in the profits of a business which are taken not, of themselves, to constitute the recipient of such a payment a partner in the business are referred to in s 2(3) as follows:

   (a) The receipt by a person of a debt or other liquidated amount by instalments or otherwise out of the accruing profits of a business does not of itself make him a partner in the business or liable as such;

   (b) A contract for the remuneration of a servant or agent of a person engaged in a business by a share of the profits of the business does not of itself make the servant or agent a partner in the business or liable as such;

   (c) A person being the widow or child of a deceased partner, and receiving by way of annuity a portion of the profits made in the business in which the deceased person was a partner, is not by reason only of such receipt a partner in the business or liable as such;

(d) The advance of money by way of loan to a person engaged or about to engage in any business on a contract with that person that the lender shall receive a rate of interest varying with the profits, or shall receive a share of the profits arising from carrying on the business, does not of itself make the lender a partner with the person or persons carrying on the business or liable as such. Provided that the contract is in writing, and signed by or on behalf of all the parties thereto;

(e) A person receiving by way of annuity or otherwise a portion of the profits of a business in consideration of the sale by him of the goodwill of the business is not by reason only of such receipt a partner in the business or liable as such.

(4) Sharing losses: a strong presumption of partnership arises in relation to any agreement under which the parties agree both to share the profits and to make good the losses from a common undertaking. This is the case even where the agreement between the parties does not describe their relationship as a partnership or either of the parties as a partner of the other; see, for example, *Fenston v Johnstone* (1940) 23 TC 29 where the court inferred the existence of a partnership from the agreement which provided that each of the two contracting parties should be responsible for half of any losses, despite an express term stipulating that the arrangement should not constitute a partnership between them. Not every agreement involving an obligation to bear losses, however, creates a partnership. Some Lloyd's managing agency agreements, for example, contain 'deficit' clauses under which underwriting losses of a syndicate in one underwriting year of account are set against the underwriting profits of following underwriting years of account before the managing agent is to become entitled to a commission. Such a provision for adjustment of the agent's commission entitlement by reference to losses in earlier years does not cause the agent to be in partnership with the syndicate; it is merely a means of adjusting the calculation of the remuneration payable to the agent.

The importance of the qualification 'of itself' appearing in the rules contained in s 2 has already been referred to. The rules simply indicate the weight to be attached to the various relationships referred to in the section when the relationships are considered in isolation. In determining whether a partnership exists, however, the correct approach is that regard must be paid to the true contract and intention of the parties as appearing from the whole facts of the case: *Cox v Hickman* (1860) 8 HLC 268. The indicia referred to in PA, s 2 are simply facts among many required to be taken into consideration.

The liabilities of partners to third parties provide an important practical incentive to clarity of analysis in determining whether a particular joint venture is to have the characteristics of partnership or not. One unfortunate example of the risks of failing to recognise the dangers involved is *Walker West Developments Ltd v FJ Emmett* (1979) 252 EG 1171. In this case a property developer and a builder entered into a series of arrangements under which land was conveyed by the builder to the developer, dwelling houses were built upon the land by the builder, and the resulting properties sold by the developer to third parties. The profits arising on sale were to be split equally.

The agreement between the parties contained no provision for the sharing of losses, and was mainly a 'prime cost' contract for building works. The Court of Appeal had to decide whether there was 'a business being carried on in common' or whether the arrangements constituted a building contract between two separate businesses, a developer and a builder.

The court held that a partnership existed. Eveleigh LJ said 'the general nature of this contract . . . appears clearly to be a joint development enterprise with a reasonable distribution of financial burden, complete with a degree of sharing of the overheads'. He went on to say that where the parties to a joint enterprise are supplying to each other their respective skill and experience 'it is not inconsistent with a partnership agreement for provision to be made for what is to happen if one of the parties, as it were, defaults in the performance of his side of the partnership business'. Eveleigh LJ also found that the reimbursement of expenses to the builder by the developer for the prime cost of the building works did not prevent a partnership from existing, as the developer would in due course have those expenses returned to him from the proceeds of sale. The absence of provisions dealing with losses was irrelevant as provision was implied by PA s 24(1) (although Goff LJ held that the builder was not liable for losses on the facts).

Goff LJ found that the strongest evidence of 'a business being carried on in common' by the parties was in the way the parties described what they were doing, calling it 'the project' and indicating that it should be advertised as a joint project.

This is a difficult case and one which it is probably right to confine to its particular facts but, nonetheless, it serves as a warning to those who fail to make clear in their joint venture agreement the intended consequences of the relationship which they are creating.

Partnership Act 1890, s 3

The provisions of PA, s 2(3)(d) (see above) should be read in conjunction with s 3. Section 3 is as follows:

> In the event of any person to whom money has been advanced by way of loan upon such a contract as is mentioned in the last foregoing section, or of any buyer of a goodwill in consideration of a share of the profits of the business, being adjudged a bankrupt, entering into an arrangement to pay his creditors less than 100 pence in the pound or dying in insolvent circumstances, the lender of the loan shall not be entitled to recover anything in respect of his loan, and the seller of the goodwill shall not be entitled to recover anything in respect of the share of profits contracted for, until the claims of the other creditors of the borrower or buyer for valuable consideration in money or money's worth have been satisfied.

Although lenders who advance loans of the type referred to in s 2(3)(d) are not, by the fact of the advance itself, to be treated as partners with the borrower, nonetheless s 3 effectively subordinates lenders to the claims of other creditors before any part of their advance become recoverable. It seems, however, that s 3 neither deprives the lenders of the benefit of security granted to them in respect of the advance nor affects their ability to foreclose on the security. In certain forms of limited recourse lending, lenders are sometimes granted a royalty or 'profit share' on the value of the asset financed or its production as additional remuneration for the risk assumed in accepting a limitation of recourse. Such forms of remuneration require careful structuring if they are not to fall within s 3.

3.3 Illustrations from the oil and gas and construction industries

Unincorporated joint ventures are common in both the construction and oil and gas industries, and the different joint venture structures encountered in these industries offer useful insights into the application in practice of the rules described in 3.2 above.

Joint ventures in the oil and gas industry

Joint ventures among oil companies are common, in relation to both the exploration and production phases of oilfield and gas field development, both onshore and offshore, and one of their main purposes is to achieve a sharing of the costs and risks, especially of exploration, among the participating oil companies. Operations on the United Kingdom Continental Shelf ('UKCS') have tended to follow this practice: licences issued to single companies are rare, and most of the licences issued by the Secretary of State for Energy under the Petroleum (Production) Act 1934 (as extended to designated areas by s 1(7) of the Continental Shelf Act 1964) have been issued to a consortium of companies.

For the purposes of this chapter, the point of interest concerns the relationship of the licensees to the Secretary of State under the licence and their relationships to each other under their joint venture agreement (usually known as a Joint Operating Agreement or 'JOA'). The licences issued by the Secretary of State are in a form primarily designed for a single licensee. The possibility of multiple licensees is recognised both in a provision to the effect that obligations of co-licensees are joint and several, and in the provisions for revocation under which the licence may be revoked against all licensees if any one co-licensee creates grounds for revocation. Licences are, however, silent as regards the position of the co-licensees inter se.

The rights and obligations of the co-licensees against each other are established in the JOA. One of the principal clauses of the JOA is that which declares the participants' respective percentage interests under the licence. By establishing a joint entitlement as against the Secretary of State on the part of the licensees together, the licence in effect establishes a joint tenancy among the licensees as a group; by specifying the percentage interests of each licensee, the JOA severs that joint tenancy and constitutes each of the participants a tenant in common of an undivided interest in the licence corresponding to its percentage interest. For the purposes of PA, s 2(1) the licensees thus fall to be regarded as co-owners of the licence, and of any petroleum won and saved under the licence.

It has been seen that s 2(1) provides that co-ownership of any property does not, of itself, create a partnership as to anything so owned, and the arrangements between the participants under a JOA are indeed structured to prevent any suggestion that a partnership may have been created between them. The aspect of the JOA which is particularly significant in this respect is that dealing with the disposal of petroleum. The practical details of offtake arrangements cannot, of course, be established until the production phase when field development plans have been finalised but, even in JOAs relating to the exploration phase, it is common to provide that each licensee shall have the right to take in kind and separately dispose of its share of the petroleum won. This approach to the disposal of petroleum makes it clear that the common enterprise of the joint venture is limited to the joint conduct of the development of the asset they hold in common; when it comes to the disposal of the resulting petroleum, each participant acts in the course of its own business, and there is no common undertaking for the joint disposal of production for mutual profit.

Such joint marketing activities are rare in the oil industry: sales of production by smaller members of a group to the larger companies possessing the facilities to lift product and process it for eventual distribution are commonplace, but they typically take place not under joint marketing arrangements, but under a straightforward contract for sale. Joint marketing arrangements are, however, encountered in hard mineral developments. It should be noted that, quite apart from complications which may arise under partnership law, significant anti-trust difficulties may be encountered with these arrangements.

Joint ventures in the construction industry

As the size and complexity of construction projects increase, it has become common for contractors to associate with one another for the purpose of submitting a tender for and, if successful, carrying out a project and carrying out the work if their tender is successful. Contractors associate in joint venture for a variety of reasons: because the size of a project would expose a single contractor to excessive risks; because the project requires the skills of a variety of specialist contractors, and each contractor wishes to pool his skills with those of other specialists in order to bid for a job which none of them alone could have handled; in the case of projects abroad, because localisation laws require the participation of local contractors or designers or to lock into the group the services of a valuable contact or agent; or, less meritoriously, with a view simply to eliminating competition from a significant rival.

Joint ventures among contractors are generally organised by reference to one of two alternative models. Although these models are not terms of art, they are widely referred to in the construction industry as integrated and non-integrated joint ventures.

Both models might share a common form of management structure. Often there would be two tiers of management; a project management committee responsible for the day-to-day co-ordination and execution of the work and an executive committee, meeting at head office rather than on site, charged with responsibility for major decisions and for resolving any matters on which consensus could not be reached in the project management committee. Representation on the committees is usually broadly pro-rata to the participants' respective interests in the joint venture.

The important distinction between the integrated and non-integrated joint venture, for the purposes of PA, s 2, lies in the relationship between the joint venture itself and its participants.

In an integrated joint venture, the venture itself is a profit centre, and its objective is to strike a profit on the project by establishing a revenue surplus of payments received from the employer over the costs of carrying out the contract. In practice, most integrated joint ventures do little of the work themselves; they are essentially project management creatures staffed by secondees from the participants. Most of the physical work is sub-contracted, sometimes to the participants, but more usually to third party sub-contractors selected by a competitive bidding process in order to achieve the lowest price, and therefore to maximise the opportunity of profit, for the joint venturers. The participants often do, but may not, take work on sub-contract from the joint venture.

The participants in a non-integrated joint venture would typically assume the same joint and several liability to the employer for the performance of their obligations under the construction contract as would parties to an integrated joint venture. In a non-integrated joint venture, on the other hand, no profit is struck at the level of the joint venture; instead, the work is divided up into discrete segments which the participants carry out severally, each bearing their own cost of performance and dividing between them the flow of payments from the employer under the construction contract. Profit is thus taken not at the level of the non-integrated joint venture, but severally by the participants, and it is possible for one participant to show a profit and another a loss on their respective parts of the work under a non-integrated joint venture.

It will be seen that the status of the two types of venture is very different for the purposes of PA. An integrated joint venture generally satisfies the test of 'the relation which subsists between persons carrying on business in common with a view of profit'; on the other hand, the non-integrated joint venture generally falls to be treated simply as an unincorporated association since the participants generally share no more than the gross payments received from the employer under the construction contract (see PA, s 2(2)).

Another important practical difference between the two types of joint venture lies in the way in which they treat default or neglect by employees of the participants in the course of carrying out the contract to which the joint venture relates. In both cases, of course, the result of any neglect or default may be to cause loss to the joint venture but how the loss is handled underlines the conceptual differences between the two types of joint venture. In a non-integrated joint venture, each participant would typically give express indemnities to the others in respect of any loss occasioned by defective performance on his part or on the part of his employees. To avoid exposing the joint venture to cash flow difficulties if the employer seeks to set loss caused by one participant off against future payments due to another participant under the contract, provision is sometimes made for a 'damages fund' to be established, under which a specified proportion of payments due under the contract with the employer will be segregated in a fund, available for appropriation in payment of claims by the employer while disputes between the joint venturers as to the extent of liability under the indemnities are being resolved. In an integrated joint venture, by contrast, things are much simpler: because the participants' employees are seconded to this type of joint venture, the participants themselves are regarded as having no control over the acts of the seconded employees during the period of secondment and, if a loss arises as a result of the neglect or default of such a seconded employee, the loss is treated as reducing the profit on the contract and is generally written off in the joint venture's profit and loss account.

3.4 Legal nature of an unincorporated association

The Partnership Act 1890 consolidates, with minor amendments and exceptions, the common law relating to partnerships. It is not a complete code of partnership law (it does not, for example, cover the question of goodwill and many of its provisions can be excluded by specific provisions in the partnership agreement) but, where PA does deal with a matter, it prevails over the pre-existing common law. The position regarding unincorporated associations is a good deal less clear-cut: there is no statute, comparable to PA, which establishes a series of authoritatively expressed propositions regarding the rights and duties of the members of an unincorporated association inter se and their liability to third parties. Rather, the general law on unincorporated associations has developed in a piecemeal fashion case-by-case, and is undigested except by private commentators.

Although there is no statutory definition of an association, judicial definitions appear in several cases. One definition commonly cited is that found in the Court of Appeal decision of *Conservative and Unionist Central Office v Burrell (Inspector of Taxes)* [1982] 1 WLR 522 where Lawton LJ thought that, in the context of s526 of the Income and Corporation Taxes Act 1970, an association meant:

> two or more persons bound together for one or more common purposes, not being business purposes, by mutual undertakings, each having mutual duties and obligations, in an organisation which has rules which identify in whom control of it and its funds rests and upon what terms, and which can be joined and left at will.

Two elements of this definition lie uncomfortably with the characteristics of unincorporated joint ventures which do not constitute partnerships: the suggestion that an association can only exist other than for business purposes since, of course, joint ventures are very much the creatures of commerce; and, secondly, the notion that an association can be joined and left at will since, in the commercial world, the personality of joint venturers is important and it would be usual to impose severe limitations on the ability of any one participant to leave a joint venture at will.

Although not apt for our purposes, this definition does illustrate the unsatisfactory state of the law in this area. Much of the difficulty flows from the use of the word 'association' to describe a wide variety of organisations and purposes. Activities as diverse as sports clubs, political parties, housing associations, trade associations, theatre clubs, campaigning groups, community associations and working men's and social clubs, as well as non-partnership trading ventures, are commonly carried on through the medium of an unincorporated association. Indeed, there are few decisions that relate specifically to those joint ventures for business purposes which do not fulfil the statutory definition of a partnership and, in practice, the legal principles applying to such joint ventures have to be extrapolated, with caution, from the rules applying to members' clubs.

A better description of the characteristics of these joint ventures can perhaps be derived from a decision of the Court of Session concerning the meaning of the term 'association' in another context. In *Re Caledonian Employees Benevolent Society* 1928 SC 633, a case concerning the winding up of an unregistered company under the forerunner of what is now Part V of the Insolvency Act 1986, the Lord President considered the meaning of the expression 'any association' in the following terms:

> No doubt the word 'association' is by itself capable of including a wide variety of much more loosely and irregularly constituted bodies of persons; but, looking to the context in which it appears . . ., I see no reason to doubt that what is meant is a society (whatever its object) based on consensual contract among its constituent members whereby their mutual relations inter se with regard to some common object are regulated and enforced.

Although of course this is a definition limited to its particular context, nonetheless it contains the essentials of the relationship created between joint venturers who are not partners in the strict sense.

The creation of an unincorporated association rests, then, on the agreement between its members. This means that, so far as the law is concerned, the creation of an unincorporated association depends on the law of contract, and in the same way the constitution of an unincorporated joint venture which does not amount to a partnership will only be enforceable insofar as it amounts to a binding agreement between the participants.

3.5 A partnership and unincorporated association compared

Liability to third parties

In a partnership each partner is treated as an agent of the firm and his other partners for the purposes of the business of the partnership, and every partner who does any act for carrying on in the usual way business of the kind carried on by the firm of which he is a member binds the firm and his partners, unless the partner so acting has in fact no authority to act for the firm in the particular matter, and the person with whom he is dealing either knows that he has no authority, or does not know or does not believe him to be a partner (PA, s 5). In consequence of the mutual agency between partners, PA, s 9 holds each partner jointly liable with other partners for all the debts and obligations of the firm.

In the case of an unincorporated association, the position is very different. There is no general implied agency among the participants. In the case of a members' club, the trustees or committee of management have only such authority to contract on behalf of the members generally as may be given to them expressly or by necessary implication in the rules of the club. The same principle applies to an unincorporated joint venture which does not constitute a partnership. The joint venture agreement might sometimes, although not typically, create an express agency. More usually, agency is expressly denied. In some situations, a more radical approach may be adopted: in contracts placed by operators under North Sea Joint Operating Agreements, it is common to see provisions by which the operator is acknowledged to be acting as a principal in respect of any obligations owed by it under the contract (so that the supplier can sue the operator alone in the case of non-performance), but by which the operator is treated as an agent for itself and the other participants for the purpose of enforcing any rights under the contract (so that the loss of all participants in the consortium holding the licence (and not just the operator itself) may be taken into account in assessing what loss is recoverable from the supplier in the case of non-performance on his part).

Termination and dissolution

Sections 32–44 of PA set out the circumstances that give rise to termination of the partnership. Section 32 provides as follows:

> Subject to any agreement between the partners, a partnership is dissolved—
> (a) If entered into for a fixed term, by the expiration of that term;
> (b) If entered into for a single adventure or undertaking, by the termination of that adventure or undertaking;

(c) If entered into for an undefined time, by the partner giving notice
to the other or others of his intention to dissolve the partnership.
In the last-mentioned case the partnership is dissolved as from the date
mentioned in the notice as the date of dissolution, or, if no date is so
mentioned, as from the date of the communication of the notice.

This section is supplemented by s 33, which provides that, in the
absence of contrary agreement, a partnership is dissolved as regards all
partners by the death or bankruptcy of any partner, or if a partner suffers
his share of the partnership property to be charged for his separate debt;
by s 34, which provides for dissolution on illegality of partnership; and by
s 35 which provides for dissolution by the court on application by a
partner alleging, inter alia, prejudicial conduct, breach of the partnership
agreement, that the business can only be carried on at a loss or that
dissolution is just and equitable.

Dissolution of the partnership does not affect the existing obligations of
the partners who have a continuing liability in respect thereof, and it is
therefore important for partners, particularly outgoing partners, to notify
third parties of the dissolution or change as soon as possible and to place a
notice in the *London Gazette* in accordance with s 36(2). Failure to do so
may mean that outgoing partners incur new liability as a result of being
apparent members of the firm (s 36(1)). An outgoing partner should also
seek an indemnity from the continuing partners against the debts and
obligations of the partnership incurred before his retirement or
resignation.

On dissolution every partner is entitled to have the property of the
partnership applied against the debts of the firm (s 39). This may not
always be welcome where a partner to a joint venture wishes to retain one
of the joint venture assets, or wishes for a distribution in specie.
Furthermore if one partner has paid a premium to another on entering
into a partnership for a fixed term and the partnership dissolves before the
expiry of that term the court may order repayment of the premium or a
part thereof (PA, s 40).

Section 44 sets out the rules for distribution of assets on final settlement
of accounts as follows:

In settling accounts between the partners after a dissolution of
partnership the following rules shall, subject to any agreement, be
observed:
(a) Losses, including losses and deficiencies of capital, shall be paid
first out of profits, next out of capital, and lastly, if necessary, by
the partners individually in the proportion in which they were
entitled to share profits;
(b) The assets of the firm including the sums, if any, contributed by
the partners to make up losses or deficiencies of capital, shall be

applied in the following manner and order:

1. In paying the debts and liabilities of the firm to persons who are not partners therein;
2. In paying to each partner rateably what is due from the firm to him for advances as distinguished from capital;
3. In paying to each partner rateably what is due from the firm to him in respect of capital;
4. The ultimate residue, if any, shall be divided among the partners in the proportion in which profits are divisible.

In the case of an unincorporated association, there is no statutory provision for its duration or termination. Like any other contract, however, an unincorporated association may at common law terminate for one of the following reasons: upon performance by the parties of all their obligations under the contract forming the association, where those obligations are not continuing; the effluxion of time where the unincorporated association is formed for a fixed period; by agreement between the parties; or by reason of frustration, by virtue of breach or by operation of law.

Part V of the Insolvency Act 1986 provides for the dissolution of unregistered companies. Members' clubs formed as unincorporated associations are not, generally, within the scope of the Companies Acts (*Re St James' Club* (1852) 2 De GM & G 383) since they do not possess the necessary element of trading to bring them within their scope (*Re Bristol Athenaeum* (1889) 43 ChD 236). Such unincorporated associations can, nonetheless, be wound up by the High Court under its equitable jurisdiction (*Re Lead Company's Workmen's Fund Society* [1904] 2 Ch 196). Although there is no authority directly on the point, it seems that, on the basis of the decision in *Re Caledonian Employees Benevolent Society* (above), joint ventures formed as unincorporated associations not amounting to a partnership would fall within the dissolution procedures provided under Part V of the Insolvency Act 1986 as being unregistered companies of the type contemplated by those provisions. The jurisdiction to wind up such unregistered companies only applies, however, in the case of compulsory winding up by the court: there is no facility for voluntary winding up or winding up subject to the supervision of the court. Nonetheless, if the rules of an association provide for dissolution, the court will not generally interfere; if there is no provision for dissolution, the court will not itself take action, at least in the case of a members club, unless either a majority of its members are clearly in favour of dissolution, or there is no practical possibility for the club to continue in being (*Blake v Smither* (1906) 22 TLR 698).

Well-drawn joint venture agreements will provide for the application of any assets held by the joint venture on termination or dissolution.

Difficulties can arise if they do not make clear provision for this eventuality. In the case of members' clubs the general principle is that, under the contract subsisting between the members, and in the absence of a rule to the contrary, a term is to be implied in the contract by which, on a dissolution, the surplus funds fall to be distributed among the then existing members. In *Re Bucks Constabulary Widows' and Orphans' Fund Friendly Society (No 2)* [1979] 1 WLR 936 Orton J held that distribution in equal shares was the correct approach. On the other hand, where there are more than one class of member, the basis on which surplus funds are to be distributed will depend upon the construction of the rules as a whole. In *Re Sick and Funeral Society of St John's Sunday School, Golcar* [1973] Ch 51 Megarry J observed that a class of members for whom the current benefits of membership are greater (perhaps in return for greater contributions) may for that reason be considered to have an entitlement to a larger share out of surplus assets on distribution but, subject to any contrary rule, neither the total amount of subscriptions paid over time by a member nor the length of his period of membership increase a member's entitlement to participate in a surplus. Different considerations clearly apply in the context of an unincorporated joint venture where the parties have been brought together for reasons of commercial rather than social intercourse but, in the absence of authority, only specific contractual provision can give the requisite degree of certainty.

Partnership property

Section 20 of PA deals with partnership property. Section 20(1) provides as follows:

> All property and rights and interests in property originally brought into the partnership stock or acquired, whether by purchase or otherwise, on account of the firm, or for the purposes of and in the course of the partnership business, are called in this Act partnership property, and must be held and applied by the partners exclusively for the purposes of the partnership and in accordance with the partnership agreement.

This provision thus brings within the partnership assets acquired and held by one of the partners if it can be said that the assets were acquired 'for the purposes and in the course of the partnership business'. In the case of unincorporated associations the position is very different. In *Jarrott v Ackerley* (1915) 113 LT 371, a case concerning an unincorporated members' club, one of its members, purporting to act on behalf of the club, took an underlease of premises executed in his own name. The head lease was later forfeited, and the club's trustees applied to the court for statutory relief. As the trustees were not a party to the underlease, they had no rights under it even though the intention of the member in taking the lease on behalf of the club was patently clear.

Rights and duties of partners and members inter se

At common law a partner had a duty of utmost good faith to those in partnership with him (*Blisset v Daniel* (1853) 10 Hare 493). This duty is reflected in ss 28–30 of PA. Under s 28, partners are subject to a duty to render to their other partners true accounts and full information in respect of all things affecting the partnership; s 29 provides, in subsection (1), that each partner must account to the firm for any benefit derived by him without the consent of the other partners from any transaction concerning the partnership, or from any use by him of the partnership property, name or business connection; and s 30 provides for a duty not to compete with the partnership business.

In the case of joint ventures conducted through unincorporated associations which do not fall to be treated as partnerships, the extent of the rights and duties of the joint venturers inter se is rather uncertain. The traditional approach is that the English courts will not stray beyond certain clearly defined limits in attempting to find an equitable solution. For example, in relation to commercial contracts negotiated at arm's length, the recent cases of *Interfoto Picture Library Limited v Stiletto Visual Programmes Ltd* [1988] 1 All ER 348 and *Banque Keyser Ullman SA v Skandia (UK) Insurance Co Ltd* [1989] 3 WLR 25 have reaffirmed the traditional refusal of the English courts to apply any implied duty of good faith and fair dealing in the performance of contractual obligations.

The English courts have therefore hesitated to follow the example of the Australian courts in enunciating a general principle of fair dealing or good faith of the type considered in the Australian case of *Brian Pty Ltd v United Dominions Corporation Ltd* (1983) 1 NSWLR 490, a case before the full Court of the Supreme Court of New South Wales. Here an agreement for property development termed a 'joint venture agreement' was negotiated between the plaintiff and others. One of the other parties gave security over the assets of the joint venturer to a third party without informing the plaintiff. Where the assets were sold, the third party claimed to be entitled to the profits due to all the venturers in satisfaction of their agreement as to security. The court held that the joint venturers owed a duty of good faith to each other similar to that which would have arisen had the relationship been a partnership. In his judgment Huttely J referred to US authority (*Meinhand v Salamon* (1928) 164 ME 545) and stated:

> The duties of joint venturers, inter se, do not appear to have been authoritatively defined in any decision binding on this court and it therefore falls upon this court to do so. A joint venture is analogous to

a partnership. The differences are not designed, as I understand it, in order to lower the standards of honour between the joint venturers. It is implied by law that parties shall be true and just in their dealings with each other, and the same rules should be laid down for joint venturers.

There is, however, one case in which the English courts have recognised obligations of good faith in the context of a contractual joint venture. In *Hampton & Sons v Garrard Smith (Estate Agents)* (1985) 274 EG 1139 the Court of Appeal considered an agreement between two firms of estate agents, not in partnership, to share a commission on a house sale for which they had been appointed joint sole agents. The property was sold by the defendant who refused to share the commission. In his judgment Dillon LJ rejected the argument by the plaintiff that he was entitled to the payment on the basis of restitution but nonetheless ordered that the commission should be shared, saying:

> It does seem to me, however, that this is a claim which lies within the field of equitable dealings between parties. It is not a partnership, but it is a joint venture, raising obligations of good faith towards the plaintiff.

This case is perhaps best regarded as decided on its special facts, as it flies in the face of the *Interfoto* and *Keyser Ullman* decisions cited above.

Even if no general duty of good faith between participants in an unincorporated joint venture can be identified, do they perhaps stand, as partners would, in the relation of fiduciaries to one another? A duty of good faith is not of itself fiduciary: good faith does not require, as fiduciary law does, that one party subordinate its interests to those of the other party (or their joint interest). It permits self-interest, but may require a party to take into account the interests of the other, and act fairly to that other in consequence. The distinction is reflected in the remedies for breach of the two duties: if the English courts were prepared to find a duty of good faith in any particular case, the remedy for its breach would, it is submitted, lie only in damages; if a fiduciary duty is breached, however, the more extensive restitutional remedies (including a duty to account) may be ordered.

There is, however, no decided case on the point and, on the contrary, there is little to suggest that the nature of the participants' relationship in an incorporated joint venture is such as to constitute them fiduciaries for each other. There does not seem to be an established practice that joint venturers are under an obligation not to act to the detriment of each other. Where particular constraints on the parties' activities are thought appropriate (such as undertakings not to compete with the business of the joint venture or, in oil and gas joint ventures, the 'area of mutual interest clauses' preventing participants from applying for concessions over adjacent areas without consent), they are heavily negotiated and may differ from venture to venture. This is not to say that, within the joint venture, one party may not owe a fiduciary duty to another in respect of property under the possession or control of that party, but duties of this sort arise by virtue of the terms on which the property in question is entrusted to the relevant party, rather than because the nature of the joint venture itself treats the participants as fiduciaries for each other in all respects.

One illustration of this approach is found in oil and gas joint ventures where cash calls received by the operator for the purposes of the joint operations may be regarded as trust monies in the hands of the operator. Another, more certain, line of authority concerns the breach of confidence cases where the English courts have intervened to protect or compensate the proprietor of confidential information from its misuse or exploitation by a party to whom it has been passed in confidence.

In *Seager v Copydex Ltd* [1967] 1 WLR 923, the plaintiff embarked upon negotiations with the defendant with a view to the development of an invention. The discussions were later terminated without any contract being concluded. Subsequently the defendant produced a competing product with the assistance of the information given to it by the plaintiff. Although much of this information was already in the public domain, some of it, such as information concerning the difficulties which had been overcome in the manufacturing process, was not. Even though the defendant was an 'innocent' misuser of confidential information in the sense that it was not consciously aware of the assistance which it had derived from the plaintiff's information, it was nonetheless held to have used the confidential information to get a head start. Lord Denning formulated the principle in the following terms:

> The law on this subject depends on the broad principle of equity that he who has received information in confidence shall not take unfair advantage of it. He must not make use of it to the prejudice of him who gave it without obtaining his consent.

Similarly, in *Coco v Clark (AN) (Engineers)* [1969] RPC 41, Sir Robert Megarry held that 'in particular where information of commercial or industrial value is given on a business-like basis, and with some avowed common object in mind, such as a joint venture or the manufacture of articles by one party for the other, I would regard the recipient as carrying a heavy burden if he seeks to repel a contention that he is bound by an obligation of confidence'.

Chapter 4

Joint venture companies

4.1 Introduction

This chapter considers the use of a company (typically newly-formed for the purpose) as the vehicle for carrying on the joint venture's business. The choice of a company is very common. For most business people it has the great advantage of familiarity and the attraction of potentially limited liability. Unlike a partnership a company enjoys its own legal identity and its liabilities are not automatically liabilities of the joint venturer. The limited liability company offers the possibility of protecting the existing businesses of the joint venturers from the consequences of the venture's failure. Particularly where the venture is high risk, that prospect may prove compelling.

Having chosen to use a corporate vehicle the parties will normally seek to characterise the company as a joint venture by applying joint venture techniques to establish a secure equilibrium for the ongoing relationship of the parties, particularly in the context of membership, management and termination. In English law, however, the parties will find their relationship circumscribed by a series of statutes relating to companies (including, most importantly, the Companies Acts 1985 and 1989 and the Insolvency Act 1986) and a vast, rather unruly body of case law. Many techniques which are used for joint venture companies have been developed to deal with shortcomings in the general law which, in some important respects, is ill-fitted to the requirements of a joint venture.

In this chapter it is not possible to examine all of the law in detail and the chapter therefore merely examines those aspects of company law which have most bearing on a joint venture company.

After a brief look at the nature of the relationship between the company and its joint venture shareholders, the chapter proceeds to examine the methods commonly used to protect the respective interests of the shareholders and the advantages and disadvantages of shareholders' agreements. The role and responsibilities of directors appointed by shareholders to the company's board are also considered, as are the

40

techniques for controlling membership of the company and finally various methods for terminating the relationship between the parties when either the joint venture has run its pre-determined course or the parties can no longer co-operate.

4.2 Relationship of the parties

Position prior to incorporation

Before proceeding to deal with the relationship between shareholders in a joint venture company it is worth reminding those who wish to conduct their business through a corporate vehicle that their relationship may commence even before the establishment or incorporation of the joint venture company, in which case some of the principles mentioned in the previous chapter may still apply.

In particular joint venturers should not start trading or developing joint venture assets until the joint venture company has been formed or else they may risk finding their relationship prior to incorporation construed by the courts as that of a partnership, although this would not happen where they are merely taking steps which are connected with the incorporation of their joint venture vehicle (*Spicer (Keith) v Mansel* [1970] 1 All ER 462).

A company's constitution

A company is a vehicle which owes its separate legal existence to CA 1985. The constitutional documents which are prescribed by that Act are the memorandum and articles of association. The former describes the objectives and personality of the company, the latter is intended to govern its internal regulation. Both bind the company and its members to the same extent as if they had been signed as a deed by each member and contained covenants on the part of each member to observe all provisions contained therein (CA 1985, s 14). For the joint venturer both of these documents, and in particular the articles of association, are therefore of the utmost importance and should always be read in conjunction with any shareholders' agreement or other documentation put in place by the parties to regulate the joint venture.

Memorandum of association

The most important term of the memorandum of association is the objects clause. This is usually drafted in a very broad manner so that the majority of acts which a company would be likely to carry out during its existence will fall within the express objects or powers set out. Potential problems caused by shortcomings in the objects clause of a company's memorandum have been reduced recently by the weakening of the ultra vires rule, and in particular by the new s 35A of CA 1985 which should protect third parties acting in good faith even if the company was acting outside the scope of its objects or powers. The memorandum of association is still important for joint venturers, however, as the objects clause can be used as a means of describing or limiting the ambit of the activities of the company as between the venturers themselves.

Articles of association

The articles of association form the contract which deals with the rights of parties amongst themselves in their capacity as shareholders. Although parties are free to adopt articles in such form as they see fit, many companies base their articles on Table A (the statutory form of articles, the text of which is set out in the Companies (Tables A to F) Regulations 1985 (SI 1985 No 805)).

For a joint venture company the articles set out in Table A will rarely suffice, and it would normally be better for long form articles to be drafted, even if based on the statutory form.

Articles of association are always a vital document in a joint venture company and, whether or not Table A is used, should never be taken for granted, both because, as a form of shareholders' agreement, it will be necessary to ensure that they do not conflict with the terms of any other shareholders' joint venture agreement, and because any one of the articles may, if not carefully considered, have unwelcome and unforeseen consequences for the parties.

Effect of the articles of association as a contract

The contract between the company and its members is generally regarded as enforceable only insofar as it relates to the shareholders in their capacity as members of the company (*Eley v Positive Government Security Life Assurance Co* (1876) 1 Ex D 88, CA). This general principle has not always been strictly applied. In *Salmon v Quin and Axtens Ltd* [1909] AC 442, for example, the company's articles vested the general management of the company's business in the directors, although certain resolutions of the directors were to be invalid if either of the two managing directors dissented. One such resolution was passed and Salmon, one of the managing directors, dissented. Salmon sued the company on behalf of himself and all the other shareholders to restrain the company and the directors from acting on the resolution. The House of Lords granted an injunction in the terms sought. Indirectly, therefore, Salmon was allowed to enforce the right given to him as managing director by suing as a shareholder for the enforcement of the relevant articles.

In *Hickman v Kent or Romney Sheep Breeders Association* [1915] 1 Ch 881 Astbury J held that 'outside rights' given to shareholders, though they cannot be enforced as part of the contract in the articles, can exist and be enforced 'by virtue of some contract between such person and the company', that is, as a result of a separate contract with the company. Such a contract can contain terms incorporated from the articles either expressly or impliedly (see, for example, *Re New British Iron Co, ex parte Beckwith* [1898] 1 Ch 324: director's rate of remuneration implied from provision in articles), but where a contract incorporates one or more of the company's articles, the terms of that contract are subject to alteration by virtue of the alterability of the articles themselves in the absence of a clear expression of the contrary intention (*Shuttleworth v Cox Brothers & Co* [1927] 2 KB 9; *Allen v Gold Reefs of West Africa Ltd* [1900] 1 Ch 656).

Any breach of the contract between the company and the members embodied in the articles may be the subject of legal action if the breach affects or concerns the members in their capacity as members (*Pender v Lushington* (1877) 6 Ch D 70, CA). Damages are the normal remedy, but either the company or the members may seek an injunction to restrain a breach of the articles (see, for example, *Hickman*) or a declaration of rights.

The courts have never satisfactorily determined how far the provisions of the articles bind the members among themselves. In particular it is unclear whether obligations of a non-personal, administrative nature are enforceable, although it would appear from the decision in *Rayfield v Hands* [1960] Ch 1 that personal obligations between members contained in the articles will be enforced. However, where there is a separate shareholders agreement between the members an injunction can be sought in an appropriate case to restrain that person from acting in a manner inconsistent with the terms of that agreement.

4.3 Protecting minority shareholders

One of the features which has been identified as common to joint ventures is an equality of bargaining power. An equality of bargaining power should result in a balance of power within the joint venture company. However, unless appropriate steps are taken, a minority shareholder may find itself severely prejudiced, not just as to participation in management, but also in respect of matters which will affect the value of its stake in the venture. The protection of the minority or the maintenance of an equilibrium between the joint venture parties is therefore something upon which a great deal of attention is generally focused.

The most common methods by which minority shareholders protect themselves are the following:

(a) by seeking to entrench their rights in either the memorandum or articles of association of the joint venture company;

(b) by separating the shares in the company into different classes, the rights of which are separately protected from variation;

(c) by obtaining contractual safeguards in a shareholders' agreement;

(d) by bringing an action in respect of unfairly prejudicial conduct under CA 1985, s 459; or

(e) by presenting a petition for the winding up of the company pursuant to s 122(1)(g) of the Insolvency Act 1986 on the 'just and equitable ground'.

The principal basis of protection afforded under each of these headings is discussed below. Protection of a minority in a joint venture may result in the use of more than one of these, but it is always better to set out express terms for the protection of the minority in a shareholders' agreement than to rely on the statutory remedies, both because the statutory remedies are in many ways unsatisfactory, and because such an exercise may result in obstacles and problems being analysed and dealt with before they can materialise. Shareholders' agreements are dealt with separately in 4.4 below.

Minorities may have other rights arising as a result of membership, but these are rarely used in a joint venture context and they are therefore not dealt with in this chapter.

Entrenchment in the memorandum and articles of association

One method traditionally used by minority shareholders to secure their rights is to incorporate those rights into the constitutional documents of the company, on the grounds that it is generally more difficult for a majority to alter rights, if so drafted, and that a majority shareholder could be prevented from acting in an unconstitutional manner. The powers to alter, or prevent the alteration of, the memorandum and articles of association are set out below:

Entrenchment in the articles
The articles of association of a company cannot be altered without a special resolution, that is a resolution passed at a properly convened meeting on which (a) on a show of hands at least 75 per cent of the members present in person and voting voted in favour or (b) on a poll, votes in favour of the resolution were cast in respect of at least 75 per cent of all the shares in respect of which votes were cast. Shareholders holding

more than 25 per cent of the voting capital of the company can therefore veto such alterations.

The power to alter the articles by special resolution conferred by s 9 of CA 1985 is a power of which the company cannot deprive itself by a statement in the articles (*Walker v London Tramways Co* (1879) 12 Ch D 705 per Jessel MR). Anything that might have been included in the original articles may be introduced into the altered articles, provided only the alteration is made bona fide for the benefit of the company as a whole. See *Allen v Gold Reefs of West Africa* [1900] 1 Ch 656; *Sidebotham v Kershaw, Leese & Co* [1920] 1 Ch 154; *Greenhalgh v Arderne Cinemas* [1951] 1 Ch 286. Thus, a provision in the articles that any specific article may only be altered with the consent of a named person may be of limited usefulness. The article which provides for such consent can itself be altered and the person named cannot prevent this or have any rights in default.

If the articles have been altered in accordance with the provisions of CA a member will have no right of action against either the company or the other member. This contrasts with the position under the general law of contract where parties (or a majority of them) are unable to alter terms unilaterally. In joint venture situations this sometimes results in the duplication of the articles in a shareholders agreement, so that any attempt to change the articles by means of a special resolution would result in an action for breach of contract under the terms of the shareholders agreement. On an article by article basis this is a somewhat clumsy approach and the most common procedure is for the shareholders agreement to provide that the parties will procure the adoption of a new set of articles in agreed terms which cannot be changed without the consent of each of the joint venturers.

Bushell v Faith clauses—weighted voting

An alternative way of preventing alteration of the articles is to provide for weighted voting. In *Bushell v Faith* [1970] AC 1099 the articles provided that on a motion for the dismissal of a director that director was entitled to exercise three votes for each share which he held. In the circumstances this meant that no director could be voted out against his will, even though CA 1985, s 303 provides that a company may by ordinary resolution remove a director before the expiration of his period of office, notwithstanding anything in the articles or in any agreement between it and him.

The House of Lords held that the weighted voting rights were legal as the articles did not attempt to provide for a stiffer majority than that required for the passing of an ordinary resolution. The decision seems to be of general application and there is no reason in principle why it should not apply to special resolutions.

A common provision found in articles where the company has two classes of ordinary shares represents another form of weighted voting. The articles provide that those members of a particular class present at a meeting shall on a poll have the same number of votes as could be cast by all members of that class if they were present at the meeting. The purpose of such a provision is to ensure that shareholders are not deprived of their rights through their unavoidable or inadvertent absence from a meeting.

Entrenchment in the memorandum of association

The general power of alteration of the articles is subject to the provisions of CA 1985 and to any conditions in the company's memorandum of association. Accordingly, any provision in the company's articles which conflicts with the memorandum is invalid: *Welton v Saffery* [1897] AC 299, HL.

If the memorandum itself prohibits the alteration of all or any of its provisions, provisions which could have been included in the articles can effectively be rendered unalterable. Such a degree of inflexibility is rarely desirable.

Different classes of shares

An alternative to weighted voting is the creation of different classes of shares for different groups of shareholders. Protection will be afforded by a provision that a resolution is only valid if passed by a requisite majority of members holding each class of shares. The scope for variation of such class rights depends on the means used to create them (CA 1985, s 125). Normally they will be set out in the articles, and if so:

- if the class rights are set out in the memorandum and it is expressly stated that they cannot be modified, they will be immutable (CA 1985, s 17);

- if the memorandum provides a mechanism for modification, that mechanism must be used (subject to CA 1985, s 125(3));

- if the class rights are set out in the memorandum and the articles adopted on the company's incorporation provide a mechanism, that mechanism must be used (subject to CA 1985, s 125(3));

- if the class rights are conferred by the memorandum and no provision is made in either the memorandum or the articles for their modification, they may be varied only if all the members agree (CA 1985, s 125(5)) or pursuant to a scheme of arrangement under CA 1985, s 425;

- if the rights are not specified in the memorandum and the articles do not provide a variation procedure, they may be varied either by written consent of the holders of three-quarters in nominal value of the issued shares of the class in question or by an extraordinary resolution passed at a separate general meeting of the holders of that class (CA 1985, s 125(2));

- if (which is the most common situation in practice) the rights are not specified in the memorandum and the articles contain provision for their variation, the procedure in the articles must be used (subject as provided in CA 1985, s 125(3)).

The rights which are afforded to shares will almost always include the right (subject in some cases to the prior rights of other classes of share, eg preference shares) to dividends (if declared) and to repayment of capital (on a winding up or otherwise). Ordinary shares will also have voting rights, while preference shares may carry a vote, or may do so in certain events. Another right which can be attached to preference shares is the right to convert such shares into ordinary shares.

A further right which can be attached to a class of shares is the right to appoint and remove one or more directors.

All of these rights can be protected by the use of different classes of share and in practice joint venture companies are sometimes found to have separate classes of share held by each venturer merely so as to entrench that venturer's right to appoint and remove one or more directors. The establishment of different classes of share can also be used to reflect the different contributions made by the various parties to the business of the joint venture.

Unfairly prejudicial conduct

Section 459 of CA 1985 entitles a member of a company to apply to the court on the grounds that the company's affairs are being or have been conducted in a manner which is unfairly prejudicial to the interests of its members generally or of some part of the members (including at least himself) or that any actual or proposed act or omission of the company (including an act or omission on its behalf) is or would be so prejudicial.

If the court is satisfied that a petition is well-founded, it may make such order as it thinks fit for giving relief in respect of the matters complained of. For example, the court may require the company not to make any, or any specified, alteration in the memorandum or articles or require the alteration of the memorandum or articles. The court may make orders regulating the future conduct of the company's affairs; requiring the company to refrain from doing or continuing an act complained of by the petitioner; authorising civil proceedings to be brought in the name of the company; providing for the purchase of the shares of any members of the company by other members or by the company itself.

Since these provisions were introduced by CA 1980 there has been a great number of cases, but very few clear decisions of principle. It is not necessary for there to be an invasion of legal rights for the protections of s 459 to be available and the general tendency of recent cases has been to construe the provisions in a broad and purposive way. The courts have been inconsistent in answering the question whether conduct by a company which prima facie affects all the members equally can ever be conduct which is unfairly prejudicial to the interests of some part of the members, but in this respect the law has been clarified by CA 1989, which amends s 459 so as to include conduct which is unfairly prejudicial to the interests of members generally, as opposed to only some part of the members.

The relationship between shareholders in the joint venture company is often described as being a quasi-partnership. The courts have been very reluctant to allow a shareholder in such a quasi-partnership to seek an order under s 459 requiring the purchase of his shares on a basis different from that provided for in the articles. This is so even where pre-emption articles do not guarantee that the price will not be at a discount by reason of the petitioner holding only a minority interest: *Re Abbey Leisure Ltd* (1989) 5 BCC 183; *Re A Company (No 006834 of 1988)* (1989) 5 BCC 218; *Re Castleburn Ltd* (1989) 5 BCC 652.

A minority shareholder would be most unwise to rely exclusively on the provisions of s 459.

Winding up on just and equitable grounds

Section 122(1)(g) of the Insolvency Act 1986 provides that a company may be wound up by the court if the court is of the opinion that it is just and equitable that the company should be wound up. The leading case of *Ebrahimi v Westbourne Galleries Ltd* [1973] AC 360 demonstrates that the court will take into account conduct of the parties which breaches some agreement between the members, even where no fraud or bad faith can be proved. This is particularly so where the company is formed on the basis of a personal relationship, where there is some understanding as to shareholder participation in the conduct of the business, or where a member cannot sell out because of restrictions on the transfer of his interest. Similarly, it seems that the breaking down of an agreement that a shareholder will participate in all major decisions relating to the company's affairs is sufficient basis for a winding-up order: *Re Noble & Sons (Clothing) Limited* [1983] BCLC 273.

Use of s 122 must be seen as a remedy of last resort. It is far better to legislate at the outset for what happens when the parties fall out rather than submit the problem for resolution by the courts. The methods commonly used to terminate joint venture arrangements are examined in 4.8 below.

4.4 Shareholders' agreements

The relationship between shareholders in a joint venture company will typically be governed by two documents, the articles of association and the shareholders' agreement. The balancing of these two documents, and the avoidance of conflict between them, are among the greater skills needed in connection with the establishment of a joint venture company.

Some joint ventures, eg those between professional partnerships, choose to regulate their day-to-day affairs by regulations and rules made pursuant to the articles of association, generally by an executive committee constituted by the members. These rules and regulations operate in a manner similar to the rules and regulations of a club, in that they have a binding contractual effect between the parties by virtue of the contract created by the articles of association. However, more commonly the agreement will be independent of the articles and have contractual force in its own right.

In many cases the details of the relationships between the parties will be highly sensitive or contain information which would be of help to commercial competitors. Shareholders' agreements have the considerable advantage of being private documents, as opposed to articles of association which are a public document.

Another reason for using a shareholders' agreement is to ensure that the rights and remedies given to each shareholder are appropriate to the contribution that that particular shareholder makes to the company. The articles of association will apply to all members alike (including new members) and the introduction of a new member may well then require amendment of the articles by special resolution.

The parties to the agreement may be some or all of the shareholders and commonly the company itself will be joined as a party so that the shareholders have contractual rights against the company which are independent of the articles and thereby can avoid the difficulties of maintaining an action under the articles as a result of the rule in *Foss v Harbottle* (1843) 2 Hare 461. The rights of parties under a shareholders' agreement are enforceable in the same manner as any contract and are not exclusive of any other remedies which might otherwise be available: *Re A & BC Chewing Gum* [1975] 1 All ER 1017.

There is some debate over whether shareholders' agreements can in some circumstances be registrable at the Companies Registry by virtue of the provisions of CA 1985, s 380(4)(c). This subsection requires the registration of resolutions or agreements which have been agreed to by all the members of a company but which, if not so agreed to, would not have been effective for their purpose unless there had been a special or extraordinary resolution passed. The better view is that such agreements, if not specifically referred to in the articles, are not registrable as they do not purport to vary the rights of the members of the company qua member and do not therefore bind subsequent members of the company who do not themselves consent to the arrangement.

It is standard practice to provide that the shareholders' agreement takes precedence over the articles where the two conflict. However, it is far preferable to avoid any conflict in the first place, thus avoiding any question of the agreement amounting to an agreement to alter the articles which could be registrable under s 380.

4.5 Controlling the membership of the company

Use of pre-emption rights

The identity of the company's shareholders is usually of critical importance to the continued success of the venture. Especially in the early years the parties will be concerned to ensure that their co-venturers are fully committed to the project. If one of them disposes of his shares, and with them his economic interest in the company, he will no longer have the same incentive to ensure the company's prosperity. It is therefore very common to find not only restrictions on transfers per se, but also rights of pre-emption in favour of the other shareholders.

The courts have traditionally given a narrow construction to such provisions and this approach stems from the basic premise that shares are prima facie freely transferable. An absolute prohibition on disposal is probably unlawful. This is the natural inference to draw from CA 1985, s 182(1)(b) which provides that the shares of any member in a company are transferable in the manner provided by the company's articles. However, there is nothing to limit the restrictions on the right of transfer which a company may impose by its articles. Such restrictions, though permanent, do not contravene the English law against perpetuities.

It will rarely be sufficient to rely on the provisions of Table A. Regulation 24 empowers the directors to refuse to register the transfer of a share which is not fully paid to a person of whom they do not approve or of a share on which the company has a lien. The absence of any restriction on the transfer of fully paid shares will hardly ever be acceptable.

If the right of transfer is to be taken away or cut down then it must be done by words of sufficient clarity to make it apparent that that was the intention (*Greenhalgh v Mallard* [1943] 2 All ER 234, 237, per Lord Greene MR).

The courts will not construe an article so strictly as to defeat its obvious intention, but recent cases have illustrated the need for careful drafting. In *Safeguard Industrial Investments v National Westminster Bank* [1982] 1 All ER 449 Vinelott J considered the effect of articles which, except in the case of a transfer to certain close relatives of a shareholder, required the shareholder to give notice of transfer to the company and then to offer the shares to the other members pro rata. If a member was willing to purchase the shares at their fair value, the shares could not be transferred to a non-member. Vinelott J held that the defendants were not proposing transferors within the meaning of the articles as 'transfer' is only apt when describing the transfer of legal title and not appropriate in the context of the transfer of a purely beneficial interest.

In *Lyle & Scott v Scott's Trustees* [1959] AC 763 the House of Lords held that a shareholder who transferred or purported to transfer the beneficial interest in a share to a purchaser for value was merely endeavouring by a subterfuge to escape from the pre-emption provisions of the articles. A sale of a share was a sale of the beneficial rights that it conferred and to sell or purport to sell the beneficial rights without the title to the shares was a plain breach of the provisions of the particular article. However, in the *Safeguard* case, Vinelott J and the Court of Appeal (affirming Vinelott J's decision) agreed that the *Scott* case was only authority as to whether or not particular shareholders were desirous of transferring their shares. Vinelott J and the Court of Appeal followed the decision of Lord Hailsham LC in *Hunter v Hunter* [1936] AC 222. There the main question was whether a mortgagee's power of sale over shares had become exercisable and, if it had, whether a purported sale by the mortgagee was in breach of pre-emption provisions. Lord Hailsham indicated that, if the mortgagee had been selling the equitable interest in the shares, none of the provisions of the article as to restrictions on the possible purchasers or as to the method of fixing the price would have been effective. It would have been a quite different transaction from a sale of the shares.

Clear drafting is therefore essential. If a restriction is to be effective, it should provide that the rights of pre-emption apply to any attempt to transfer or otherwise dispose of any interest, whether legal or equitable, in the shares. An appropriately drafted clause should prevent disposal of control over the voting rights attaching to the shares and also of the right to receive dividends. It is desirable to include the restrictions on transfer both in the articles and, either verbatim or by reference, in the shareholders agreement.

4.6 Management of the joint venture company

Appointment of directors

The shareholders will wish to ensure that the joint venture company is run in accordance with their wishes. Although they may not wish to be involved in the day-to-day operations, they will wish to be kept fully informed and to have some assurance that the directors will not act against their interests. Commonly, therefore, the board will be drawn directly from the major shareholders, each of whom will have a right to nominate their own officers. The usual and most convenient way of conferring this right is through the rights attached to the shares.

There are certain drawbacks associated with such class rights. The directors will have to work together and they should therefore be acceptable to each other. It is clearly undesirable that the best available person should not be chosen or that the promotion of employees from within the venture should be restricted unnecessarily.

The duties of nominee directors

The directors of a company are under a fiduciary duty to exercise their powers for the benefit of the company as a whole, and not for the benefit of the directors themselves, or for a section of the shareholders, or for employees of the company, or for the company's holding company or subsidiary, or for outsiders. This is so even if the directors in question are nominated by outsiders or by a particular shareholder or group of shareholders to represent his or their interests.

That is not to say that it is necessarily unlawful for a director to exercise his powers in accordance with the instructions of an outsider, or otherwise with a view to protecting an outsider's interests, provided that in doing so he pays proper regard to the interests of the shareholders as a whole.

Directors must not put themselves in a position where there is a conflict (actual or potential) between their personal interest and their duties to the company. If a director makes a prior engagement with an outsider (for example, the company nominating him to the board) to vote in the outsider's interests on particular transactions, thereby leaving himself no independent discretion whatsoever to consider the company's interests in the matter, he is in breach of duty. Such a director would be liable for any consequent misapplication of property. However, the status of nominee does not of itself give rise to such a conflict: any breach of duty must be proved on the facts of the particular case.

Control of the board by a shareholder through its nominee directors may also amount to unfair prejudice under CA 1985, s 459. Thus, where a holding company deliberately and successfully pursued the policy of starving out its partly-owned subsidiary on whose five-man board it had three nominee directors, the minority members successfully brought an action for oppression under CA 1948, s 210 (s 459's rather narrower predecessor): *Scottish Co-operative Wholesale Society v Meyer* [1959] AC 324. Lord Denning held that the nominees had put their duty to the holding company before their duty to the subsidiary and, although they honestly thought that as nominees of the holding company their first duty was to the holding company, in this they were wrong. In subordinating the interests of the subsidiary to those of the holding company and in failing to do anything to defend the company's interests where they ought to have taken some action they had conducted the affairs of the subsidiary in a manner oppressive to the other shareholders.

These constraints on the actions of nominee directors are often unwelcome in the context of a joint venture, but reflect a general rule of equity stated by Lord Cranworth LC in *Aberdeen Railway Co v Blaikie Bros* (1854) 1 Macq 461, 471:

> No-one, having [fiduciary] duties to discharge, shall be allowed to enter into engagements in which he has, or can have, a personal interest conflicting, or which possibly may conflict with the interest of those whom he is bound to protect . . . no question is allowed to be raised as to the fairness or unfairness of a contract so entered into.

Directors may sometimes be placed in a position where, although their interest and duty conflict, they can properly and honestly give their services to both sides and serve two masters to the great advantage of both. However, in no circumstances is it open to the fiduciary to relax the rule. But, since the rule is one essentially for the protection of the person to whom the duty is owed, the person entitled to its benefit may relax it to such extent as he thinks proper: *Boulting v ACTAT* [1963] 2 QB 606, CA.

Directors who blindly follow the instructions of the shareholder without giving any thought to the propriety of the proposed action will be liable for any loss which results to the company and may even be guilty of misfeasance: *Re London & South Western Canal Ltd* [1911] 1 Ch 346. A director is put into an impossible position where his two loyalties conflict. He must either put the interests of the company first, or resign his directorship. If he is not to be in breach of his duty, the director must preserve a substantial degree of independent discretion as to how he will exercise his powers.

The question arises: how can joint venturers ensure that their own interests are protected? The solution frequently adopted is to withdraw areas of potential conflict from the authority of the board.

Reserving important decisions

A number of methods are available to ensure that important decisions are not made without the consent of all the parties. However, the corollary to that control is the increased risk of deadlock.

Some matters will always be of critical importance to the parties. If there is any likelihood of dividends becoming payable, the parties will wish to establish a distribution policy which can only be changed with the consent of all the shareholders. Particularly sensitive will be the issue of new shares and the introduction of new shareholders. Other issues may be important because of their effect on ancillary contracts in which a member is interested, or because they impinge on the business activities of the company itself (for example, the authority to purchase major assets or to borrow money above a certain level), or, more importantly, because they affect the value of the participants' shares in the joint venture company.

Subject to the law relating to fraud on the minority and the remedies available under CA 1985, s 459 and the rather extreme action of seeking a winding up on the 'just and equitable ground', the majority will always govern the minority. Both positive and negative restrictions can be invoked to protect the shareholder. Stringent quorum requirements can be imposed or a vote in favour of the proposal by the affected shareholder can be required.

Probably the most effective method of structuring a decision-making process in a joint venture company is to restrict the authority of management, reserving the most important matters to the parties themselves. The objective should be to ensure that those decisions which may affect the value of the venturers' stakes in the joint venture company are reserved to the parties themselves, but that such restrictions do not prevent the day-to-day management of the business of the company.

The articles of association generally contain provisions delegating authority to manage the business of the company to the board of directors. Once this power has been delegated it is not open to the members to seek to manage the company themselves by resolution (*Breckland Group Holdings Ltd v London and Suffolk Properties Ltd* [1989] BCLC 100). These terms will therefore, in the case of a joint venture company, need to be adapted so that there is reserved from the general power of management delegated to the board of directors, those matters which the shareholders feel are particularly important. As the parties may not always wish to set out these matters exhaustively in the articles of association, it is not uncommon for the articles to contain a summary of those matters to be reserved which are capable of affecting third parties, and for a fuller list, including those matters and matters which are relevant as between the shareholders themselves, to be set out in the shareholders' agreement.

Dealing with the reservation of important matters in this way prevents them being raised at board meetings where the directors may face problems by virtue of their fiduciary duties.

A clause operating by restriction of quorum may take effect by providing that no vote may be taken upon an issue unless a particular director or member attends the meeting. If unanimity is required the clause should prevent the board (or company) from taking action without the consent of the minority shareholder or its representative. It will not alter the majority in such a meeting but may prevent a decision being taken. As with any restriction on the management of a company the ability of one party to cause deadlock should be avoided and, in cases where a restriction by quorum is stipulated, provision should be made for an 'empty chair' clause to prevent the dissenting shareholder from obstructing the business of the company by non-attendance at meetings.

If the company is unable to carry on its business because meetings of shareholders are inquorate the court has power under CA 1985, s 371 to convene meetings on such terms as it thinks fit and the courts have shown themselves willing to use these powers where otherwise deadlock will ensue: *Re Opera Photographic Ltd* (1989) 5 BCC 601. Such obstruction of the company's business may also bring the provisions of CA 1985, s 459 into play on the grounds that such behaviour is unfairly prejudicial conduct.

Usually the appropriate place for such restrictions is in the articles where they will automatically affect new members. However, certain matters may be of such a nature that the shareholders' agreement will be the more appropriate place, for example decisions affecting ancillary agreements between the company and the member or restrictions of a confidential nature.

Day-to-day management

If a managing director has been appointed, he will be responsible for the day-to-day management of the company. Similarly, committees will be delegated many decision-making tasks. At some point it may be deemed expedient to demand that particular decisions be taken by the entire board of directors, or that some decisions should lie with the shareholders in general meeting. If one party has a majority of directors or a majority of the votes available to be cast in general meeting, the other party can protect its position by demanding that no resolution affecting particular issues should be deemed to have been passed unless there is either unanimity or a specified majority.

Joint ventures involving foreign parties pose their own special problems. In particular, it is important to ensure that directors based abroad receive adequate notice of board meetings, both in terms of notice period and in the details of the business to be transacted at the board meeting. The provisions of Table A will certainly require amendment. Regulation 88 provides that it is not necessary to give notice of a meeting to a director who is absent from the United Kingdom. There is also no specific notice period required.

Dealings with third parties

The Companies Act 1985 provides substantial protection to third parties in their dealings with a company and despite extensive controls over management incorporated into the articles or the shareholders' agreement, a party may find that the company is bound by a contract with a third party even though a particular director had no actual authority to conclude the contract on behalf of the company. The Companies Act 1989 has improved the position of third parties who seek to enforce a contract which has been entered into by a director without proper authority. The new s 35A of CA 1985, inserted by s 108 of the Companies Act 1989, provides that, in favour of a person dealing with a company in good faith, the power of the board of directors to bind the company, or authorise others to do so, is to be deemed free of any limitation under the company's constitution. A person is not regarded as acting in bad faith by reason only of his knowing that an act is beyond the powers of the directors under the company's constitution (CA 1985, s 35A(2)(b)) and such third party is not bound to inquire as to whether there is any limitation on the powers of the board of directors to bind the company or authorise others to do so (CA 1985, s 35B).

In addition, CA 1989 has added a new s 711A to the 1985 Act. The new section provides that a person is not to be taken to have notice of any matter merely because of its being disclosed in any document available for inspection at the Companies Registry or at the company's registered office.

In order, therefore, to avoid a contract with a third party it will be necessary to show that the third party not only knew of the relevant restriction, but also was aware that the transaction in question was being entered into improperly.

The rule in Turquand's Case

The common law has also long afforded protection to third parties. The rule in Turquand's case (*Royal British Bank v Turquand* (1856) 6 E & B 327) is designed to protect outsiders in their dealings with the seemingly authorised agents of the company. Even where a person dealing with a company has notice of its constitutional documents, he is not affected by matters of 'indoor management'. He is entitled to assume that the internal procedures of a company, both at directors' and shareholders' meetings, have been regularly conducted in the absence of actual notice to the contrary.

Deadlock: how to break it

The corollary to reserving control over important decisions to each of the shareholders is the increased risk of deadlock. In the event of deadlock the parties need to have available a mechanism for resolving the impasse.

It is not always clear when a deadlock has occurred as the parties may disagree on this issue. Consideration should therefore be given to defining the situations in which the members will be considered to be in deadlock.

There are several, more or less extreme, methods of resolving a deadlock.

(a) Turn to an independent third party
This is not a very satisfactory method of resolving an impasse as the disagreement may not turn upon a question of sound business judgment but rather contrary interests or business preferences. For example, one shareholder may need a large cash dividend while the other wishes to reinvest, expand and capitalise on an advantageous market position. How is the outsider to weigh these conflicting elements of self-interest?

(b) Give a casting vote to a member of the board
This may have advantages where the director is independent of the parties and familiar with the joint venture, although the difficulties identified in (a) above may still apply. Where the director is an appointee of a shareholder his lack of impartiality is rarely likely to be acceptable. In any event, if he is an active member of the board he may decide an issue in favour of one party before both parties have had sufficient opportunity to work out a compromise. Sometimes it is provided that such a person will only vote in cases of 'serious' deadlock, but such a provision leaves him with insufficient guidelines by which to determine his role.

(c) Arbitration
Arbitration is more appropriate for deciding the legal rights of the parties than for resolving matters of policy. An arbitration mechanism may be used for deciding whether those rights have been infringed (eg a resolution improperly passed) but an alternative mechanism should be available for resolving policy deadlocks, with arbitration (or court proceedings) as a last resort.

(d) Termination: buy out or sell out
These sorts of provisions are the most common way of breaking a deadlock and frequently constitute the most difficult part of joint venture negotiations. They are considered in more detail in 4.8 below.

4.7 Voting agreements and voting trusts

Generally a shareholder may exercise his vote as he pleases, for as Lord Maugham said in *Carruth v Imperial Chemical Industries Ltd* [1937] AC 707:

> The shareholder's vote is a right of property, and prima facie may be exercised by a shareholder as he thinks fit in his own interest.

Thus, he is quite free to enter into an agreement with others as to how he will exercise that right and such an agreement will be enforceable between the parties by an injunction: *Greenwell v Carter* [1902] 1 Ch 530; *Puddephat v Leith* [1916] 1 Ch 200. This general proposition has only limited application in the case of directors who cannot bind themselves to vote qua director except bona fide in the interests of the company as a whole.

A voting trust involves the voting rights of all or some of the shares in the company being settled upon trust. This has been a practice much more common in the United States than in the United Kingdom, but such trusts can be a very flexible instrument of control. The trustees may be given a wide or a very limited discretion. It is, however, a more formal device than a shareholders agreement since the trustees get title to the shares. This may have disadvantages for the original shareholder who may lose his membership rights and not be able to control the trustees.

A similar device, but one which avoids the shareholder losing title to the shares, is the grant of an irrevocable proxy to exercise voting rights on behalf of the member. To be irrevocable the proxy must be coupled with a security interest, but this probably requires no more than that the proxy is given for a valuable consideration.

4.8 Termination and transfer of shares

Reasons for termination

The termination provisions are of crucial importance. The reasons for the parties wishing to terminate their relationship fall under five principal headings:

(a) one of the parties wishes to transfer his interest to another party or to an outsider;

(b) the agreement has achieved its purpose;

(c) there has been a breach of the agreement and the innocent party wishes to withdraw;

(d) the parties are in deadlock;

(e) events have made further collaboration undesirable or impracticable.

The aim should be to provide a flexible response whatever the reason for termination. There should be scope for the joint venture business to continue and also an effective means of dissolution. Whether the business continues or is dissolved, a method of valuing the parties' interests will need to be devised and the impact on connected agreements will have to be considered, together with the extent to which any rights or duties ought to survive termination or new rights and duties ought to be imposed.

The shareholders' agreement will commonly restrict the right to terminate at will in the earlier years by providing that there should be no termination for a fixed period after formation.

Where one of the parties is to withdraw from the venture, but the business itself is to continue, a procedure for transferring that party's interest either to an existing party or to a new party must be available. A distinction has to be made between voluntary and compulsory transfers.

Voluntary transfers

Restrictions on voluntary transfers will reflect the respective roles played by the parties to the shareholders' agreement. If one party possesses critical skills and facilities, the withdrawal of that party in the early years of the joint venture would effectively mean dissolution and an absolute prohibition may be appropriate. If withdrawal is not so serious because a new partner would be able to provide a like facility, then a requirement of consent may be all that is necessary.

By far the most popular type of restriction on transfer is that of first refusal. Rights of first refusal carry with them a built-in valuation mechanism and give to the remaining parties the greatest possible number of options. Because many joint ventures are highly speculative and in rapidly growing fields of research, the parties may be reluctant to commit themselves at the time of formation to any fixed formula for valuation. However, if the scope of the joint venture's activities can be predicted with reasonable certainty a formula may be chosen and the non-selling party may be given an option to buy either at the price determined by the formula regardless of the offer, or at the lower of the offer and the formula price. The mechanism for first refusal is very flexible.

To take an example: a joint venture company has been formed by two parties. If A wishes to sell, it must first negotiate with B to set a fair value for its shares; if they cannot agree the issue is submitted to an expert for determination. B then has an option to purchase at this price. If B decides not to purchase, A then has six months to sell its shares to a third party for a price that is at least equal to this figure. If A finds that it must sell at a price below that originally offered to B before the six months expires, B has first refusal at this lower price.

The disadvantage of this method from B's point of view is that B has no control over the identity of its new partner if A finds someone to purchase at the option price. However, this may put added pressure on B to buy A's shares and thus encourage a prompt resolution of the problem.

Compulsory transfers

Typically the right to compel transfer will arise when one of the parties is in breach of the shareholders' agreement. The non-defaulting party is given the option of buying out the defaulter or of disposing of his own interest to the defaulter (or to a third party). Some of these methods can also be used as part of a deadlock breaking mechanism, but in such cases there is not normally an 'innocent' and a 'defaulting' party, so that the terms, particularly in respect of valuation, have to operate more even-handedly.

Put and call options

Put and call options are very common and receipt of a notice expressing a wish to exercise the option will oblige the recipient to comply with the terms of the option either to buy the other shares (in the case of a put option) or to sell them (in the case of a call option) at the agreed value. The means for determining the value of the shares will normally mirror those applicable to voluntary transfers. Such options, unless contained in the articles, are subject to the rule against perpetuities.

If foreign laws prohibit an outsider holding more than a certain percentage of the shares, it will be futile to include provisions which allow the foreign partner to buy out the resident partner. The clauses should either allow or require the resident partner to purchase all the shares.

Russian roulette provisions

Russian roulette provisions are only really appropriate where there are only two parties and they do not mind whether they sell their own interest or buy that of the other party. The procedure is said to have had its origins in Justinian's Code, the idea being that one divides and the other chooses. Although it provides a reasonable guarantee that each party will receive a fair value for its shares, the uncertainty and risk are unattractive. A form of Russian roulette clause is included in the specimen shareholders' agreement in Appendix 2.

The procedure normally works as follows:

1   If A wants to sell:
    (a) A offers his shares to B for a price specified by A.
    (b) If B does not wish to buy at that price, A then is obliged to buy B's shares at the same price.

2   If A wants to buy:
    (a) A offers to buy B's shares at a specified price.
    (b) If B does not wish to sell, B is obliged to buy A's shares at the same price.

There are many variations of this basic concept. For example, the parties may be given time to attempt to reach agreement on a price and in default a fair value for the shares will be determined by an expert. Thereafter the appropriate party will have the right within a specified period to purchase all of the other's shares. Failure to exercise that right will entitle the other to purchase the former's shares. If neither right is exercised, each party may by notice to the directors require the convening of a general meeting for the purpose of considering a resolution to wind up the company. The agreement will provide that at the meeting no member will vote otherwise than in favour of the resolution unless all members present otherwise agree.

Auction provisions ('shoot out')

Auction provisions are useful where one party no longer wishes to participate, but both parties are interested in acquiring the joint venture's shares or assets.

The agreement will provide for service of a notice by the terminating party indicating whether he wishes to buy the other's shares or the company's assets. The other party is then given a specified time in which to serve a counter notice indicating his interest in buying the terminating party's shares or the company's assets.

If both wish to buy, each submits a sealed bid to a person acting as auctioneer. If they cannot agree upon a choice of an auctioneer, he will be nominated by a third party. At this stage it is open to either party to withdraw from the auction, in which case the assets are transferred at the price stated in the other party's bid. If both make bids, an auction will be held.

The terms upon which the auction is to be conducted can be set out fully in the agreement or a broad measure of discretion may be conferred on the auctioneer. In either case it is highly desirable to consult with the appointer or auctioneer to ensure that the method of conducting the auction is one which is workable. In some cases the terms provide that the terminating party's bid is disclosed to the other, who has to exceed such bid (if any) by a fixed percentage. This method is often used to ensure that each party will be reluctant to terminate, as it will place the other party in a much stronger position.

Auction provisions are only effective if it is absolutely clear what shares or assets are subject to auction and what each party is bidding for. Where, before termination, the parties have unequal shares in the assets, or have shares carrying unequal rights, care needs to be taken to ensure that the bids are comparable.

Chapter 5

Collaboration agreements

5.1 Introduction

Meaning and advantages

In recent years there has been a tendency towards the increased use of collaboration agreements as a means of bringing together companies, public sector organisations, scientific and educational establishments and individuals, both on a national and international scale. While the variety of collaboration agreements is manifold, the common thread uniting them is the *combination* they create through *contract*. Each party brings to the collaboration a different resource, whether it be assets, finance, expertise or otherwise. The parties will perceive that they can add value to their own resources through the collaboration. While the price for this will be, in part, the loss of independence through the obligations of collaboration, this will be seen as more than counterbalanced by the gains to be made from the collaboration. Further, while combination might be effected through a joint venture company or some formalised unincorporated association, often this will not suit collaborators who will see collaboration through contract as presenting a more flexible method of bringing the parties together. In this way, they are not faced with the constraints of a corporate vehicle or the unfamiliarity of an unincorporated association. They can avoid not only the cost of establishing, running and liquidating the company, but also the bureaucratic culture that companies or unincorporated associations spawn, such as the need for 'board' meetings and meetings of shareholders or the members of an association.

Collaboration agreements are essentially contracts for services and will contain many of the characteristics of such contracts, although some joint venture techniques may also be applied to the parties. They may, however, constitute partnerships if they result in the carrying on of a business by the collaborators (see for example, *Walker West Developments Ltd v FJ Emmett* (1979) 252 EG 1171)) and therefore should also be considered in the light of the cautions set out in Chapter 3.

Examples of collaboration agreements

As mentioned above, there are many varieties of collaboration agreements. Thus, one case may involve a manufacture and sale agreement whereby a manufacturer of a product and a party with expertise in selling that product combine. Alternatively, two or more parties might set up a forum where they exchange ideas or know-how or pool together similar assets with a view to exploiting jointly or severally that which is seen as worth exploiting. This leads to, perhaps, the paradigm example of collaboration, namely collaborating in research and development ('R&D collaboration').

R&D Collaboration

The rest of this chapter will analyse R&D collaboration agreements. As it would not be feasible in a chapter of this length to consider all varieties of collaboration agreements, the R&D collaboration agreement has been chosen as a model for analysis. This is for a number of reasons. First, there is considerable experience to date on these agreements. Secondly, they may be more familiar to readers. Thirdly, with the continual exhortation by government and others to invest in R&D and the growing willingness of 'institutions' to collaborate (such as universities, other higher education establishments and the public sector), an increase in the demand for R&D collaboration agreements is likely. Finally, it is thought that the R&D collaboration agreement encompasses many of the concepts and problems that will be applicable to most other collaboration agreements.

Even within the concept of the R&D collaboration agreement, there are a number of varieties. Some R&D collaborations are conducted through incorporated joint ventures. This might typically occur in projects involving a university, where the university forms a subsidiary which is funded through external parties. The shareholders might include the university (or its R&D subsidiary), individual scientists working on the project plus possibly the financiers and external industrial or commercial participants in the project. The joint venture company will solicit ideas from scientists and engineers working within the university with a view to funding to the point of development those ideas that seem the most promising. The financiers might take their reward either through a combination of a straight repayment of their advances plus a share in the income received from the commercial exploitation of the chosen ideas to give them some 'profit' (although, of course, they would have to be careful not to create a partnership) or the ability to develop the chosen ideas themselves.

A second example is the so-called 'club' where a number of parties (predominantly industrial companies), often numbering ten or more, will sponsor a programme of work by an establishment (again, for example, a university) and in return for their sponsorship they will receive, on a non-exclusive basis, the results of the programme of work.

A third example is where a party (generally, a financier) agrees to collaborate with another in a particular field of endeavour on the basis that the latter will put forward proposals to the former (and no others) involving particular projects within the field. The former then has the opportunity of either funding that project on terms previously agreed or allowing the other to seek third party support.

In the rest of this chapter, this final variety is taken as the model for analysis. First, the general business considerations facing the collaborators are considered. Secondly, the provisions that might be included in a collaboration agreement will be examined. A specimen collaboration agreement is set out in Appendix 4.

The analysis is considered primarily from the point of view of the party providing finance because, generally speaking, it will be this party that prepares the documentation. For convenience, this party is referred to as 'the company' and the other party as 'the contractor'. This is not to say that one may not find more than two parties to a collaboration or that 'the contractor' must be one of the many industrial organisations providing a R&D service. Indeed, as mentioned below, many trans-national collaborations will involve one or more contractors and the contractors themselves will include public sector organisations (such as laboratories, research councils and dedicated R&D establishments together with universities, polytechnics and technical colleges). Equally, the company should not be seen as the stereotype provider of finance. Often, the contractor will be looking for a collaborator who provides more than just finance. It may be looking for a party with the ability to exploit commercially the fruits of the work it produces. Thus, the company may not be a bank or the traditional venture capital organisation. Instead, it might be an industrial conglomerate or one of the growing number of companies funding R&D projects on a 'hands-on' basis, ie providing the contractor with not only funds but also advice on the direction of the projects funded.

What follows considers the research and development phase rather than the exploitation phase. The latter is beyond the scope of this chapter. Exploitation will take predominantly one of three routes. First, the assignment to a third party of the fruits of the work of the contractor. Secondly, the establishment, by the company and possibly the contractor, of a company to manufacture, market and sell the product arising from the collaboration. Thirdly, the licensing to a third party of the product or process developed. The reader will find examples of these agreements in other publications.

5.2 General business considerations

Before looking at the provisions that might be included in R&D collaboration agreements, it would be worthwhile noting some of the general points that the parties might consider. These considerations can conveniently be looked at by reference to the logical phases of the collaboration, namely selecting a collaborator, agreeing the structure for the collaboration, determining which projects to undertake and then, finally, considering the external finance that might be available.

Selecting a collaborator

5.1 above touched on the nature of the company with which the contractor might contract. The company, for its part, will need to consider carefully with whom it should be collaborating, especially if the collaboration is to last for a reasonable period of time.

It is a trait of research and development work that not all projects commenced will, in the final analysis, progress to a product or process that may be successfully exploited. This is especially so where the work is more 'research' than 'development'. As a result the company is likely to be looking for a collaboration over a number of projects. It should not base its selection therefore by reference to one particular project. It needs to choose a contractor that either has a successful 'track record' in the proposed area of collaboration or a contractor that has the necessary 'experts' in that area.

It will want to assure itself that the contractor has not only the necessary personnel but also the necessary facilities to undertake the work. The company will be particularly concerned to obtain as much comfort as possible that the facilities of the contractor will be available for the project and will not be diverted to other concerns. Furthermore, as regards the personnel to work on the project, it has to be anticipated that one or more individuals may leave the contractor, and it is therefore important that not only should the contractor have a team of people on hand (so that the loss of one individual can be accommodated) but also the contractor must be of sufficient standing that it is able to attract replacements with the necessary qualifications, experience and expertise. Often, the company will find that initial contacts leading to the collaboration are engineered through the scientists. If this is the case, the company will wish to check that the 'management' of the contractor is prepared to demonstrate an equal commitment to the collaboration.

In the final analysis, notwithstanding the legal documentation, whether or not the collaboration works will turn upon the willingness of the parties to work together. The cultures of the company and the contractor may be vastly different. It therefore behoves the company to select from its own staff those employees who are most likely to work effectively with the scientists **at** the contractor. There will be a need for periodic meetings in order to ensure from the company's point of view that the project is proceeding in the direction most likely to achieve commercial success. It is to be noted that scientific success is not necessarily the same thing as commercial success.

Finally, as important as choosing a collaborator is selecting the area of collaboration. On the one hand, the area of collaboration should not necessarily be commensurate with the initial project that the parties have in hand, on the other hand the area should not be so broad as to lack focus. Ideally, the company should be seeking to collaborate in a particular market area using a particular type of technology. Thus, for example, agreeing to collaborate 'in biotechnology', apart from being without focus is also unlikely to be acceptable to the contractor if the collaboration restricts collaborating with others. It would seem more efficacious to define the collaboration as, say, 'developing kits for diagnosing x, y, z diseases through the use of monoclonal and polyclonal antibodies technology'.

Structure

A number of structures for the collaboration are possible. The paradigm example has two features. First, the parties agree to collaborate in a defined field and the contractor puts forward proposals within the field for the company to fund. Secondly, the contractor undertakes the particular projects which the company agrees to fund. As will be seen, these two features are reflected by two separate documents—the collaboration agreement and the project contract. One or other of these documents will establish the principal objectives of the contractor with regard to the work to be undertaken, dates for completion, costs and standard of work.

In agreeing a structure to suit their purposes, the parties will have to consider whether there are any external constraints. In particular, regard must be had to fiscal and anti-trust considerations together with other legislation that may affect what the parties can undertake (particularly relevant in the field of R&D will be government regulations on health and safety and other environmental matters).

Selecting the projects

Once the collaboration has been established, the contractor will bring forward projects for consideration by the company. The next section suggests a helpful format in which the contractor may put forward these proposals. On receipt of the proposals, however, the company will have to consider how best to analyse the projects. This may be undertaken in a

67

number of ways. First, the review may be undertaken jointly by representatives of the company and the contractor. This has obvious disadvantages, the most notable being that the contractor is the person least likely to be able to give an objective and unbiased view on the proposal. Secondly, the company might refer the proposal to some external body for review—a 'peer group'. While this has an advantage in that the eminence of the peer group may be such that the contractor would find it attractive and acceptable to have the project reviewed by such an august body, on the other hand, the company would be sacrificing its control of funding to a third party. However such a group might also have an ongoing involvement. This could materially assist the company in supervising quality control and the direction of the project once under way. The third possibility is for the company to determine whether to fund, having taken into account the views of its own eminent consultants. This allows the company to have the 'science' of the project reviewed by consultants, while retaining to itself a review of 'business' factors.

In totality, the review will need to address many factors. Particularly critical will be a risk analysis of the project. Six key risk factors might be contemplated. First, whether the project can achieve technological success. Secondly, the strengths and weaknesses of the personnel working on the project with particular reference to the possibility of one or more employees leaving the contractor. Thirdly, in so far as one can, one needs to consider whether third parties are undertaking the same work and, if so, how advanced are they and how strong a competitor are they likely to be? Fourthly, one needs to be assured that there is a market for the projected product or process and, in particular, whether the sales forecast will meet the project costs and the desired return on the investment. Fifthly, bearing in mind that, by definition, one is creating a novel product or process, one needs to assess the potential for products being defective or leading to injury or loss to purchasers, ie product liability. Finally, R&D projects are notorious for their expenditure overruns. The possibility of this happening needs to be evaluated.

External finance

The importance placed by governments on R&D is often reflected in their willingness to fund or make grants available to R&D collaborators. In Europe, this funding may be available not only at the national level (for example in the United Kingdom through the Department of Trade and Industry) but also at European Community level. Thus, the company and the contractor should consider whether state finance is available and whether they want this. Inevitably, government funds or grants will come with strings attached. The benefit of the cash will have to be weighed against the restrictions the government will place on the parties.

As an example, in October 1987 the EEC adopted a framework programme with a budget of 5.3 billion ECU for specific programmes in research and development for the period from 1987 to 1991 (see (1987) OJ L302/1, 24 October). However, three central constraints applied. First, to obtain such funding, the collaboration had to involve organisations in two or more member states; secondly, the parties had to enter into a standard form contract produced by the EEC which was likely to include restrictions on exploitation; and thirdly, a considerable amount of effort had to be expended on pushing through the application for funding, with success not being guaranteed.

5.3 Typical provisions of an R&D collaboration agreement

Appendix 4 contains a specimen R&D collaboration agreement and project contract. Although finely balanced, the agreement in Appendix 4 is slightly more in favour of the company than the contractor. The provisions that might be included in such documentation are considered here.

The documentation is structured on the basis that the parties would first enter into the collaboration agreement which seeks to achieve two objectives. First, it sets out the long-term collaboration intended by the parties, together with the opportunity for the contractor to put forward project proposals for consideration by the company. Secondly, where the company accepts the proposal, the agreement sets out the terms that will govern the project (unless otherwise agreed). It is then contemplated that the parties will, in respect of each project, enter into a project contract that incorporates the terms of the collaboration agreement and all other special terms dictated by the nature of the individual project. In this way, having invested some time in agreeing the collaboration agreement which, in effect, sets out a standard form project contract, all project contracts should be able to be entered into with the minimum of negotiation and delay.

An alternative is entering into similar service contracts for collaboration between the company and different contractors. This reduces the risk that the parties are held to have carried on a business 'in collusion' where there are many collaborators. The resulting structure as a whole will be that of a total collaboration, but if dissected will be made up of individual contracts.

Parties

As noted above in 5.2, the selection of collaborators will have been an important initial consideration. Generally speaking, therefore, the draftsman of a collaboration agreement will only need to be concerned to name the parties correctly. However, there are three exceptional circumstances to note.

First, where there are a group of contractors, ie different persons undertaking work for the collaboration. Here, thought will have to be given to whether all contractors should be made a party to the agreement or whether one contractor will 'represent' the other contractors. This consideration will have to include whether the contractors are to be made directly liable to the company under the terms of the collaboration agreement or whether the signatory to the agreement will be exclusively liable for the acts or omissions of its fellow collaborators.

Secondly, where the contractor is a company established under CA 1985, there should be little difficulty in establishing that it has capacity to enter into and perform the collaboration agreement and the ensuing project contracts. On the other hand, where the agreement and contracts are to be entered into with public sector organisations (including, in particular, universities, polytechnics and technical colleges) reference will have to be had to the Acts, statutes, charter and so forth establishing the organisation in order to check the contractor's capacity to enter into and perform the agreement and contracts.

Thirdly, again where the contractor is a public sector organisation, bearing in mind the amorphous nature of these bodies, the draftsman will need to identify the particular legal person involved. Generally speaking, the company will regard itself as having a relationship with the particular part of the organisation (such as a university department), but of course, the collaboration agreement will have to be entered into with a legal person. A mismatch between the legal entity and the department or other non-legal entity with whom the company is dealing may, in practice, have ramifications for other aspects of the collaboration agreement. Thus, for example, the contractor may find it difficult to enter into commitments that cover all of the activities that are undertaken by the legal body (for example, the university) as opposed to the activities undertaken by the body of individuals (for example, the physics department) with whom the company is in contact.

Collaboration

The type of collaboration in contemplation is one where the contractor is putting forward to the company proposals for undertaking projects within a particular field. An obligation to produce so many projects a year might be placed on the collaborator although such a provision may prove counter-productive. An onus might also be put upon the contractor to offer all proposals that it contemplates within the field to the company before offering the same to a third party. It will be necessary to have regard, depending upon the circumstances, to whether any anti-trust legislation penalises, prohibits or renders unenforceable any such undertaking. In any event, as a matter of practice, it will be difficult to agree with a contractor (especially a public sector organisation) a too 'exclusive' collaboration. The spirit of the collaboration rather than the strict letter of the collaboration agreements will dictate the flow of project proposals to the company.

Fundamental to this process will be an agreement as to the 'field' within which the parties will collaborate. The desirability of selecting a field that is neither too broad nor too narrow has been mentioned. The ambit of the field is likely to be driven by the extent to which the contractor feels able to 'restrict' itself to only putting forward proposals to the company. On the other hand, the company will more often than not be viewing the collaboration as a series of projects over a defined period whereby it will build up a team at the contractor dedicated to producing a series of products and processes. Indeed, as the first product or process is marketed, it is as likely as not that improvements will be required or a second generation of products and processes will be quickly identified. In this event, the company will be looking to the team at the contractor to take forward their initial work to this next phase. If this is to work in practical terms, then the team will need to be focused towards the commercial goal of their work, ie a market for the product and process. Thus, the definition of the field should reflect the market sector to which the parties are aiming and the type of technology they have in mind.

The duration of the collaboration will need to balance the potentially conflicting interests of the company and the contractor. The company will want a fairly long period of collaboration (say, five years) so as to give the team at the contractor sufficient time to develop a series of successful projects leading to exploitable products or processes. On the other hand, the company will not want to be 'committed' to fund beyond the foreseeable future. The company is unlikely to be prepared to enter into a commitment that is binding in law to fund all projects proposed under the collaboration agreement. Nevertheless it will find itself impelled to fund the majority of proposals put forward by the contractor; otherwise it risks losing the goodwill of the contractor and the team in place. From the point of view of the contractor, while welcoming a steady flow of funding for R&D, it will not wish to find itself bound to one party for too long a period of time. This will be especially so when the collaboration represents the first time that the two parties have worked together.

The company would be well-advised to set out a standard format upon which it desires that proposals should be submitted to it by the contractor. This has the double advantage of first, focusing the attention of the contractor on the issues that the company wants to address and secondly, having the proposals submitted in a consistent format with which the parties will have increasing familiarity. The manner in which the company might seek to review such proposals has been discussed under 'Selecting the projects' above.

Set out in the specimen collaboration agreement (Appendix 4) is a list of matters to be covered in the proposal (see clause 4). Briefly, the proposal might look at the following:

(a) A description of the proposer for the project and his experience in the field.

(b) An account of any work undertaken to date on the project and a statement of the proposed duration of the project, together with details of the resources to be used and any pre-existing intellectual property rights.

(c) A statement of the proposed management and budgetary controls for the project.

(d) If feasible, a plan for the commercial exploitation of the project (this may well be something that is more in the domain of the company than the contractor).

(e) A fair assessment of the strengths and weaknesses of the technology, production and design capabilities of the contractor, the ability of the contractor to provide marketing and sales support and the management the contractor has in hand to oversee the project.

(f) The projected commercial success for the project.

There are a number of ways that the company might seek to protect the 'integrity' of the collaboration. The possibility of placing an obligation upon the contractor to offer proposals within the field has already been considered. Assuming the successful completion of one or more projects, the company would be wise to seek a commitment from the contractor that it would not, for a defined period, assist a third party with the development of any product or process likely to be competitive with any product or process developed for the company. This is because of the risk that the contractor will be using technology 'bought' by the company for the benefit of a third party. However, specialist anti-trust advice would have to be taken on whether such a covenant from the contractor will be rendered ineffective or be undesirable by reason of the rules of competition law. See Chapter 12 for an outline of domestic and EEC competition law as they may affect these agreements.

The work to be undertaken

The specimen agreement proceeds on the basis that the contractor will produce, in consultation with the company, a protocol describing the work that will be undertaken. It will be imperative that the description is as complete as possible, leaving no margin for dispute as to what tasks the contractor agreed to perform. The company will prefer to describe the project work in terms of products or processes to be developed. On the other hand, the contractor will prefer simply to list the tasks that it will perform, giving no commitment to the results of those tasks.

If projects are to be of a significant duration, then it may prove feasible to introduce 'break points' into the project whereby the project can be assessed stage by stage. If the contractor has dedicated equipment and personnel to a project on long-term contracts, it will seek some level of compensation from the company if the project is determined at a particular phase.

The company will wish to monitor progress on the project. A method of doing this will include the submission of reports by the contractor to the company at regular intervals. To ensure the timely supply of such reports, the company may tie in payments to reports. Reports might also be tied in with the 'break points' fixed for the project in order that the report can contain sufficient information to enable the company to determine whether to go to the next stage.

In addition if the company has appointed a 'peer group' to approve projects they may take up a role of continually reviewing progress and direction of the project. Moreover, in complicated collaborations a management committee may be installed, but in more simple cases a 'company's representative' will suffice.

The protocol or the project contract should detail the equipment, materials and personnel that are to be used on the work. This might be conveniently set out in the payment schedule to the project contract as payment will normally be related to costs incurred.

The company will wish to confirm, in the contractual documentation, the standard of work required of the contractor. In addition, it will want some reassurance as to the state of art to which products or processes to be developed will be taken. A convenient yardstick against which to assess the fruits of projects will, of course, be agreed product or process specifications.

Finally, the projects should state precisely what is to be delivered to the company upon completion, eg not only a final report detailing all work undertaken but also items such as prototypes, models and other equipment or works produced.

Payment

One of the most difficult terms for the principals to resolve will be the payments due under the project contracts. It is undoubtedly the case that the funding of R&D work is not cheap because the work is labour intensive and generally undertaken by higher paid employees.

The company, for its part, will wish to be protected against cost overruns. Thus, it will look for a fixed price contract.

From the point of view of the contractor, it will only be able to accept a fixed price contract if it is able to forecast accurately the costs that it will incur. This will prove more difficult the longer the project is to run and the more the project work is defined in terms of products or processes to be developed rather than tasks to be undertaken. The contractor will generally wish to have a prompt reimbursement of its costs and, therefore, will require payment at short intervals. Further, where the salary (and other benefits) of employees are beyond its control (particularly so in the case of universities and other public sector organisations), it will want to be protected by the company against increases in the salary and other remuneration costs of those working on the projects.

Both parties will need to consider the VAT implications of the payment mechanism they set up. Generally speaking, payments will be subject to VAT but this is not necessarily the case for some research projects that are established on a reimbursement only basis. Specialist tax advice should be taken on the matter.

Fruits of collaboration

The company will wish to provide that the fruits of the collaboration belong to it. However, it will also wish to require the contractor to undertake steps to protect the fruits of the collaboration. This will involve giving assistance in relation to the obtaining of patent or other forms of protection. Further, the company may require the contractor to assist in proceedings either brought by the company against alleged infringers or in proceedings brought by third parties seeking the revocation of the company's patents or other forms of protection.

Much technology is incapable of being protected through patents, designs or copyrights. However, the fact that the technology comprises information not in the public domain may make it nevertheless valuable and marketable. The classic example is the trade secret. To protect such information, the company will want confidentiality undertakings from the contractor and maybe, if feasible, also from those individuals undertaking the project. Furthermore, if the contractor is sub-contracting part of the work, confidentiality undertakings will be required from the sub-contractor.

Often, the contractor is involved in R&D work for a number of reasons which include publishing the results of the work (particularly in the case of public sector organisations) or utilising the results for the purposes of further work which may or may not be done with a view to profit. Here, the interests of the company and the contractor may appear to conflict.

However, as regards publication, it should be possible for the company and contractor to agree what should or should not be published. Once the company has the protection of patents, designs or copyrights then it should be possible for the contractor to publish, with the agreement of the company, details of the project. The ultimate test for publicity is whether the disclosure would be of commercial value to the competitor.

As regards the contractor using the results of the work, it should be possible for the company to agree that the contractor may use the fruits of the project for its internal research purposes. Indeed, a quid pro quo for such a licence would be for the contractor to make available to the company a non-exclusive licence to use that further research by the contractor. If the contractor wishes to go further and use the fruits of the project, for example in consultancy work for a third party, this may well be acceptable to the company if the contractor pays a sum on account of this to the company.

Exploitation of the fruits of collaboration

The parties will have determined from the outset who will be responsible for the exploitation of the fruits of collaboration. The specimen documentation in Appendix 4 proceeds on the basis that this role will fall upon the company. The company will seek out assignees or licensees for the arising technology or may even set up its own manufacturing, marketing and sales entity. Whichever route is adopted, it is to be anticipated that further support will be required from the contractor and this ought to be catered for in the collaboration agreement or project contracts. Thus, for example, the contractor may be involved in discussions with prospective assignees or licensees of the technology. Further, there may be a requirement for technical ongoing support from the contractor. The contractor may also be concerned to require the company to exploit the fruits of collaboration. He will not wish to expend time and effort developing new technology which the company may, possibly for its own internal reasons, or for change of policy, fail to exploit.

Sharing the fruits of collaboration

Increasingly today, contractors undertaking R&D projects will be looking to receive more than a lump sum payment from the company for undertaking the work. A collaboration where the work and interest of the contractor does not end with the termination of the project, leads to the need for the principals to agree the share of the money arising from the commercial exploitation of the projects. The varieties of arrangements that the parties might agree are legion. We can, perhaps, divide them into four broad categories.

First, there will be the situation where the company promises to make some (unspecified) reasonable payment to the contractor if the project is a success. This, however, from the point of view of the contractor, is somewhat unsatisfactory as there may be much debate as to what would be a reasonable payment to the contractor and if the parties are unable to reach an agreement, the courts are unlikely to determine that agreement for them. On the other hand, the company will not be keen to pass the determination of this issue to a third party.

A second category is the possibility of making available to the contractor an equity stake in a joint venture vehicle set up to exploit a successful project. An attractive feature of such an arrangement is the ability to issue shares to those individuals working on the project and therefore tie them in to the continued success of the project. However, such a structure is only likely to be justifiable in those situations where the project is leading to a demonstrably successful commercial product or process.

The third category would be the payment of a fixed sum to the contractor on a once-and-for-all basis. This is only likely to be in prospect where it is anticipated that the company will 'assign' outright the fruits of the project. Again, one will have the difficulty of determining what is an equitable share between the parties although, as the assignment will take place usually not too long after the completion of the project, a split may be agreed by reference to the respective contributions of the parties to the success of the project; this being, in particular, as far as the company is concerned, an amount necessary to repay the funding of the project plus an agreed rate of return on that expenditure together with the costs incurred by the company in effecting and agreeing the assignment.

The fourth category is for a sharing arrangement arising from the exploitation of the project. In its simplest form, this can be just a royalty on sales of products or processes developed from the project. However, this approach will be seen to be over-simplistic in the common situation where the fruits of the project will require further expenditure before being turned into a product or process capable of commercial exploitation. In this situation, what would be more equitable between the parties is a revenue sharing arrangement that takes into account the total expenditure on the project and divides the 'net income' arising from the project on an agreed basis. This mechanism permits a number of ways for the parties to share the fruits of the collaboration. Thus, one might have a system whereby the contractor would receive an initial payment and thereafter an agreed percentage of net income. The company might have a first 'charge' on the receipts of the project through being paid back its payments expended on the project together with a levy but leaving the balance to the contractor. Yet another situation would be for the parties to agree a split of the receipts from the project after the company had received, out of the project receipts, reimbursement of its expenditure together with an agreed rate of return on that expenditure. This mechanism can be used where expenditure continues to be made on the project by providing that, at the end of each year, the parties would calculate whether the company had received its reimbursement and agreed rate of return as at that time and, if it had, then the receipts outstanding would be shared in the agreed proportions.

Whichever of these varieties is used, it will be important for the draftsman to ensure that the documentation encapsulates provisions covering, first, the description of all income and expenditure to be taken into account and, secondly, a procedure whereby the contractor can be satisfied that it is receiving its agreed return on the project receipts.

Warranties and indemnities

Consideration should be given to the warranties and indemnities that the company will expect from the contractor. On the warranties side, the company may want the contractor to warrant that it has capacity to enter into the collaboration agreement and the ensuing project contracts, there are no adverse third party patents, designs, copyrights or other intellectual property rights and there will be no claim against the company from the contractor's personnel or consultants for a share of the receipts from the projects. The contractor, for its part, may want a warranty from the company that it has capacity to enter into the agreement and the contracts.

Turning to indemnities, an issue to be resolved between the parties will be who is to bear the risk arising from the work of the contractor on each project. As the contractor is best placed to control the work and to obtain insurance, prima facie the liability should fall on it and the company should take an indemnity. However, when a project moves to the phase of exploitation, product liability needs to be considered. Here, prima facie, the company will be best placed to obtain the necessary insurance or to obtain indemnities from assignees or licensees of the fruits of the project. In these circumstances, the contractor may seek an indemnity from the company although the company will wish to exclude liability arising from the acts or omissions of the contractor in the research and development phase.

Other matters

A collaboration agreement would also include the standard terms that one would expect to see in any commercial agreement. Thus, the agreement should include provisions dealing with grounds for termination and the consequences of termination, force majeure, the assignability of the agreement and a governing law provision. Examples of these clauses are contained in the specimen collaboration agreement in Appendix 4.

Chapter 6

Technology joint ventures

6.1 Introduction

What is special about a technology joint venture?

The pooling of technological resources is often the reason for the formation of a joint venture, and so a large proportion of joint ventures are technology joint ventures. A technology joint venture (which in this context should be taken to mean a joint venture created in order to develop, promote or market technology) gives rise to special considerations over and above those set out in the rest of this book. This chapter sets out the questions most often encountered, and gives practical solutions.

Matters which are particularly relevant in the context of a joint venture are:

(a) the basis upon which technology which may originally be the property of one of the parties is used by the joint venture;

(b) the consequences, both for the provider of technology and for the joint venture, of termination of a joint venture or the withdrawal from the joint venture of the party providing the technology;

(c) the effect on the parties of the development or improvement by the joint venture itself of technology contributed by one of the parties.

The relevance of the special considerations applicable to technology joint ventures will depend on the nature and extent of the technology involved. This chapter begins, therefore, with a description of the rights involved and then how they might be dealt with, referring also to the constraints most frequently encountered. There then follows a discussion on how the rights might conveniently be grouped together. With all that information, this chapter considers some typical arrangements.

6.2 Identification and protection of rights in technology

There are five main ways in which rights in technology can be protected in this country. These are by means of patents, copyright, registered and unregistered designs, and confidentiality. In some other countries, additional rights exist such as utility models, separate topography rights in semi-conductor products, petty patents, and others. This chapter is, however, confined to the five main topics. Use of these rights, and trade marks, is often a vital element of a joint venture. But trade mark rights are not peculiar to technological products and are therefore dealt with separately, in Chapter 10.

These various rights in technology are different in nature. A detailed analysis of each of them is beyond the scope of this book, but an outline will provide the background for the discussion which follows. The differences are such that these various rights should not automatically be bundled together and thought of as one right which can be dealt with in one way only. The UK position is described below; details will vary from jurisdiction to jurisdiction but the main features will be similar in most countries. In important cases, local advice should be sought.

Patents are national rights. So any act done in a country other than that in which a patent has been obtained, cannot be an infringement of that patent. A patent may be obtained for an invention and for that invention to be patentable it must be novel, involve an inventive step (ie must not be obvious to a person skilled in the art), be capable of industrial application and must not fall within a list of statutory excluded subject matter. Novelty and inventiveness are determined by reference to the 'state of the art'. The state of the art is made up of all matter available to the public anywhere in the world any time before the priority date of the application (rather than at the date of the invention). Patents currently last for 20 years from the date of application (not grant). Although the inventor can be the applicant for a patent (or the patent holder), he need not be. Generally, the inventor is entitled to the patent rights, subject to rules about employee-inventions or any contract made by the inventor. An invention made in the course of an employee's normal duties, or duties specifically assigned to him where an invention might reasonably be supposed to result (and in certain other specified circumstances), will belong to the employer, otherwise the invention belongs to the employee. Any term in a contract of employment which diminishes the employee's rights in such inventions will be unenforceable.

Copyright subsists in, amongst other things, original literary works. Computer programs are treated as literary works. Copyright comes into existence automatically when an original work is recorded or fixed in tangible form. The United Kingdom is party to two international conventions (the Berne and the Universal Copyright Conventions) which provide that works of authors who are nationals of another country, party to either Convention, which are first published in such a country, are entitled to the same protection in all other countries which are party to the relevant Convention as are nationals of such countries. There are no marking or registration requirements in order for copyright to subsist in a work created in this country, but the presence of a copyright notice on the work is useful because, amongst other things, it gives rise to evidentiary presumptions of authorship. The author (ie the person who creates the work) is generally the first owner of copyright. In the case of computer-generated works, the author is the person who makes the arrangements necessary for making the work. Copyright in a work made by an employee in the course of his employment is originally owned by his employer. It is possible to assign future legal (as well as equitable) interests in copyright even before the work to which such copyright relates has been created. In the case of literary works, copyright lasts from the creation of the work until 50 years from the end of the year of the author's death. Copyright in computer-generated work lasts 50 years from the making of the work.

A *registered design* provides protection for certain new and original designs which do not fall within a statutory list of excluded items. Like a patent, it is a national right. It protects shapes, configurations, patterns or ornamentations which have 'eye appeal'. Novelty and originality are determined by reference to designs which have been published, registered or were otherwise available to the public in the United Kingdom at the time of application. The first owner of a registered design is the person who created it, his employer or assignee. Registered design protection can now last up to 25 years from registration.

The *unregistered design* right, introduced by the Copyright, Designs and Patents Act 1988, subsists (without the need for registration) in any original and non-commonplace aspects of the shape or configuration of an article which do not fall within a list of excluded items. Semi-conductor topographies are protected by this right. The right lasts 15 years from the end of the year in which the design was first made but if articles made to the design are marketed within five years from then, the design right lasts only ten years from the date of marketing. The right is similar to copyright; so, for example, it is possible prospectively to assign design rights in a work not yet created. The rights in an unregistered design belong to the employer where an employee creates the design in the course of his employment.

Confidentiality: technological information (or secret 'know-how') may be protected by means of the law relating to misuse of confidential information. The requirements for protection of confidential information are: first, that the information must have the necessary quality of confidence (ie it really must be confidential); secondly, it must have been imparted in circumstances importing an obligation of confidence (ie the person receiving it must know, or have reasonable grounds for knowing, that it should not be disclosed to third parties), and lastly there must be an unauthorised use or disclosure of it (or threats to do either of them) to the detriment of the person who owns it. No contract is necessary to protect confidential information but the obligation of confidence may arise out of one. The rights to protect confidential information and ensure it is not misused can last for so long as the information remains confidential.

Patents, copyrights, design rights and rights of confidentiality are often referred to collectively as intellectual property rights.

6.3 How can intellectual property rights be dealt with?

The rights used by a joint venture can be rights it owns (itself alone or jointly with others) or rights licensed to it from the joint venturers (or third parties). Naturally, there will often be less freedom to deal in rights merely licensed.

Intellectual property rights in a joint venture can be dealt with by assignment, licensing, and joint ownership and by way of security over intellectual property. Assignment, licensing and co-ownership are by far the most frequently encountered, while security, in this context, is only very rarely adopted. Some joint ventures will require a combination of these techniques: for instance, to ensure that the joint venturers can use, in other parts of their business, certain technology which may be assigned to the joint venture. (This aspect is discussed later in this chapter.)

Patents, copyrights and registered and unregistered designs can be assigned, licensed, jointly held or mortgaged. Confidential information cannot, in the strict sense of the word, be 'assigned' because it is impossible to 'unlearn' information which may be in people's heads forming part of their general skill and knowledge. However, an effective assignment can be made by the transfer of the information coupled with a restrictive covenant by the original owner not to use it. Confidential information can be 'licensed' in a similar way. It is possible (and often desirable) to record dispositions of patents and registered designs at the relevant Patent Office or Designs Registry. The effects of assignment, co-ownership and licensing are considered below.

6.4 Assignment, co-ownership and licensing

Assignment

The assignee stands in the shoes of the assignor and is fully entitled to deal with the rights as the original owner could. Provision can be made for assignment back at the end of the venture; but even so, the absolute quality of an assignment does not suit many types of joint venture.

Co-ownership

Co-ownership entitles the joint owners to an equal undivided share in the relevant intellectual property rights. Because of the complexities involved, an agreement between the co-owners is advisable. Particular issues need to be addressed, for each of the rights. These include: whether a licence can be granted, or a mortgage or assignment made, without the consent of the other co-owner(s); whether each co-owner needs to account to the other(s) for any revenue derived as a result of exploitation of the right; and who should be entitled (or obliged) to take action to protect, maintain, enforce or defend the right.

Co-ownership may be appropriate in certain circumstances; often, however, it is encountered as a compromise solution causing uncertainties and disputes over the issues identified above.

Licensing

There is no such thing as a standard licence. There will be many key issues to resolve, which cannot be dismissed as mere details. What features are judged to be suitable will depend on the type of the venture and the respective contributions of the parties (and their bargaining power).

Among the more important issues are the following (readers may refer to a work on licensing for a fuller list): whether the licence is to be exclusive, sole or non-exclusive; whether it is to be limited to a particular field of technical application or a product market; whether a separate consideration or royalty is to be payable; its transferability; its duration; rights of termination and rights upon termination (or expiry); and the territory of the licence.

As to the meaning of 'exclusive' and 'sole', unfortunately usage varies. An 'exclusive' licence is normally taken to mean one which allows the licensee to exploit the subject matter of the licence and excludes everybody else (including the licensor) from doing the same thing; whereas a 'sole' licensee has the rights to the exclusion of everybody else *except* the licensor (who therefore has concurrent rights). The expression 'sole *and* exclusive' is therefore contradictory and should be avoided. It is good practice to insert a clear definition in the agreement.

An *exclusive* copyright, design right (registered and unregistered) or patent licence holder has statutory rights to take action for infringement (although normally the licensor has to be joined as a party); but a non-exclusive licensee has no such rights. A non-exclusive licensee will, if it is possible to do so, have to have that right specifically assigned to it, for it to be able to take such action.

As mentioned, a licence can be limited in scope to particular fields of technical application or even product markets. So, for example, an exclusive patent licence may be given for a specified field and the licensor may retain rights outside that field. This sort of arrangement is common in technology joint ventures.

6.5 Constraints affecting the treatment of intellectual property rights

The joint venture will need to ensure that its intellectual property rights are sufficient for what it wishes to achieve. As has been said above, the rights it has can be owned by it or given to it (by way of assignment or licence) from the joint venturers (or third parties). Acquiring the rights from the joint venturers may not be as simple as it seems. There are two areas of concern here: first, where there are existing licences and, secondly, where governmental or quasi-governmental regulatory approvals are required.

Licensing agreements with third parties

Sometimes the joint venturers themselves will have intellectual property rights licensed 'in' from third parties under existing contracts, which the joint venturers may wish the joint venture to use. (There are likely to be third party computer programs, if nothing else.) Similarly, the joint venturers may have already granted licences of intellectual property rights to third parties. If the joint venture is to exploit such rights, the difficulty which may arise, in either case, is similar. In the first case, the terms of these already existing licences may preclude their transfer or sub-licensing to the joint venture; whilst in the second case the original licence 'out' may restrict any further licensing by the licensor. Careful consideration of the terms of the existing contracts will therefore be required. Even if there is no express ban in the existing contract, the contract may be 'personal' in nature to the original party (or parties). Many intellectual property agreements have this character.

Regulatory approvals

Various fields of technology are subject to governmental regulation. Three approvals commonly encountered are telecommunications licences (under the Telecommunications Act 1984), cable licences (under the Cable and Broadcasting Act 1984) and product licences (under the Medicines Act 1968). The effect of these Acts is to make it a criminal offence to conduct specified activities without the appropriate licence. Apart from the obvious point of ensuring that the joint venture has whatever approvals it needs, there is a more subtle point involved here. That is, whether one of the joint venturers who already enjoys such an approval can assign it to the joint venture, thereby avoiding the long delay that otherwise might be caused if the joint venture were to apply for the full approval from scratch. Most types of approvals (including each of the three referred to) are not generally assignable from one legal entity to another. Another route must be found. One to examine is this: where shares of the entity holding the approval are transferred to another entity, the new shareholders may not need to apply for a full new approval, but instead it will only be necessary (if at all) to obtain approval to the change in control (usually a quick and straightforward matter). The practical effect of this is important to appreciate. It means that where regulatory approvals are required and cannot be transferred, it will not usually be possible for the joint venturer to dispose of the business to the joint venture in such a way that the joint venture is able to use the approvals. Conversely it may be practicable to strip out those assets of a company which are *not* required for the joint venture (leaving the approval in place), and selling the shares in the company to the joint venture.

6.6 Some useful labels

It is usually helpful to group together different kinds of intellectual property rights. First those which already exist, as opposed to those which arise during the venture from the efforts of the joint venture or the joint venturers. But that distinction is not enough. Other distinctions are usually made, for example, 'background' vs 'foreground' and distinctions relating to particular businesses or technical fields of application (ie the uses to which the various intellectual property rights may be put). 'Background' describes that intellectual property which is of broad application, but only incidentally relevant to the activities and efforts of the joint venture, whereas 'foreground' technology relates directly to the activities of the joint venture. The distinction is often not clear cut, and refinements may be called for in suitable circumstances.

We now consider some typical arrangements.

6.7 Examples of typical arrangements

It may be trite to say, but it is often forgotten (to the distress of many joint venturers) that clear provision needs to be made for what is to happen to the various categories of intellectual property rights not only, (a) in order to establish the joint venture, and (b) while the joint venture is operating, but also (c) after termination of the joint venture or upon the disposal of one party's interest in it. It is not usually fitting for the intellectual property rights to be treated as simply another asset to be disposed of at the end.

Establishment of the joint venture

The possibilities for allocating the intellectual property rights are endless. However, from what has been said above, it will be seen that where a joint venturer has intellectual property rights to be used by the joint venture, the 'foreground' intellectual property may be assigned to the joint venture for use in the field of the joint venture, with a licence back to the joint venturers for use of that intellectual property outside the field of the joint venture. An assignment may not be necessary and a licence of the foreground intellectual property to the joint venture may suffice. Whether foreground intellectual property be assigned or licensed, it is usual, where the joint venturers have relevant intellectual property, to license the 'background' intellectual property to the joint venture (perhaps exclusively for the particular purposes of the joint venture) making it clear that the joint venturers can continue to use those rights outside the field of the joint venture.

During the operation of the joint venture

Here, 'arising' intellectual property generated by the joint venture and the joint venturers needs to be dealt with. The joint venturers may obtain licences of the joint venture's arising intellectual property and vice versa. The licence might be only for use outside the field of the joint venture or the joint venturers, as the case may be. Sometimes the joint venturers will want to provide for ownership and licensing of intellectual property rights arising out of contract research with the joint venture (or the other way round), although it is often dealt with on a case-by-case basis when the time comes.

Termination of the joint venture or disposal of a joint venturer's interest

Parties are often reluctant to consider what should happen on termination or expiration of the joint venture or on the disposal of one party's interest in it. What happens to the technology in such circumstances is crucial. However amicable relations were between the parties at the start, at termination or on a disposal, litigation over the continued use of the rights is a distinct possibility; because the parties may have fallen out, the joint venture may not have been as successful as was hoped for and the documentation on this point may not be as helpful as it might have been.

The professional adviser's role is, however, to minimise the scope for litigation by ensuring that this subject is considered during the negotiations. Two different scenarios need to be considered and specifically addressed: first, expiry or termination of the joint venture and, secondly, one of the joint venturers buying out the other's (or another's) share. Some suggestions for the first scenario might be that the foreground intellectual property, previously assigned to the joint venture, will be re-assigned to the respective joint venturers and any licences of the background intellectual property may be terminated. The parties will need to consider and negotiate over the question who might own and be able to use the arising intellectual property rights generated by the joint venture. Some questions for the second scenario include whether the departing venturer should nonetheless be required to keep its foreground or background rights licensed to the joint venture (to enable the joint venture to continue operation) and whether the departing joint venturer should be entitled to continue to have the benefit of any licences granted to it by the joint venture.

6.8 Confidentiality

Protection of confidential information exchanged by the parties prior to the formalisation of joint venture arrangements has been referred to in Chapter 2. Nonetheless, there will usually be separate provisions governing the disclosure and use of technical information during the term of the joint venture.

It should be borne in mind that if the confidential information is not properly safeguarded, the value of confidential information, and opportunities to apply for patent or registered design protection, could be lost. Particular care needs to be taken in the drafting of any licences between the parties as, for example, a licence to 'use' intellectual property can result in its disclosure to third parties, causing a diminution in its value. In such circumstances, consideration should be given to requiring either that such disclosure is not made or, if it has to be, that relevant confidentiality/secrecy obligations are in place.

6.9 Management of the intellectual property portfolio

The portfolio of intellectual property rights needs to be properly managed to preserve (and increase) its value. Numerous issues will fall to be determined, some having a great impact on the future value of the portfolio. For example, what practical steps should be taken to safeguard the joint venture's trade secrets? For which inventions should patent protection be sought, and how widely should applications be filed? Which patents and design registrations should be maintained and which allowed to lapse? Who should be entitled (or obliged) to take enforcement proceedings against an infringement by a third party of the joint venture's intellectual property rights, or to defend a key patent against revocation proceedings? Whilst the administrative aspects of such decisions will often be taken care of by the parties' existing patent and licensing departments, responsibility for the basic decisions needs to be allocated between the joint venturers and the joint venture itself.

6.10 Other considerations—tax and competition law

Issues of tax (particularly on royalty payments) and EEC and domestic competition law are often particularly relevant to technology joint ventures. Both of these areas are dealt with, generally, in other chapters of this book. On tax, specifically, stamp duty at the rate of 1 per cent will generally be payable on assignments of intellectual property rights (except pure know-how assignments) and the granting of exclusive and non-revocable licences. On competition law, EEC competition law (particularly) is usually of more fundamental importance in a technology joint venture than in an ordinary joint venture. A full analysis of the application of EEC and domestic competition law to technology joint ventures is beyond the scope of this book (and specialist advice should always be sought). A few key features of competition law are, however, outlined in Chapter 12.

Chapter 7

Property joint ventures

7.1 Introduction

This chapter focuses on joint venture arrangements relating to property development. Obviously the key element in any such joint venture is the land involved in the proposed development. This may already be in the ownership of one of the joint venturers; two or more parties may pool their holdings to form an attractive whole; or the land in question may be acquired from one or more third parties. The developments which occur will vary substantially, but most of the principles being examined apply to the whole range of property development joint ventures including residential developments, major town expansion and new town developments, out of town retail and industrial developments, town centre redevelopments and city office developments.

7.2 What is a property joint venture?

Property joint ventures may be divided into two main types:

(1) *Agreements between developers* to carry out a major project. These fall into two sub-groups as follows:

    (a) Agreements to purchase a large development area with a view to breaking up the land between the parties. This can be used for major town expansion projects or inner city regeneration. The parties will purchase the land, put in the major infrastructure and then partition the development land between them.

    (b) Agreements to combine to carry out major development projects and to share the profits. The parties carry through the development and the end product results in a one-off profit if the development is sold or a joint investment if the development is retained.

(2) *Agreements between developers and other participators* in a development to co-operate in and achieve the carrying out of the development. This is the form of property joint venture which is most commonly encountered and most of what follows will be applicable to this type of property joint venture. On a large scheme, a number of developers may be involved and there will inevitably be overlap between (1) and (2) above.

The parties likely to be involved in these types of development projects are as follows:

- landowner

- fund/institution providing finance

- builder/contractor

- purchaser/occupier

These parties may become involved in a variety of ways, and the joint venture agreement will reflect their different interests in and expectations of the project, and in particular their participation in its management, their share of the profits and their short and long-term goals.

Property joint ventures may be distinguished from construction joint ventures, where typically a number of contractors will agree to share the construction work of a project, but none of the contractors will usually have any interest in the land which forms the site of the project. They will effectively be employed by a third party to carry out the construction project. Thus, whereas a property joint venture is concerned with the property, normally a construction joint venture is concerned with the rights and obligations as between the parties employed on a project. The two can, however, co-exist.

7.3 Other arrangements distinguished

A number of other arrangements relating to the financing of land development, falling short of joint ventures, have been devised, and for completeness the more important arrangements of this nature will now briefly be described.

- *Debt financing.* In simple terms, debt financing involves the developer borrowing funds which sooner or later have to be repaid. The lender will have fairly limited involvement in the development.

- *Equity financing.* This can be effected in two ways. One method, often referred to as forward funding, is where an institution acquires a site from a developer before development begins and pays the developer to put up a building on that site. In addition to development costs, the developer may also be entitled to a share of profits dependent on the success of the scheme. A second method, called forward purchasing, is not strictly a means of funding the development but is where the institution agrees to pay a particular price for the property once development has been completed and would expect to impose tight controls on the design, building and letting processes which will take place before it completes its purchase. Again, the price may be variable according to the scheme's success.

- *Equity kickbacks.* These give a lender a financial participation in the development by varying the return on the loan according to the success of the end-product, eg tied to the amount of developable land realised and rents achieved.

- *PINCs, SPOTs and SAPCOs.* A number of 'unitisation' vehicles, notably Property Income Certificates ('PINCs'), Single Property Ownership Trusts ('SPOTs') and Single Asset Property Companies ('SAPCOs'), have been developed (but not yet extensively used) in order to provide an alternative type of long-term ownership of large buildings by creating multiple public ownership of property in a liquid form, the liquidity being provided through a Stock Exchange listing. Their aim is to establish vehicles as long-term owners of the property with investors buying and selling units in those vehicles as they would shares in a public company or property unit trust.

7.4 Why are property joint ventures attractive?

For a landowner
Rather than selling his land at the outset, the landowner can rely on the expertise of the developer and participate in the profits of the developed land, taking land value and a share of any development profit.

For a developer
The developer will have access to development opportunities with the possibility of spreading its risks and burdens.

For a fund
Rather than charging interest on finance as the development proceeds, the fund will often roll up the interest and take a more lucrative share of development profit at the end.

For a builder
The builder will often agree to forego payment against a monthly certificate and will fund its own building work, taking an eventual share of the proceeds of sale.

For an occupier (eg a retailer)

The main advantage to an occupier is the achievement of a tailor-made development plus a share in profits or realisation of capital growth.

7.5 Types of property joint venture

Unincorporated joint venture

Apart from the general points referred to in Chapter 3, the following matters require special consideration when the joint venture takes the form of an unincorporated association:

— No hive-down—as an unincorporated association, the entity cannot hold assets. The joint venturers will retain their land holdings and agree to sell them at the optimum time to realise development profits; or grant a building lease to the developer immediately or on completion of the development; or enter into option agreements to dispose of the land in phases.

— Public bodies—local authorities and quangos may be restricted in their ability to participate in an unincorporated association of this nature, or may lose grants or funding if they derive profits or capital receipts under such an arrangement.

Joint venture company

Chapter 4 covers the basic matters that have to be considered if the parties decide to form a company to carry out their property joint venture. Additional matters peculiar to property joint ventures include the following:

— Hive-down—it may be advisable to vest the title of land held by a particular landowner in the property joint venture company at the inception or creation of the company or later. This will depend on (inter alia) the amount of stamp duty which would be payable by the joint venture company, and the borrowing requirements of the joint venture, ie whether the land will be required as security. A transfer of the property naturally brings about a loss of the landowner's control over the land but this may be regarded by the other participators as a necessary commitment by the landowner to the project.

— Public bodies—local authorities and other similar bodies may be restricted in their ability to subscribe for shares in a joint venture company. The Local Government and Housing Act 1989 regulates the powers of the local authorities both to set up and to participate in companies and makes such arrangements less attractive to them than before the 1989 Act came into force.

Partnership

Chapter 3 covers joint venture partnerships in general, but again there are a number of matters in relation to property joint ventures that should be emphasised, inter alia:

— Property-holding by the partnership: any land held by a partner-ship will be held on trust for sale for the parties as tenants in common. This means that on sale of the property or dissolution of the partnership, each party will be entitled to his agreed share. This will apply whether the property is legally held in a single name or joint names. However, it is possible to control the level of interest which is enjoyed by the partnership. For example, a freehold owner can arrange for only a leasehold interest or tenancy to be enjoyed by the partnership.

— Public bodies—local authorities and other similar bodies may be restricted in their ability to enter into a straight partnership agreement.

The partnership vehicle is in practice rarely encountered in property joint ventures, although it may be a useful structure to adopt if a large property is to be held jointly and managed and developed over a long period. Also, it is sometimes tax effective for landowners to combine to sell a joint development site where the trading implications of a partnership are not detrimental.

Co-ownership agreement

This arrangement relates to co-venturers acquiring and developing property simply as co-owners. Each co-owner would own an agreed share of the property and would be entitled to an agreed share of the profits arising on an eventual sale. The interest in the property would be held on trust, either by themselves beneficially or on behalf of them by a trust company.

It is very unusual for a mere co-ownership route to be adopted in the case of the development activities of a property joint venture. If an unincorporated association is not a preferred alternative, then the more appropriate medium would be for a partnership or company to be formed.

The following additional factors need to be taken into account:

● *Marketability.* A co-ownership share will be an interest of a less marketable type and this would be reflected in the valuation of the co-owner's share. A special purpose subsidiary could be created to hold the co-owner's share in the assets and ultimately for the purposes of selling off its interest to third parties, ie by sale of shares in the subsidiary.

- *Trust for sale.* As the interest in land is to be held by more than one person, ie two or more co-venturers on trust, English land law rules will impute a trust for sale (if no express obligation of trust exists) ie a legal obligation to sell the property, unless all the owners agree that the disposal should be deferred. This makes the viability of a shared ownership situation dependent on the continued co-operation of all the owners. Even if the co-owners attempt to agree alternative arrangements, the court has an inherent jurisdiction to override such provisions under s 30 of the Law of Property Act 1925 and order a sale, contrary to the wishes of one co-owner.

Longer term investment structures

The parties to the property joint venture may require a structure which enables the parties to unlock profits generated over a longer period. Thus, rather than allowing the developer to pay the landowner his share in expected capital receipts (so that the developer alone takes all the income from the scheme later) or, as is common, the joint venturers disposing of the scheme on its completion, the landowner and/or developer may wish to retain their interest and participate in income growth. These structures are particularly attractive to local authorities and quangos who may be constrained from entering into the usual types of property joint venture with parties in the private sector. There can be substantial advantages to such local authorities in taking profit in income rather than capital form.

Although it could be difficult to generate income from residential developments where freehold sales or leases of units for capital payments are the norm, an equity sharing leasehold structure for the income to be generated from an office retail, or mixed office/retail scheme can be devised.

Consideration of the following issues will be relevant:

(a) fixed rents guaranteed to the landowner;

(b) percentage equity sharing arrangements as between the landowner and developer;

(c) top slicing, bottom slicing preferences indicated;

(d) options for the landowner to sell its share to the developer at or following specified dates (these may be put and/or call options);

(e) building obligations placed on the developer;

(f) landlord and tenant type obligations, duties and stipulations, eg full repairing and insuring terms to be imposed on undertenants. A model form of occupational lease may be attached to the equity sharing lease;

(g) controls on disposals (including sublettings and sales) by either party, particularly the developer;

(h) management committee delegated with future maintenance and management obligations;

(i) the precise definitions of gross income, net income and expenditure arising from the scheme;

(j) the collapse of the structure if the parties agree to dispose of their interests to third parties.

7.6 How to choose the appropriate vehicle

Chapters 2 to 4 cover certain of the advantages and disadvantages of particular types of joint venture vehicle. In the context of a property joint venture there are certain other relevant considerations, some of which have been identified above. In general, the administrative arrangements should be as simple as possible, consistent with effectively achieving the objects of the property joint venture. Thus, in practice the parties should start by asking whether the object can be achieved by a simple agreement. If it is essential for land to be jointly owned, then it may be necessary to superimpose a trust. A partnership would normally be created only if the trading circumstances dictated. It might be advisable to form a company if the size, complexity and duration of the project dictate that the nuisance of the initial administrative formalities and dissolution problems on termination of the property joint venture are outweighed by the long-term benefits of providing a co-ordinating centre with formal administration and accounting.

In practice, the choice of vehicle will be determined by a combination of the following:

(a) The property involved
In the case of a sizeable property or a property involving particular difficulties (eg decontamination of polluted land) a more formalised vehicle may be appropriate.

(b) The complexity of the project
Whether the parties desire a short/long-term involvement in the project will be relevant. If the parties envisage a short-term involvement, then

forming a joint venture company might not be the best option because of the problems associated with dismantling the corporate structure. It might be more appropriate to have a simple joint venture agreement.

(c) Parties involved

There may be statutory constraints on a particular body participating in the property joint venture. For example, a local authority's ability to enter into a partnership agreement or a co-ownership of land arrangement, or to form a joint company, is constrained.

(d) Financing

Wherever the property joint venture parties rely on external financing, it will be essential to ensure that the security value of the assets which are the subject matter of the joint venture is retained. Thus, there is little point transferring land into a joint venture company if the transferor is to retain a first charge over it for future performance by the company. In these circumstances, it is far simpler to leave the land with the owning party and to create an agreement for sale or an option in a form which enables the land itself to be mortgaged.

(e) Ownership

Where there is a joint venture for the development of a site involving a developer and an owner, the owner will not usually wish to sell his land to the developer until the latter has completed his side of the bargain. Thus, in practice the developer is often given a licence to build on the owner's land and the owner agrees to transfer the freehold or grant a long lease on completion of the development. In this way, the owner retains security for the performance of the developer's obligations through the value of the construction on his land, while the developer knows that if he performs his obligations the owner will be required to transfer the land or grant the lease.

(f) Property taxation

Detailed consideration of property taxation is outside the ambit of this book but the following points should be considered.

(1) It is normally important that the owner of land does not make a disposal of the land for tax purposes before the proceeds of sale are available for payment of the resulting charge to tax.

(2) If two or more parties holding separate interests in land enter into an agreement obliging them to pool their interests and take an agreed share of the prospective joint holding, each owner will for tax purposes be treated as having sold his land for a consideration equal to its agreed share of the prospective joint holding. Thus if its

land was originally acquired at a low price, it could trigger a charge to tax before the full value of the joint holding is realised.

(3) Wherever shareholders in a joint venture company agree to provide benefits through the company at less than market value, there is always a danger that the Revenue will tax the company as if it had received full market value for the benefit. If a joint venture company acquires fragmented land at less than the eventual marriage value and then transfers land out to its members at cost rather than the enhanced market value, the Revenue could tax the company as if it had made a profit on the receipt of full market value, leaving the members who had received the land with a low base value for the purpose of taxation when they eventually sell.

(4) Where land is acquired by a joint venture company, and later sold, liability to stamp duty can arise on both transactions.

(5) VAT on construction costs and dealings with the land and buildings will always require careful consideration.

(6) Capital allowances can be important for developments in certain areas eg enterprise zones, or for certain types of development.

7.7 The form of the property joint venture agreement

As with all joint ventures, the choice of vehicle will dictate the form of the main agreement. For example, a trust agreement will incorporate particular provisions relating to the administration of the trust, and a partnership agreement will incorporate all of the essential requirements for the effective running of a partnership.

However, all property joint venture agreements will cover the following basic matters (in addition to those discussed in earlier chapters):

(a) Objects of the property joint venture
Whatever structure the parties decide to adopt, they should be encouraged specifically to agree the objects of the joint venture and to prohibit variation without consent. Thus, if they know the property to be acquired, they should identify it and its ultimate use. Any further details which have been agreed such as an established or a required minimum lettable area, and any preliminary plans and descriptions which describe the project, should be included.

(b) Conditions precedent

These will include, as necessary,

(1) the grant of planning permission in respect of the development land;

(2) confirmation of road closure orders and compulsory purchase orders;

(3) modification of restrictive covenants affecting the development site;

(4) provision of finance;

(5) pre-lettings; and

(6) confirmation of taxation treatment.

The agreement should specify which party is responsible for satisfying the different conditions. Each party will usually accept responsibility for satisfying the condition most closely under its control. Thus, a developer might undertake to obtain planning permission, listed building consent, a road closure order, etc; whereas only a local authority could accept responsibility for securing and confirming a compulsory purchase order. The land owner would normally accept responsibility for perfecting its title (although he could lend his name to the developer to conduct proceedings in this respect). Taxation clearance would be the responsibility of the party or parties directly affected.

In dealing with the planning condition, some provision should also be made for dealing with any 'planning gain' required by the local authority (typically under s 106 of the Town and Country Planning Act 1990, s 111 of the Local Government Act 1972 or s 33 of the Local Government (Miscellaneous Provisions) Act 1982).

Under s 106, an agreement may be entered into for the purposes of restricting or regulating the development or use of the land, and it may contain positive covenants as incidental or consequential provisions. Such agreements are intended to enable a local authority to control aspects of a development, or to counteract any adverse effects, where this could not be achieved by way of conditions attached to the grant of planning permission. Local authorities have used these powers, however, to require from developers benefits which do not relate to the particular development proposed, or sums of money to be used by the authority for works or services having no relation to the planning permission. Typical examples of such 'planning gain' include provision of community or leisure facilities, and highways improvements or financial contributions to highways improvements. Advice on planning gain is contained in Department of the Environment Circular 22/83, which lays down guidelines to ensure that what is required of the developer fairly and reasonably relates in scale and kind to the proposed development, and what the developer is asked to provide or pay for is a reasonable charge on him rather than being something which the public purse should more properly bear. However, an applicant for planning permission will often find it commercially more attractive to give the benefit asked for in return for an early grant of permission, rather than resisting the local authority's demands and having to fight an appeal at a public inquiry. Developers should bear in mind however that a permission granted in consideration for an improper inducement will be open to attack by a third party by way of judicial review.

The negative and positive covenants contained in a s 106 agreement will bind successors in title as well as the original parties to the agreement. The participants to the property joint venture should therefore take care to insert a clause into the s 106 agreement securing the release of the original parties from the covenants once they have parted with all interest in the land, or try for a time limited s 106 agreement. Agreements may be modified or discharged by the Lands Tribunal under s 84 of the Law of Property Act 1925. The Tribunal will not lightly discharge a covenant freely entered into, especially if it is of recent date. It will normally require to be satisfied that the covenant is obsolete, or would impede the reasonable use of the land, and that no injury would be caused to the person having the benefit of the covenant. It is always open, of course, to a developer (or his successor) to negotiate a release with the local authority, but this may be time-consuming, apart from which the authority may simply not agree.

The question of enforceability of s 106 agreements has been considered by the courts. In *Abbey Homesteads (Developments) Ltd v Northamptonshire County Council* (1986) 278 EG 1249, the s 106 agreement reserved land on a housing estate for the purposes of a school. Argument was submitted that the covenant did not run with the land and was of limited duration, expiring on completion of the housing development. The court however, held that the covenant was restrictive of user and since no period was prescribed under s 106, it must be taken to have been intended to run in perpetuity.

(c) The obligations of the respective parties

All of the components of the property joint venture project should be allocated between the parties, either to be performed directly or by an arrangement with a third party.

For example:

(1) A landowner would agree to grant a licence to allow development to be carried out on his land and to grant a lease at the end of the development.

(2) A developer would agree to procure that the development is properly designed, that all necessary consents are applied for, that the development is properly constructed, and that the accommodation is let to suitable tenants.

(3) The agreement will need to specify who is to be responsible for obtaining finance for the joint venture. This will usually be the party with the greatest financial muscle or experience.

In a joint venture between developers, each developer might agree to co-operate by sharing the cost of joint acquisitions, agreeing a plan for the development, and the provision of joint infrastructure works.

(d) Matters requiring the consent of all the parties

As with all joint ventures, there will be a list of matters requiring the consent of all or a majority of the participants. In the case of property joint ventures, the following may also be appropriate:

- acquisition of further properties

- approval of planning applications/consents

- choice of contractors, project managers etc; their appointment and removal

- disposal of the joint venture property

(e) The management of the project

The parties to a property joint venture will need to appoint a project manager. In practice, a development project is often run by a manager seconded from one of the participants. A seconded manager can be in a difficult position, often having to strike a balance between the interests of the project and those of the organisation to which he hopes to return. Project management may be a 'perk' offered to a subsidiary or associate of one of the participants—eg many developers will be looking for 'in-house' project management (at a fee of between 2 and 5 per cent of development costs) as distinct from their prospective return from the project itself. Sometimes developers see their project management fee in any event as a guaranteed return for participating in the venture.

Conflicts of interests may also pose a problem for the other parties if developers seek to place contracts for the joint venture with their own subsidiaries. Participants trying to defend a special deal will prove distinctly intractable in adapting their terms to the needs of the evolving structure and, almost invariably, these deals are harmful to the project because they pre-empt part of the project's revenues or reduce its contractual protection. The contract price may not be competitive in the overall market place, and an insistence on handicapping the property joint venture with a captive source of supply may represent a drag on the joint venture's profitability.

Managing conflicts of interest requires the clear segregation of the competing interests within the management structure of a participant. Proper reporting lines within the joint venture and the appointment by it of separate representatives to conduct the commercial negotiations with the developer and its sub-contractor subsidiaries should help to mitigate the strains on loyalties.

(f) The termination arrangements

It is essential for the parties to agree at the outset a mechanism for establishing when the property joint venture has either been satisfactorily completed or alternatively terminated following breach by one of the parties. The same problems arise as with all joint ventures but the following considerations are peculiar to property joint ventures:

(1) The parties should consider at the outset the position as to the eventual sale or letting of the development. Often the parties will have differing views as to whether they wish to keep the completed development as an investment or to sell it on. If there are conflicting desires amongst the parties then it is usual to incorporate 'put and call' options ensuring that the party wishing to realise its investment will transfer its interest in the land or its shares in the joint venture company at an appropriate fair value to the party wishing to retain a stake in the development in the longer term.

(2) Similarly, in the event of a dispute which cannot be resolved or the breach of a substantial provision by one participant, the joint venture agreement may contain put and call options for the transfer of the land or, in the case of a joint venture company owning the land, for the transfer of shares in the company, from one party to another. For example, if more money is needed to be put into the property for refurbishment or redevelopment, but one party does not wish to increase its investment, the joint venture agreement might provide in this situation for an adjustment to the relative shares, or it might allow the willing party to lend to the joint venture on terms generous to the lender, or it might provide for a forced sale. If there is a deadlock in decision-making, one of these courses may be inevitable, the most likely being the forced sale. Indeed, as we have seen above, the law implies a forced sale in the case of a trust for sale. Such situations are of course open to abuse: an argument could be manufactured to force a sale, and so it is crucial that the joint venturers can trust each other. They will also want to approve any replacement of a joint venturer.

(3) Dealing with construction and other contracts in these circumstances can be problematical. In the case of a joint venture company there should not be a problem provided the joint venture company is the employer. Where, however, one party, who was the employer under the relevant contract or contracts, wishes to drop out, the contracts cannot normally simply be assigned to the other party. The contracts will have to be novated to ensure that the benefit and burden of the contracts become vested in the remaining participant or participants. Collateral agreements should be made available at the outset between the contractors and other participants to the joint venture for the benefit of the joint employers allowing them to step in as employers at a later date.

Options are mentioned above and at various other places in this chapter. Their use is very common in property joint venture arrangements. Insofar as the options relate to land (as opposed to shares) particular problems are caused by s 2 of the Law of Property (Miscellaneous Provisions) Act 1989. Section 2 requires that agreements for the disposal of an interest in land, including freehold and leasehold sales and the creation of charges, must be incorporated in a document containing all the terms of the disposal (this can be done by including express reference to other documents) which is signed by both parties to the contract. It has hitherto been common to provide that the option is exerciseable by one party giving notice to the other. This may not be sufficient for the purposes of s 2 of the 1989 Act, as the recipient of the notice will not have signed any document (other than the option agreement, and case law—eg *Helby v Matthews* [1895] AC 471—indicates that a contract will not arise until exercise of the option). Various ways have been suggested to cover this problem. For instance on entering into the option agreement the grantor of the option could hand over a document incorporating all the terms of the sale agreement duly signed by it, so that the grantee can on exercising the option merely countersign the same document. Alternatively the grantee could be given an irrevocable power of attorney to sign a contract on behalf of the grantor when exercising the option. This does not, however, address the problems which may face option holders under options granted prior to the 1989 Act coming into force.

(g) The profit-sharing arrangements

The profit-sharing arrangements will depend upon the type of property joint venture:

(1) Commercial developments—These usually provide for the parties to benefit as follows:

- Owner—receipt of land value plus a share of overage (this term is defined below).

- Fund—repayment of costs, payment of basic return and possible payment of a share of overage depending on the level of risk undertaken by the fund.

- Developer—developer's profit as priority yield (perhaps 10–20 per cent) plus a share of the balance of overage.

(2) Residential developments—

- Owner—agreed price for any unit plus a share of any super profit.

- Developer—building costs plus developer's profit plus a share of any super profit.

In the case of a property joint venture between developers, profit-sharing would generally be on the basis either of agreed shares of the eventual profit or on an agreed allocation of developable land.

Wherever the parties share in the profits of a development, the distribution formula will depend on the concept of 'residual value'. This is calculated by taking the capital value of the development (usually found by capitalising the actual or anticipated rents) and deducting the cost of known factors (eg land costs and development costs) to leave a residue representing the value of the unknown element.

'Overage' is the share of the residual profit left after the developer has taken a priority return or a fund has taken a basic return or an owner has taken an agreed land value. The joint venture agreement will usually provide for the sharing of this overage.

Whether there is a property joint venture company, partnership or other contractual agreement governing the joint venture, the parties must decide how much profit to distribute and when. If the joint venture is for a single project, should distributions only take place once all the developed properties have been sold? This could result in the joint venture having large amounts of money in the bank and, particularly for the smaller joint venturers, potential cash flow problems in the meantime. The solution may therefore be to require profits to be distributed after an appropriate date eg practical completion. However, practical completion may not be appropriate if the developed units have still to be marketed as opposed to forward financed. Another possibility would be for distributions to be triggered once the property joint venture becomes cash positive, ie it has received sufficient revenue to cover known project expenses. In any event, the parties should provide in appropriate instances, for instance a phased development, for earlier distributions by agreement. Directors of a joint venture company who wish to pay dividends before completion of the development will need to have regard not only to the rules in CA 1985 as to distributable profits, but also to the finance that will be required to complete the outstanding phases and to corporation tax liabilities that will be incurred. This is inevitably less of a problem for a partnership or a contractual property joint venture where shares of the profit will automatically be attributed to the parties as each participant is credited with an apportioned share of revenue and expenses.

7.8 Property joint ventures with local authorities

In the present economic and political climate, joint ventures with local authorities are becoming increasingly common. Local authorities have a number of powers relating to land which can be of assistance in this context, notably powers to purchase land, both by agreement and compulsorily, and to develop and dispose of it, under the Local Government Act 1972, the Town and Country Planning Act 1990 and the Local Authorities Land Act 1963. It should not be forgotten, however, that there are also constraints to which local authorities are subject, notably under the Local Government and Housing Act 1989, which restricts capital expenditure by local authorities, and it is recommended that specialist advice be sought in relation to any joint venture with a local authority.

Chapter 8

Management buy-outs

8.1 Introduction

What is a management buy-out?

The concept of a management buy-out ('MBO') is now very familiar. Typically, the senior management ('the management team') of a company ('the target') will negotiate the purchase of the target from its parent company ('the vendor') or the business (or part of the business) of the target in which case the target will be the vendor. The acquisition will be carried out by a newly incorporated vehicle ('Newco') in which the management team will have an equity participation but which will in large part be financed by a combination of equity provided by outside, often institutional, investors ('the investors') and debt provided by banks and other financial institutions ('the lenders').

Variations on the theme of a MBO include leveraged buy-outs ('LBOs') and management buy-ins ('MBIs'). A LBO involves the acquisition of an existing company or business, with or without management participation but with a large element of debt financing. A MBI is a buy-out in which the existing management are replaced by a new management team brought in by the investors for the purpose. Many of the considerations which are relevant to MBOs are also relevant to LBOs and MBIs.

MBOs, and other forms of venture and development capital investment, may be regarded as a species of joint venture between the management team and the investors and, to a lesser extent, the lenders. The task of the lawyers is to create a commercially workable structure within which the different interests of each group will be respected. This is likely to be achieved by establishing a system of checks and balances using joint venture techniques.

In order to understand the dynamics of such a joint venture, it is necessary to consider the different commercial objectives of each group.

The management team

By undertaking a MBO, the management team will have the opportunity of running a business in which they will be part owners free from the constraints of operating as part of a larger group. If the business is successful, they will be rewarded by the possibility of realising their shares at a very significant profit.

On the other hand, they may well be taking considerable personal risks. The management team will often be abandoning the security of working for a large organisation or group. They may well have to find a significant capital sum, often by personal borrowing secured on their homes, in order to finance their equity participation in Newco.

The investors and lenders

The investors and lenders will be looking for an adequate return directly related to the degree of risk which they will be taking. The investors who will be taking only an equity participation in Newco will generally be looking for a high internal rate of return. The return which the lenders will be seeking will depend on the quality of the security which Newco and the target are able to provide and also the target's cash-flow.

The sheer burden of debt with which Newco and the target will be encumbered is normally such as to make such a financing riskier than normal corporate bank lending and so justify a higher interest rate. Lenders of 'mezzanine' debt which may be unsecured or rank behind primary debt will be looking for a still higher return and, often, some equity participation as well.

Market development

In the United Kingdom, the record of MBOs has until recently been good and failures have been relatively rare. Thus a MBO has been a very attractive proposition both from the point of view of the management team and from that of the investors and lenders. The MBO could, however, yet be a victim of its own success. On the one hand, there is an increasing scarcity of quality transactions and on the other there is ever increasing competition for those transactions which are available. It is possible that this situation may lead to more highly leveraged (or geared) transactions, thus carrying a higher degree of risk, than have yet been seen in the United Kingdom. Furthermore, there have been some well-publicised recent examples of debt laden companies (whether or not resulting from a MBO) encountering financial difficulties.

8.2 Conflicts of duty and interest

Duties as directors and employees

A MBO gives rise to considerable scope for conflicts of duty and interest for the management team. In fact, the initiation of a MBO (other than by the vendor) will almost inevitably give rise to actual or potential conflicts of this kind. The management team will be placed in an impossible position if they try to reconcile their duty to their employer (ie the target and/or the vendor) when considering whether and on what terms to recommend or approve a MBO with their own interest in securing the best possible deal.

The duties of fidelity, loyalty and good faith owed by the management team whether in their capacity as directors or employees of the target and/or the vendor may be broken when they make the first move towards organising a MBO unless they have obtained prior consent. Soliciting support for a MBO from among their colleagues may put them in breach of such duty. It may be difficult to present a convincing proposal to potential investors without divulging confidential information which will again be in breach of their duty. The consequences for the management team of taking such steps without consent could include summary dismissal, claims for damages and injunctive relief.

The investors should also tread cautiously. They could be held liable for inducing, procuring or facilitating breach of contract or duty by the management team and they could be restrained from using or disclosing confidential information which the management team have divulged to them.

When acting for either the management team or the investors, relevant contracts of employment should be reviewed to determine whether they contain any provisions which could be breached as a result of the proposed transaction. These could include notice periods and post-termination restrictive covenants (eg not to disclose confidential information, not to entice away fellow employees and non-competition covenants). In a typical MBO, these provisions are likely to be relaxed by agreement with the vendor to the extent necessary to enable the transaction to proceed. However, they could be very relevant in hostile situations.

Where the management team are directors of the vendor (or, in the case of a public MBO, the target), they should disclose the full extent of their interest to the board of directors of the vendor (or, if appropriate, the target) and exclude themselves from any consideration of the proposed MBO from the point of view of the vendor (or the target). It will not generally be sufficient to rely on provisions of the articles of association of the relevant company which enable directors who have made full disclosure of their interests to take part in the discussions relating to, and to vote on, contracts in which they are interested.

Class 4

If the target is part of a group listed on The Stock Exchange, it will be necessary to consider whether the MBO is a Class 4 transaction as defined in Section 6, Chapter 1 of the Stock Exchange Yellow Book. This will be the case if the MBO involves an acquisition by (or certain other categories of transaction with) a director, substantial shareholder or associate of either.

If the MBO is a Class 4 (or indeed a Super Class 1) transaction, it will be necessary (unless the Quotations Committee decide otherwise) for it to be approved by the relevant listed company in general meeting and for a circular (which will contain a notice convening an EGM) to be sent to its shareholders containing information, which is likely to include an accountants' and/or a valuer's report, with a view to demonstrating the reasonableness and fairness of the transaction. An independent expert's opinion to this effect will also have to be included in a Class 4 circular. Those involved in the MBO would normally be excluded from voting on the resolution to approve the transaction.

Companies Act 1985, s 320

Whether or not the target is part of a listed group, the requirements of s 320 (as amended) should not be overlooked. Shareholders' approval (unless the company concerned is a wholly-owned subsidiary) will be required where a director of a company or its holding company (or a person connected with him) acquires one or more non-cash assets of the requisite value (ie exceeding the lesser of £100,000 and 10 per cent of the company's net asset value) from the company.

Persons connected with a director include his immediate family, the trustees of related trusts, partners and any company in which the director and persons connected with him are together interested in 20 per cent or more of the equity share capital or in respect of which they are entitled to exercise or control the exercise of more than 20 per cent of the voting power at general meetings.

8.3 Advising the management team

Conflict

First and foremost the management team will need to be advised as to the conflict of duty and interest which is likely to arise when initiating, or in the course of, a MBO. As indicated above, it will, in many cases, be impossible to avoid such conflict altogether if the MBO is to get off the ground. The management team should, however, be advised as to the consequences.

Information memorandum

As a first step the management team may produce an information memorandum which will be used in order to solicit offers of finance from investors and/or lenders. To the extent possible, the contents of the information memorandum should be verified since, despite any exculpatory language to the contrary, the management team are likely to be asked at some stage to warrant its accuracy.

The information memorandum and related material may constitute an 'investment advertisement' for the purpose of FSA 1986, s 57 which it would be an offence for the management team (who will not be authorised persons for the purposes of FSA 1986) to issue or cause to be issued unless its contents have been approved by an authorised person as defined in FSA. If this is not possible, the management team may be able to rely on the exemptions contained in para 6 or 9 of the Financial Services Act 1986 (Investment Advertisements) (Exemptions) Order 1988 (SI No 316) which exempts certain investment advertisements issued by a participator or potential participator in a joint enterprise to another participator or potential participator in the same joint enterprise or issued to authorised persons.

Confidentiality/exclusivity

The management team are likely to wish to require confidentiality undertakings from the investors and/or lenders in order to protect so far as they are able confidential information which is provided to them. In return, the management team may be required to enter into an exclusivity undertaking to discourage them from seeking finance elsewhere. Normally there will in any case be a document setting out the principal terms on which finance is to be provided to Newco before the management team makes any approach to the vendor.

Costs

The question of costs is likely to figure prominently in the thinking of the management team. Due to its inherent complexity, the costs of a MBO can be very significant. If successful, the management team may expect the costs to be borne wholly or partly by Newco. However, they will be looking for ways to minimise the costs if the MBO does not proceed. The professional advisers are quite likely to be asked to work on a contingency basis (with a very much reduced, or no, fee if the MBO is not concluded). However, a generous (or desperate) vendor or investors who are exceptionally eager for the business in an increasingly competitive market may agree to absorb the costs of an unsuccessful MBO.

8.4 Advising the investors

Due diligence

The investors will wish to carry out as much preliminary due diligence as possible with respect both to the target and the management team. The former will of course depend on the willingness of the vendor to allow access to the target before the acquisition agreement is entered into. Ideally, the investors will wish to commission an accountants' investigation in order to have a more objective view both of the target's business and of the past performance of the management team.

Negotiation of the acquisition agreement

The investors and their legal advisers will normally wish to play a major role in (or even take exclusive responsibility for) negotiating the acquisition agreement under which Newco will acquire from the vendor the share capital of the target or (where the target is the vendor) the business (or part of the business) of the target. The management team are likely to have much less experience in negotiating such agreements. Furthermore they may be inhibited when dealing with their existing employer or parent company and, indeed, simply be over eager to do the deal on whatever terms are offered.

Warranties

The subject of warranties is likely to give rise to a debate on the following lines. The vendor will resist giving warranties on the footing that the management team know the business better than the vendor. The management team will be unwilling to incur further personal liability by giving warranties but will be seeking some protection from the vendors as regards matters not within their knowledge or control. The investors will wish to take warranties both from the vendor and from the management team.

The result is usually a compromise. Given the inside knowledge of the business which the investors will be acquiring through the management team, the investors may be prepared to accept a more limited set of warranties from the vendor than would otherwise be the case. They may also accept that the vendor should have no liability for matters which are outside its knowledge but within the knowledge of the management team. Such matters should be covered by warranties given to the investors by the management team. Both the investors and the vendor should consider very carefully whether the vendor should preserve or exclude the right to sue the management team where reliance has been placed by the vendor on information supplied by the management when giving the warranties. In most cases, the warranties would be accompanied by a thorough 'due diligence' investigation of the target by the investors.

On occasions, the management team and/or Newco may be asked to give warranties to the vendor to the effect that nothing has been done or omitted to be done (including the manner in which items have been accounted for) by or with the knowledge of the management team during the period leading up to the buy-out which could damage the performance of the target. For example, the management team might seek to depress profits artificially where the purchase consideration is based on a multiple of profits. The value of such warranties to the vendor may be doubtful since it is unlikely ever to discover whether or not they have been breached other than—possibly—as a result of a completion audit.

8.5 Structuring the MBO

Establishing Newco

The vehicle used to effect the acquisition will almost invariably be a new company formed for the purpose of carrying out the acquisition of the target. Newco is likely to be promoted by the management team who will hold one class of shares and largely financed by the investors who will subscribe for another class of shares (possibly at a large premium) and may also provide some debt financing.

The key documents to establish Newco are its articles of association and a subscription and shareholders agreement. These documents will govern the relationship between the management team and the investors in very much the same way as in any other joint venture. Thus the documents will deal with such matters as the right to appoint and remove directors, management of the Newco group, restrictions on transfers of shares and control over certain key matters.

However, there are a number of special features of MBOs which will also need to be reflected in such documents. These may include 'ratchets' or arrangements under which the shares held by the management team are enhanced (or diminished) in value depending on the performance of Newco after the acquisition and arrangements for providing the investors with a minimum Internal Rate of Return on their investment. These provisions are commonly found in the articles of association of the company used to effect the buy-out (ie Newco), which will set out in full the rights attaching to, and the ranking of, the investors' shares and shares held by the management team. The variety of such share rights is limited only by the ingenuity of the persons devising them.

Although typically day-to-day management of Newco will be left in the hands of the management team, the investors will normally require the right to take control in certain circumstances—eg where Newco defaults under the loan documentation or fails to achieve certain performance targets or, perhaps, where there is a material breach of warranties given by the management team to the investors, which cannot be satisfied by the management team out of their own personal resources.

The original intention of the management team and the investors may be to float Newco on The Stock Exchange within a given period after the MBO has been completed, if market conditions permit. However, the investors will require the freedom to dispose of their shares to a third party purchaser as an alternative to flotation. The management team are likely to wish to protect themselves either by requiring the investors to use their best endeavours to ensure that any third party offer which would result in a change of control is extended to the management team or by requiring that the management team would have the right to put their shares on the investors in such circumstances. In addition, the investors will commonly either require that no shares held by the management team may be transferred without their consent or will require that members of the management team who wish to sell their shares must first offer them to other shareholders or persons selected by the directors. Frequently, the management team will be obliged to offer their shares for sale on ceasing to be employees of Newco (other than as a result of injury, sickness or retirement).

If the assets and cash flow projections of the Newco group (including the target and any subsidiaries it may have) are insufficient to enable the MBO to be financed entirely from straight debt and equity, it is likely that the gap will be bridged by 'mezzanine' debt, which encompasses a variety of financial instruments, but in the UK commonly takes the form of convertible redeemable preference shares, or subordinated convertible loan stock, in Newco. Whilst found in a variety of different forms, such instruments tend to have common characteristics which distinguish them from senior debt and equity; the investment is usually unsecured, ranks behind the senior debt, carries an intermediate rate of return (of, say 15–20 per cent, between the senior debt which would yield a return related to prevailing interest rates and equity which would yield a return of 30–40 per cent compound per annum) and carries an equity interest participation in Newco through, for example, conversion of preference shares or loan stock, or warrants to subscribe equity. Chapter 9 contains further information on the types of security which Newco may find itself issuing.

Tax

Chapter 11 deals with taxation in the context of joint ventures generally. Tax issues arising on MBOs are likely to be particularly complicated. It is not intended to do more here than to mention one or two points which are often relevant to the management team.

Management are likely to wish to obtain tax relief on the interest which they pay on borrowings raised to finance their investment in Newco. This can be achieved if the relevant loan is made to an individual and is used to acquire ordinary share capital in a close company (other than a close investment holding company). A further requirement is that the individual claiming relief must either have, alone or with associates, a material interest in Newco (broadly 5 per cent of its ordinary share capital) or must have worked for the greater part of his time during the period from the raising of the loan to the time the interest in question is paid in the actual management or conduct of Newco or its associates.

Alternatively, relief may be obtained for interest on a loan used to acquire ordinary share capital in an 'employee controlled company'. If relief is to be sought on this basis, careful consideration should be given to the definition of 'employee controlled company'.

The other key tax concern for the management team used to be s 79 of the Finance Act 1972. This, however, has been replaced by new provisions contained in ss 77–89 of the Finance Act 1988. These apply to shares which employees acquire in connection with their employment. In such cases, a charge to income tax can arise in three different circumstances:

(1) A 'growth in value' charge in respect of shares in a 'dependent subsidiary' may arise on the earlier of the disposal of such shares and the expiry of seven years from their acquisition (even if they are not disposed of). If the company becomes a 'dependent subsidiary' after the shares are acquired, a 'growth in value' charge may arise on the earlier of seven years after it became a 'dependent subsidiary', the disposal of such shares and the time at which the company ceases to be a 'dependent subsidiary'.

(2) A charge on any special benefit received by virtue of ownership of the shares. The scope of this provision is unclear, but it is generally thought that the operation of a ratchet should not constitute a special benefit for these purposes.

(3) A charge where shares are increased in value by a manipulation of rights attached to those or other shares. The critical question is

whether the operation of a ratchet constitutes such manipulation. There is no clear answer to this question, which will depend on the form of the ratchet, although there are good arguments that, in most cases, it should not do so.

8.6 Financial assistance

General

A MBO is likely to require a high level of debt financing with the result that the new Newco group (ie incorporating the target) will probably be much more highly geared than an equivalent non-MBO company. The lenders will be interested in the target's cash flow and/or assets. The former represents the means by which Newco's debt obligations will be serviced and the latter may provide security for such obligations.

In either case, CA 1985, s 151 will need to be looked at closely. This prohibits a company, such as the target (or its subsidiaries) from giving certain forms of 'financial assistance' directly or indirectly for the purpose of the acquisition of shares of the company before or at the same time as the acquisition takes place or for the purpose of reducing or discharging a liability incurred for the purpose of such acquisition.

Newco is free to charge the shares of the target as security for its debt obligations, but this is unlikely to be sufficient security for the lenders since they will rank behind the unsecured creditors of the target in the event of the target's liquidation. There should be no problems under s 151 if the MBO takes the form of the acquisition by Newco of the target's business or assets (or part thereof). In this case, the relevant assets will become the property of Newco which is free to use them as security for its borrowings.

Where the MBO takes the form of the acquisition by Newco of shares in the target from the vendor, the lenders will generally require the target (and any subsidiaries it may have) to guarantee (or assume) the debt obligations of Newco and to give security by means of fixed and floating charges over its (or their) assets. Unless a relevant exemption applies (which is unlikely in these circumstances) execution of such guarantee and security documents will amount to prohibited 'financial assistance' by the target (and its subsidiaries, if relevant).

There may well also be other varieties of 'financial assistance' involved (for example, if the target puts Newco in funds by way of a dividend, loan or gift in order to enable it to discharge, say, a short-term loan raised for the purposes of the acquisition or to pay deferred consideration to the vendor). It will be necessary to analyse carefully what kinds of 'financial assistance' are involved and, in each case, whether a relevant exemption is available.

Even if what is proposed does not contravene s 151 or if there is an available exemption, it may be necessary to amend the articles of association of the target (and/or any relevant subsidiary) to remove a restriction (which may be incorporated by reference to an earlier version of Table A) based on CA 1948, s 54.

A detailed examination of these sections is outside the scope of this book, but by way of summary it may be said that a private company which is a wholly-owned subsidiary may, so long as it complies with certain solvency tests and the directors can give a statutory declaration which is supported by its auditors, give financial assistance to its parent company by way of bank guarantee or loan.

8.7 Other aspects of financing

Introduction

Even if the involvement of the target in the acquisition financing organised by Newco does not infringe CA 1985, s 151 or there is an available exemption (eg under s 155), any arrangements entered into by the target (or any subsidiary it may have) for such purpose may be liable to attack either under the Insolvency Act 1986 (hereafter 'IA') or under the general law.

Insolvency Act 1986

It may well be that any guarantee in respect of Newco's borrowings or any other obligation incurred by the target (or a subsidiary) in connection with the acquisition of the target by Newco constitutes a 'transaction at an undervalue' for the purposes of IA. If so (depending upon the availability of possible exemptions in the circumstances concerned) an administrator or liquidator of the target (or a subsidiary) could apply to the court under IA, s 238 (within the appropriate period) for an order to set aside that guarantee or other obligation.

Whether the period of risk is six months or two years will depend on whether or not the other parties to the relevant transaction (for example, Newco and/or the lenders) are 'connected' with the company which incurs any relevant obligation.

The reason why any such guarantee or obligation may be vulnerable to attack under IA, s 238 is because it may well be questionable what consideration (if any) the target (or its subsidiary) is receiving for it. A 'transaction at an undervalue' is defined in IA, s 238(4) to cover a situation where a guarantee or other obligation is 'on terms that provide for [the target or the subsidiary] to receive no consideration, or . . . [is] for a consideration the value of which, in money or monies worth, is significantly less than the value, in money or monies worth, of the [guarantee or other obligation]'.

If, as is quite likely, any guarantee or other obligation given by the target (or its subsidiaries) in these circumstances is given 'at an undervalue', possible exemptions from successful attack by an administrator or liquidator are available if, in broad terms, the court is satisfied either (a) that the target (and any relevant subsidiary) entered into the transaction in good faith and for the purpose of carrying on its business and, when doing so, there were reasonable grounds for believing that the transaction would benefit it, or (b) that the target (and any relevant subsidiary) was able to pay its debts at the time of the transaction and has not become unable to pay its debts in consequence of that transaction.

It may, in practice, be difficult to prove that either of these exemptions applies: for example, it may be difficult to demonstrate that the purpose of a guarantee or other obligation given or incurred by the target (or any subsidiary) is given for the purposes of carrying on its business and could reasonably be believed to benefit that business.

A person is 'connected' with the target (or its subsidiaries) if he is a director or shadow director of the company concerned or an associate of the company. Newco will almost certainly be 'connected' with the target (and its subsidiaries) and it is possible that an investor or lender may also be so connected.

If the transaction (ie guarantee or other obligation) has been entered into with a person who is 'connected' with the target (or its relevant subsidiary):

(1) the onus of proof that those companies are able to pay their debts at the time of the transaction and have not become unable to pay their debts in consequence of the transaction is on the 'connected person'. If no other party to the transaction is so 'connected', the onus of proof would be on the administrator or liquidator; and

(2) the period of risk of attack if an administration order is made or the relevant company goes into liquidation is two years from the date of the transaction as opposed to six months in other cases.

General law

In giving any such guarantee or incurring any other such obligation or otherwise becoming involved in the acquisition financing (eg by paying an extraordinary dividend), the directors of the target or the subsidiary must act in what they believe to be the interests of the target or the subsidiary and not those of the Newco Group (including the target and any subsidiaries) – *Rolled Steel Products v British Steel Corporation* [1985] 3

All ER 52. However, a guarantee by a company conferring no obvious conceivable commercial benefit on the company but which is within its stated objects and unanimously approved or ratified by its shareholders may be valid provided that the interests of its creditors are not thereby harmed. Whilst it is by no means certain what the force of that (obiter) statement is, it is not unusual for the lenders to seek unanimous approval of relevant guarantees or other obligations by the target (and its subsidiaries) in circumstances such as these (see also 8.6 above).

Chapter 9

Funding techniques

9.1 Introduction

Arrangements to fund a joint venture's operations take a variety of forms. The choice of funding technique is predominantly influenced, of course, by the legal nature of the joint venture, but tax considerations play an important part as do the financial objectives of the participants, the nature of the joint venture's investment programme and the profile of its cash requirements over time. In the case of an unincorporated joint venture, the absence of any separate corporate entity means that the funding techniques are relatively straightforward. In an incorporated joint venture, on the other hand, the issue of shares with differing class rights and of different types of debentures allows the funding arrangements to be tailored to meet the expected roles and economic objectives of the different classes of participant. This chapter summarises the various funding techniques encountered in practice.

9.2 Funding an unincorporated joint venture

The simplest structure is that often encountered in a partnership. The joint venture participants agree to make initial contributions to the joint venture, in cash or in kind, and the value of their contributions is stated in their capital accounts in the partnership. In addition, there is likely to be an express obligation to bear or make good the losses as they arise and/or to provide working capital insofar as needed for the operations of the joint venture.

Many joint ventures in the construction industry (of both the types noted in 3.3) follow this pattern. In balancing the payment terms in their contract with an employer against the flow of payments which they will be required to make to carry out the works which they have agreed to construct, contractors seek either to remain cash-positive or, at least, to minimise the working capital which they will have to contribute to the joint venture in order to allow it to carry out the works. Working capital obligations of this type are common in both forms of joint venture: in both the integrated and non-integrated forms of joint venture working capital contributions may be required to finance the expenses of the joint project management or project co-ordination capability at the level of the joint venture and, in an integrated joint venture, the working capital contributions may be required in addition to meet payments due to suppliers and sub-contractors of the joint venture insofar as payments due from the employer under the construction contract are insufficient for this purpose.

Perhaps because the general expectation of contractors is that working capital calls will be relatively few in number and small in amount, joint venture agreements between contractors frequently address the possibility of non-payment by one party in only scanty detail. Sometimes default interest will be provided on the basis that the defaulting participant can put himself back in good standing with the other members of the joint venture by repairing the default within a certain stated time period, but often the only sanction for non-payment of a working capital call will be the termination of that party's participation in the joint venture for breach, a blunt and frequently inappropriate sanction in view of the additional costs likely to be incurred by the innocent parties if they are forced to mobilise a new consortium member previously unconnected with the project in order to replace the resources brought to the joint venture by the defaulting party.

A different procedure has grown up in relation to joint operating agreements in the oil industry and in the mining sector. Projects in these industries are typified by an intensive capital investment programme involving the disbursement of substantial amounts over a period of development of the hydro-carbon or mineral deposits concerned which may last several years. Participants in such a venture will usually have an obligation to make cash contributions to the joint venture in proportion to their percentage interests in the underlying project. In view of the regularity of cash calls and the extent of the capital commitments undertaken by the operator on behalf of the joint venture, prompt payment has always been regarded in these industries as being a key feature of operating agreements. The typical structure of the cash call machinery in such a joint operating agreement for the UK sector of the North Sea would involve:

- budget approval by the operating committee on behalf of the participants in the joint venture, combined with a system of authorities for expenditure (usually referred to by the abbreviation 'AFE') in relation to specified items for which provision is made in the budget;

- a system of regular cash calls made by the operator on all participants (including itself in respect of its own retained percentage interest) to fund items for which AFEs have been issued;

- a short period of grace during which default interest will apply to the payment of any defaulting party, followed by an obligation on all non-defaulting parties to make up the share of any defaulting party in order to ensure that the operator has the funds necessary to proceed with the development and that the development itself is not delayed as a result of the default of any one party;

- a suspension of the voting and other rights of the defaulting participant (including its right to petroleum) for so long as the default continues, with the opportunity to cure the default by paying up the amount in default together with interest at a default rate within a specified cure period (typically 60 days) after the date on which the cash call is due for payment; and

- ultimately, forfeiture of the defaulting party's share in the joint venture in favour of one or more of the other parties.

9.3 Funding an incorporated joint venture

The ability to attach differing rights to equity and loan capital issued to different classes of participants in an incorporated joint venture gives rise both to great flexibility and a range of structures potentially of considerable complexity, culminating in the structure of some management buy-outs which may include three or four levels of equity each with different rights and two or more levels of debt of different priorities.

At the simple end of the spectrum lie joint ventures in which the participants simply subscribe ordinary shares, or perhaps shares carrying special class rights as regards the appointment of directors or voting rights at general meetings but otherwise ranking for dividends and capital as if they were ordinary shares, for contributions in cash or in kind proportionate to their respective interests in the joint venture. Plain vanilla joint venture arrangements of this sort are by no means uncommon, especially when the joint venture participants are companies from the same sector of business of approximately equal bargaining power. Joint ventures structured in this manner may be appropriate, for example, if companies (whether from the manufacturing or service, especially financial service, sectors) are combining their activities in the same or complementary businesses with a view to increasing their overall market share.

Joint ventures of this type may also contain escrow machinery to provide a framework within which substantial increase of capital in the joint venture company can be arranged. Unlike the classic hydro-carbon or mineral development unincorporated joint venture referred to in 9.2 above, this species of joint venture may not have the need for a regular flow of cash contributions over time to meet the expenses of developing a fixed asset. Instead, the concern of the joint venturers may be to ensure that, if the joint venture agreement provides for an increase of capital or the parties agree on such an increase, no one party irrevocably commits itself to the increase of capital by paying up its share before it is clear that the other parties will perform their own obligations in relation to the increase of capital. It may be the case, for example, that no one party would wish to make up the increase of capital due from a defaulting party, but it is a condition of being able to proceed with the development for which increase of capital is required that all parties should promptly honour their own obligations. Some joint venture agreements, therefore, provide that in such a case the participants will have a period of, say, 21 days to subscribe their increase of capital to an escrow account opened in the name of the joint venture company. Once all parties have paid their subscription, the increase of capital becomes unconditional and the funds are released from escrow to the joint venture company. If any one party defaults, the increase of capital is rescinded; any participant which has paid its share of the increase to the escrow account is reimbursed the amount so paid; and the party which is in default in payment of its share of the increase in capital is susceptible to expulsion from the joint venture.

More complex share capital structures are frequently encountered in joint ventures which are used as venture or development capital vehicles or for management buy-outs or buy-ins. Many of these transactions involve balancing the interests of a management group, usually employed full-time in administering the affairs of the joint venture but with an investment in its capital of modest proportions, with those of one or more financial institutions whose concerns may relate more to the protections of their return on investment in the short to medium term, than to the long-term interests of the company itself. In an investment sector carrying much higher risks than portfolio investment in quoted securities, financial institutions will seek high compound rates of return on their participation (40 per cent per annum is not an uncommon target) and a secure exit route which can make venture capital and, perhaps to a lesser extent, development capital seem extremely expensive to an unsophisticated management team. The building blocks in structuring these transactions are different types of preference shares or convertible loan stocks, although deferred shares, too, may also be encountered. The different rights attached to these instruments, and their objectives in these types of joint ventures, are as follows:

(a) Cumulative: cumulative preference shares (which may provide for a fixed or, occasionally, floating rate of dividend) entitle the preference shareholders to payment of arrears of preference dividend before distributions are paid to any other class of shareholders. The rate of dividend attached to such shares is an important part of the financial institution's overall return; it is generally fixed at a market rate or above, and the rights to cumulation offer the institution some element of protection against the risk of a passed dividend in a bad year.

(b) Participating: participating preference shares give the financial institution the right, ahead of the holders of the ordinary shares, to a participating dividend (almost invariably a cumulative dividend and in addition to any fixed dividend) usually expressed by reference to a percentage of the company's annual pre-tax profits. For the purposes of calculating the participating dividend, adjustments to the normal basis of calculation of pre-tax profits may be agreed, for example so as to disregard directors' remuneration. The combination of fixed and participating dividends is a common approach adopted by financial institutions where a running yield (as opposed to a return based predominantly on the realisation of capital gains) is sought from the investment.

(c) Redeemable: preference shares may be made redeemable, at the behest either of the company itself or the preference shareholders. Redemption rights may accrue at a date certain or on the occurrence of specified circumstances affecting the company, and may be at par or at a premium. The purposes for which redemption rights may be provided in these types of transactions include the following:

— in conjunction with conversion rights, to maintain the financial institution's stake in the company at an agreed level. In this case, redemption may be at the company's option (often subject to the achievement of pre-set performance targets) to forestall conversion of preference shares into, and the consequent dilution of, valuable ordinary equity;

— to achieve part of the financial institution's required return. Redemption at a premium at a future date affords the financial institution an alternative means of securing its investment in lieu of fixed preference dividends and may offer advantages in relation to companies where profits are expected to increase sharply after a number of years at a lower rate (once, perhaps, the benefits of a specific investment programme start to be felt);

— to protect the institution's investment against external circumstances. The institution may have power to require redemption if, for example, a third party acquires more than a stipulated proportion of the company's ordinary equity, or the ordinary equity is subsequently listed on a stock exchange.

It should be noted, however, that the redemption of shares is subject to significant constraints under the Companies Acts. The detailed restrictions affecting redemption of shares are outside the scope of this book: briefly, however, a company may redeem shares only out of distributable profits or the proceeds of a new issue of shares.

(d) Convertible: convertible preference shares carry the right to convert the preference shares, at the behest of the holder, into shares of another class (usually ordinary equity, pari passu or with enhanced voting rights) in specific circumstances. Like redemption rights, conversion rights are employed for a number of purposes:

— as a sanction. The management group may be required to accept conversion, and therefore a corresponding dilution of their ordinary equity, if the company fails to redeem the securities or to pay dividends on an agreed date; and

— in conjunction with redemption rights, to adjust the institution's stake in the light of the company's financial performances. Commonly, these transactions include a mechanism (known as the 'ratchet'), the effect of which is to permit conversion of all or a part of an institution's holding of preferred shares if pre-determined performance targets (set perhaps by reference to annual pre-tax profits) are not achieved. Sometimes the ratchet may apply to the management's equity stake (instead or as well as the institution's). In this case, the management may hold convertible deferred shares which will convert into ordinary equity if the stipulated targets are met.

Loan stocks can be devised which mirror the effects of these class rights of preference shares: convertible loan stocks are commonplace, and participating debentures are also encountered, although only rarely. The choice between a loan stock and a preference share involves complex issues of financial evaluation. One feature commonly cited as an advantage of loan stock does, however, require comment here: the tax treatment of dividends on preference shares and interest on loan stock is different. In the hands of the paying company, loan stock interest may in some circumstances be deductible or (more commonly) allowable as a charge on income in computing the profits and gains of the company subject to UK corporation tax. Preference share dividends will be treated as distributions subject to the rules regarding advance corporation tax.

The ability to offset loan stock interest against other chargeable income is sometimes claimed as an advantage, but only companies which enjoy a strong and assured positive cash-flow can be confident of servicing loan stock interest, and few venture or development capital investments fall into this category. For them, uncertain profitability may make preference shares carrying a fixed and participating dividend more suitable, except in the instance of companies likely to become asset-rich but income-poor, where preference shares redeemable at a premium may be appropriate.

Chapter 10

Ancillary contracts

10.1 Introduction

In most joint ventures the parties will be contributing goods, services, know-how or capital and in respect of such contributions they will prima facie have a conflict of interest with the joint venture itself.

Although the joint venturers' contributions will be vital to the success of the joint venture itself, some of the benefit which they will obtain from the joint venture will be the consideration they receive for the goods or services they provide to the joint venture.

A party providing such goods or services should have a contract with the joint venture covering such matters. It is better for this contract (which is referred to in this chapter as an 'ancillary contract') to be separate from the main joint venture agreement although referred to in it.

The terms of the ancillary contracts themselves should not usually be incorporated into the joint venture agreement, as this should primarily be restricted to matters relating to the management and operation of the joint venture vehicle. To do so is to risk difficulties in enforcement (particularly if the joint venture vehicle is not a party) and in disentangling the rights and obligations of the parties (especially if covered by the same termination or deadlock provisions).

Although it is better to have ancillary contracts signed (or at any rate agreed) at the same time as the main joint venture agreement, it is vital to do so where the supply of goods and services or other matters are crucial to the success of the joint venture. Where it is necessary to establish the joint venture at high speed, the joint venture agreement can be signed before the ancillary contract, but the basic principles to be incorporated in the ancillary contract should always be agreed and incorporated in a clause or schedule to the joint venture agreement itself, as negotiation of the ancillary contract can cause as many difficulties as negotiation of the joint venture itself. Problems may arise as the parties begin to realise the actual cost of their contribution to the joint venture and the amount they expect to receive from it.

The lawyer's task in relation to ancillary contracts is to ensure that the joint venture will have the legal right to use everything which it will require to achieve the commercial aim of the parties.

The most common ancillary contracts found in joint ventures relate to the following areas:

10.2 Funding agreements

Many joint ventures derive their initial finance from a third party provider of venture capital who will itself participate in the joint venture, and whose attention is normally directed less at the management of the joint venture than at capital growth and the financial return from the joint venture.

The method of funding of joint ventures is dealt with in more detail in Chapter 9 but whatever method is used there will be a separate funding agreement. This will set out the terms on which the funding is to be made available, including the repayment arrangements, the restrictions to be imposed on the management of the joint venture, the financial covenants to be complied with by the business and the joint venturer's participation in the joint venture itself. The covenants and restrictions can be extremely onerous; providers of venture capital are notoriously inflexible in their demands. They are the party least likely to get carried away by the initial enthusiasm which sometimes prevents joint venturers from critically analysing all the risks at the start of a joint venture.

Sometimes the funding agreement itself will be preceded by a facility letter setting out the terms upon which the funds are to be provided to the joint venture, including any warranties and further information required.

10.3 Property rights

Suitable arrangements should be made for the licence, lease or purchase of the property where the joint venture is to conduct its business, even if this is to be at the offices of one of the participants.

The premises of the joint venture should if at all possible be kept physically distinct from those of the joint venturers as failure to do so can lead not only to adminstrative problems but also to disputes as to the charging of overheads for facilities used by the joint venture.

Where the joint venture is unincorporated, care should be taken to prevent the inadvertent operation of PA, s 20, which provides that all property and interests in property brought into the partnership stock or acquired, whether by purchase or otherwise, on account of the firm, or for the purposes and in the course of the partnership business are called partnership property. This may lead to disputes as to the precise ownership of items on the premises used by the joint venture. The independent identity of the property of the joint venture can become important in the context of insolvency, where the parties will not wish to leave it to the insolvency practitioner to decide which property belongs to whom.

As the parties may feel it unwise to commit themselves to a long-term lease or the purchase of freehold premises at the beginning of the venture, it is not uncommon for the joint venture to operate from the premises of one of the joint venturers. In that event the joint venture should at least take a licence from the occupier of the premises. An occupier who is himself a tenant under a lease should make quite certain that the establishment of another business on his premises does not put him in breach of the terms of his own lease, or give rise to any other problems in the context of planning, covenants to adjoining landowners or any mortgage arrangements which he might have.

Where a separate property is to be bought for the joint venture, it will be necessary for the solicitors to investigate title, planning restrictions, etc, in the usual way.

10.4 Protection of name and trade marks

As with any new business, thought will have to be given to the protection of the joint venture's name and trade marks. It is often (mistakenly) thought that registering the name of a company at the Companies Registry is enough to stop anybody else setting up a company with a similar name or selling products or services under the same or similar names. The position is that, although the Registrar of Companies has a discretion, which he may exercise within 12 months of registration, to direct a company to change its registered name if it is the same as or 'too like' a company name already registered, that discretion is rarely exercised. Even then, that of itself would not prevent the rival from *trading* by reference to a conflicting name or mark. But remedies are available through the law relating to trade and service marks.

These may be either registered or unregistered. Registered trade (or service) marks are protected by the statutory action for trade mark infringement. Unregistered trade marks are protected by the common law action for passing-off, one condition of which is to show established goodwill in the mark in question. This may present a problem for a newly formed joint venture.

The joint venture will often derive its service or trade marks from either (or both) of the joint venturers and it will be necessary to protect those marks. How to do this will depend on whether the marks concerned are

127

registered or not. If they are registered, it would be usual (and in most circumstances necessary) for the joint venture to be a licensee of the marks and for the licence to be registered (at the Trade Marks Registry) for each relevant registration. This licence is called a 'registered user agreement'. Over and above the ordinary requirements, a registered user agreement for a joint venture will normally provide that the right to use any of the joint venturers' marks expires if that joint venturer ceases to have an interest in the joint venture. Consequently, if one venturer disposes of his interest, the joint venture may have to change its corporate name and product marks. But such provisions are necessary to preserve the value of the venturer's established names and marks, if the outgoing venturer is not to be left in control of the use of the marks by the joint venture. Where the joint venture comprises a group of companies, subsidiary companies wishing to use the mark should enter into an agreement (again, to be registered) direct with the owner of the mark.

Where the marks are unregistered, the position is much more complex, although broadly the desired result will be more readily achieved if there is a transfer to the joint venture either of associated *registered* trade marks or of the whole of the relevant business.

10.5 Contracts for the supply of goods

If the joint venture is being set up to manufacture or market particular goods, then it may need to have a contract to ensure the supply to it of the goods, or the commodities or components that will make up the goods.

Pricing will obviously be of particular importance in this context, as will the term of the supply contract. Ideally this should be for a term of not less than the anticipated life of the joint venture, or if the joint venture is intended to be continuing, for as long a term as possible.

In settling the supply contract it will be important to agree an appropriate retention of title clause specifying the time at which the articles become the property of the joint venture. Where goods have to be shipped from abroad it will be necessary to provide for the currency and manner of payment as well as transport arrangements, with particular attention being paid to the risk of damage in transit and arrangements for the back-up supply of goods in case transport problems develop.

10.6 Contracts for the provision of services

Next to funding agreements, the most common type of ancillary agreement encountered in a joint venture is a contract for services.

One type of contract for services which is frequently entered into between joint ventures and their constituent members is the distribution or agency contract, particularly where the joint venture is being used as a means of penetrating a new market. In respect of these types of contracts many of the principles discussed in 1.4 will be relevant.

Another common example is the management or administration contract. Such contracts will often be used in the early stages of a joint venture, when it may be considered unwise to employ staff strictly for the purposes of the new vehicle.

In this way the joint venture can avoid incurring the dismissal and redundancy costs which may arise if the continued employment of people directly by it becomes no longer viable. On the other hand, the managing party in a management contract should be careful to ensure that it can require the employees to undertake the new duties for the joint venture within the terms of their existing job descriptions and that similarly no claims would arise if subsequently they were no longer required to work for the joint venture.

Whether or not an overall management contract is used a joint venture company will normally require staff from its parents, who will often be provided by means of secondment agreements, either in support of management contracts or directly between the party concerned and the company.

Secondment agreements raise particular problems, and in view of their importance and frequency in joint venture arrangements they will now be analysed in further detail.

10.7 Secondment agreements

If the joint venture is to be successful this will be helped by having skilled and experienced people working on it. One or more of the participating companies are likely to have skilled and experienced personnel whom they would like to work on the joint venture. How then should this be arranged? Should the employees be offered employment directly with the joint venture? Or alternatively, should they be seconded from the companies participating in the joint venture?

In its widest possible sense secondment connotes a situation where a person retains some kind of lifeline back to a company which employed him up to his going on secondment. It can therefore cover a situation where a person becomes employed for a particular period of time by another body, but who will usually have a contractual right, 'a lifeline', back to his former employing company after his spell working away for someone else. More usually however the expression suggests a situation where a person remains employed by the same person but spends his time working or performing duties for another. In other words, the employing company can still exert some control over the employee. The extent to which he does so during the secondment can vary enormously, and at the end of the day a court or industrial tribunal would need to determine as a matter of fact whether or not an employment arrangement had actually continued to exist during the secondment with the original employer or whether a new employment relationship has unwittingly been created with the company to whom the employee had been seconded. Factors such as reporting lines, continued participation in pension schemes or other benefit plans, salary payments and reviews are all likely to be factors which would influence the decision. If a new employment relationship has arisen then a further relevant consideration may be the ownership of intellectual property created during the new relationship. This could (at least in part) be owned by the new employer and not the original employer. For the purposes of this chapter it has been assumed that in most cases it will be the wish of all parties that the employee remains employed by the former employing company whilst working for the joint venture.

One of the main reasons why secondment is often chosen as the way for getting the people the participating companies want to work on the joint venture is that the employee's statutory continuity of employment with his employing company can be maintained. Unless the joint venture falls within the definition in the Employment Protection (Consolidation) Act 1978 of an associated employer the employee will not be able to count the period of service which he had accumulated with the participating company as part of the period of his continuous service with the joint venture. It may be particularly difficult for a 50/50 deadlock joint venture company to fall within this definition.

The definition has come in for some recent judicial attention in the case of *Pinkey v Sandpiper Drilling Ltd* [1989] ICR 389. Until this decision it had been thought that the definition of associated employers only applied as between limited companies. In other words the reference in the definition in the EPCA to 'company' had to be read literally to mean just a limited company so that it was only limited companies which could be associated. However, in *Pinkey* it was held that a partnership of limited companies should be viewed as though it were a company. This decision clearly has important implications in the context of joint ventures, particularly where one is considering a joint venture partnership arrangement.

Secondment may also be a preferable option for the joint venture in any event. It may be difficult for the joint venture to offer the same sort of contractual benefits which had been enjoyed by employees with a participating company.

A further preliminary consideration for a participating company will be whether or not the employee's contract of employment allows it to second the employee to another company without his prior consent. Whilst it would not be uncommon for the employment arrangements, particularly for senior people, to provide that the employer may second the employee to 'group companies' without his further consent being obtained first, the definition of these in the contractual arrangements will need to be considered to see whether or not the joint venture falls within them. If not, then the secondment may only take place, without risking claims for constructive dismissal, if the employee specifically consents.

There is not really one correct way of documenting secondment arrangements. Several possible ways may need to be considered. For example, where say only a couple of key employees are to be seconded and there are no particularly confidential matters regarding their secondment arrangements to be agreed between the participating company and the joint venture, a tripartite agreement between the participating company, joint venture and the employee(s) to be seconded may be the most appropriate document. This document should make it clear who owns the intellectual property arising out of the work done by the employee whilst on secondment. Where several or a large number of employees are to be seconded it may be appropriate to prepare an agreement between the participating company and the joint venture making it clear, as between them, who owns what and then have the participating company write to the employees explaining the terms on which they are to be seconded. Since this arrangement will not result in any undertakings being given directly by the employee to the joint venture a further document may be needed between the employee and the joint venture for example to ensure that the joint venture is in the best position to protect its confidential information.

It is similarly difficult to generalise about the contents of agreements to second employees to joint ventures as arrangements are likely to vary considerably depending on such factors as the nature of the joint venture, where it is situated and where the participating company is situated. The specimen agreements set out in Appendix 6 should provide a useful starting point. There are however, probably four major problem areas with secondment arrangements which deserve some more detailed attention. These are namely tax, pensions, continuance of contractual benefits and what happens at the end of the period of secondment.

Tax

In circumstances where a person is employed and paid by one company but works for a second then in general the first company is treated as making a supply of staff to the second company and the consideration for that supply is the payment by the second company, whether on a cost or on a cost plus basis on which VAT will be chargeable at the standard rate, unless the two companies are members of the same VAT group, or unless the joint venture is outside the United Kingdom in which case the supply of staff is zero-rated.

In most cases, therefore, where a joint venture is situated in the United Kingdom and where the joint venture reimburses the participating company for the salary and probably also other employment costs of the people seconded to it, VAT as well will be payable by the joint venture on reimbursement of these expenses.

It may be possible for the joint venture to minimise the VAT cost by arranging to pay the salaries direct to the employees on secondment to it. With careful drafting it should then only be liable for VAT on payments which it makes to the participating company. The joint venture should also arrange to pay the PAYE and National Insurance contributions due on the salaries direct to the appropriate authorities. An offshore joint venture may not be under any obligation to account for PAYE. The employee could stand to benefit from this because he could be paid gross subject only to deductions for any local taxes.

However, if payments of salary are made direct to the employee on secondment by the joint venture company then this may have unfortunate knock-on effects for the employee's pension arrangements: see further below. In addition the Revenue may decide that the employee has in reality been employed by the joint venture notwithstanding the identity of the other party to the contract of employment. Whilst again such a finding may be better from the VAT point of view it may not be so from the employment and pensions point of view. Caution should therefore be exercised before entering too enthusiastically into any arrangement to minimise VAT liability.

Pensions

Membership of an approved pension scheme must be confined to employees of employers participating in the scheme. Practice Note 3.9 of the Inland Revenue Practice Notes indicates that an employee may remain in full membership of an approved pension scheme when he is seconded to another employer provided that he does not become a member of another retirement benefit scheme during his period of secondment and provided that there is the definite expectation that he will return to service. If these conditions can be satisfied the rules of the scheme may give the employer or administrator discretion to permit continued membership for up to three years in any case or for longer with the Inland Revenue's consent.

There is no definition however of what the Inland Revenue consider secondment to be. Probably though, on the basis of current practice, for there to be a secondment in the eyes of the Inland Revenue a real employer/employee relationship must continue to exist. What constitutes such a relationship for these purposes is not entirely clear but factors such as whether the employer retains any element of control over the employee whilst he is on secondment, whether he still pays the salary to the employee and whether he provides their contractual benefits are likely to be considered by the Inland Revenue. There would also still, most importantly, need to be a clear expectation that the employee would return to performing duties full-time for the employing company at the end of the period of secondment.

Where the secondment is known at the outset to continue for more than three years the Inland Revenue should be consulted in advance to see whether a special arrangement can be agreed. Similarly, if at the end of a three-year period the parties wish the secondment to continue, the Inland Revenue should be consulted to see if the employee's right to remain in the employing company's scheme could be extended.

If the employee is or is to be regarded as employed by the joint venture then his continued membership of the pension scheme could be achieved by the joint venture itself becoming party to the scheme of that employer from whose employment the employee has transferred. The Inland Revenue will permit this if the degree of association between the two bodies is sufficiently close as it would normally be in the case of a joint venture.

If the joint venture is not resident in the United Kingdom then Inland Revenue Practice Notes 17.7, 17.8 and 17.9 provide that the employee's continued membership of the United Kingdom employer's scheme may continue in certain specified circumstances including secondment as it is described in Practice Note 3.9. The other circumstances are:

(a) where the employees are sent abroad in circumstances which cannot be regarded as secondment, to serve with non-resident companies in a group of which the parent company is resident in the United Kingdom, but the parent company retains control over the movements of the employees within the group, ie remains in a position to recall them or to direct them elsewhere; or

(b) where employees remain effectively chargeable to United Kingdom tax under Case I of Schedule E because they do not work overseas for a period of 365 days or more.

The problem in the joint venture context for the first of these exceptions is that, whilst the three-year time limit for secondment as set out in Practice Note 3.9 does not seem to apply, the exception only applies where employees are sent to work for other group companies. As has already been explained above this is likely to cause problems where the joint venture is not part of the employing company's group. If the employee is to be employed or regarded as employed by the joint venture directly then an overseas joint venture also could participate in the former employing company's scheme as explained above as an alternative solution for ensuring the employee's continued membership of the pension scheme. At the end of the day, if the employee's continued membership of the employing company's pension scheme is crucial it will be necessary to tailor the secondment arrangements so that they fit within the relevant Inland Revenue Practice Notes.

Continuance of contractual benefits

An employee's continued participation during a period of secondment in benefit schemes run by his employer may need to be considered. The rules of these should be checked to ensure that membership is not prejudiced by the secondment. The effect on pension scheme membership has already been discussed above. Particular thought may need to be given to an employee's continued participation in a bonus scheme where his share may depend in some way on his contribution to the profits of the employing company. He may not be able to make this contribution whilst on secondment. If however participation in the bonus scheme is part of the employee's contract of employment, then removal of the right to participate will not easily be done without giving rise to claims for constructive dismissal.

Further problems may also be encountered under, for example, Inland Revenue Approved Share Option Schemes where the entitlement to participate depends on working for the participating company for not less than 25 hours per week. The Revenue however appear to take the view that whilst employees who are on secondment may be providing their services to the joint venture they are still to be treated as working full-time for the participating company. The rules of individual schemes should still however be carefully checked as these may still insist on employees actually working for their employing company or at least another group company.

Employees who are on secondment should also not be forgotten when new bonus or share participation shemes are introduced by the employing company.

Return at the end of the secondment

For the pension reasons outlined above it may be necessary to provide clearly that the employee will return to performing duties full-time for the participating company at the end of the period of secondment. It may be more straightforward to do this where the secondment to the joint venture is for a fixed period. Even if the employee is seconded indefinitely he may insist on it being made clear that whenever the secondment does end he will return into the fold of the participating company. The participating company will need to consider what job he will be given to do on his return. If the secondment has been for a long time then the employer may not be able to offer the employee the same job back and if there is a risk of this then the participating company should build into the secondment arrangement for itself sufficient flexibility to enable it to redeploy the employee without risking giving rise to a claim for constructive dismissal.

Chapter 11

Taxation

11.1 Introduction

Tax considerations will often have a significant influence at the outset in determining the choice of joint venture vehicle. However, in practice, the most suitable tax structure and commercial necessities will often not coincide. In such cases the most appropriate or efficient tax structure may have to be compromised in favour of a structure which more adequately suits the commercial necessities. Nevertheless, tax considerations are extremely important and in the same way that one should not lose sight of commercial aims in the midst of an intricate tax planning exercise, so tax should never be forgotten when deciding how best to achieve those commercial aims.

This chapter considers in turn the treatment under UK tax law of: an incorporated joint venture; a partnership; and an unincorporated association. Particular tax aspects relating to property joint ventures, management buy-outs and secondment arrangements are discussed or referred to in Chapters 7, 8 and 10 respectively.

11.2 Joint venture companies

For brevity it is assumed that the joint venture vehicle will be a UK resident trading company and that its shareholders are all UK resident companies holding their shareholdings in the joint venture company other than as trading stock.

Corporation tax

A joint venture company is a separate legal and taxable entity. As such it will be assessable to UK corporation tax on its total profits (including chargeable gains) wherever those profits arise, under normal corporation tax principles. A discussion of those general principles is outside the scope of this book. However, there are a number of specific points which frequently arise in the context of a joint venture and which therefore merit particular consideration in this chapter.

Losses

Particularly in the early stages of a joint venture careful consideration will have to be given as to how any losses arising in the joint venture company can best be utilised. Similarly, consideration will have to be given as to how any profits arising in the joint venture company can best be sheltered. It need hardly be said that this point should be considered at the time that the structure is put into place and not when the losses or profits arise.

In the absence of the availability of group or consortium relief, losses arising in the joint venture company will, in accordance with normal corporation tax principles, be available for set-off against the profits of the joint venture company. Thus, losses may be tied up in the company for a number of years whilst its participants are paying corporation tax on their own profits. Alternatively, the joint venture company may pay corporation tax whilst tax losses are tied up in its participants. This situation should be avoided and, depending on the circumstances, this may be possible by using one of two reliefs.

Group relief

Broadly, current trading losses incurred by a company and certain other amounts eligible for relief from corporation tax may be surrendered by that company to another company which is within the same group. Two companies are treated as part of a group for these purposes if one is a 75 per cent subsidiary of the other or both are 75 per cent subsidiaries of a third company. A company is a 75 per cent subsidiary of another company if not less than 75 per cent of its ordinary shares (that is all shares other than fixed rate preference shares) are beneficially owned by the other company. Accordingly, where a joint venture company is a 75 per cent subsidiary of one of its corporate participants then, subject to anti-avoidance provisions in ICTA, ss 410 and 413 any losses which it incurs may be surrendered to that participant. Similarly, losses of the participant may be surrendered to the joint venture company.

In practice, most joint venture companies will not be able to take advantage of the group relief provisions either because no participant will hold 75 per cent of the ordinary shares of the company, or because there are arrangements in existence in relation to the joint venture company, possibly embodied in the company's articles or in a shareholders' agreement, which will fall foul of the anti-avoidance provisions in ICTA, ss 410 and 413 restricting the availability of group relief in certain circumstances.

Consortium relief

Consortium relief is simply a form of group relief whereby current trading losses and certain other amounts eligible for relief from corporation tax can be surrendered by the company that is owned by the consortium to its members in proportion, subject to anti-avoidance provisions, to their shareholdings. Further, the consortium losses etc available for surrender to a consortium member may also be surrendered to a company within the consortium member's own group. Losses of a consortium member and companies in its own group may be surrendered to the consortium owned company for offset against the consortium member's 'share' of the consortium owned company's profits.

For these purposes, a company is owned by a consortium if three-quarters or more of its ordinary share capital is beneficially owned by UK resident companies, none of which has a holding of less than one-twentieth of that capital. Anti-avoidance provisions apply if a genuine consortium relationship does not exist. The relief is not available where the consortium owned company is a 75 per cent subsidiary of any company (in which case group relief may be available) except where the consortium company is a 90 per cent directly held subsidiary of a holding company which is owned by the consortium. Nor is relief available where the anti-avoidance provisions of s 410 of ICTA apply. These relate to situations where 'arrangements' exist for the consortium company to cease, in various ways, to be a consortium company. The Inland Revenue has issued a Statement of Practice on the subject (SPS/80, 26 March 1980).

Group income and charges on income

Where more than 50 per cent of the ordinary shares of a joint venture company are held by one corporate shareholder or where the joint venture company is a company owned by a consortium, then an election may be made under ICTA, s 247 to pay part or the whole of its dividends without accounting for advance corporation tax. Dividends paid under such an election are not regarded as franked investment income in the hands of the recipient corporate shareholder, and as they are paid out of taxed income, no further tax is payable on this group income by the recipient.

A similar election can be made for charges on income to be paid by the joint venture company to its shareholders, or by a shareholder which holds more than 50 per cent of the ordinary share capital of the joint venture company to that company, without deduction of tax by the payer.

Anti-avoidance provisions introduced by the Finance Act 1989 ensure that an election can only be made where a genuine group or consortium relationship exists. In addition, a consortium election will no longer be possible if the consortium owned company is or may, by virtue of arrangements, become a 75 per cent subsidiary of any company.

Advance corporation tax

Surplus advance corporation tax (ACT), that is, ACT which has been paid but which cannot be set off against the payer's mainstream corporation tax liability and which has not been repaid, may be surrendered by a company to any other company which is its 51 per cent subsidiary provided that such subsidiary was a 51 per cent subsidiary of it or (in relation to accounting periods ended on or after 14 March 1989) of its parent company throughout the accounting period during which the surplus arose. Again, anti-avoidance provisions exist denying the ability to surrender surplus ACT where arrangements exist by virtue of which any person has or could obtain control of the subsidiary company but not of the parent company (ICTA, s 240(5)). Again, care should be taken in structuring the joint venture to ensure that these provisions are not breached.

It should be noted that surplus ACT may only be surrendered to a 51 per cent subsidiary.

If a consortium member has surplus ACT, then it may be advisable for dividends to be paid by the joint venture company to that consortium member outside of a group income election. This will give rise to a liability to pay ACT on such dividends but will mean that the consortium member receives franked investment income out of which it may pay dividends without increasing its ACT surplus.

Value added tax

A joint venture company will be subject to VAT under normal VAT principles, a discussion of which is outside the scope of this book. If the joint venture company is a member of the same group of companies as a corporate participant, then it may be included in a VAT group registration with that participant. Two companies are treated as members of the same group for these purposes if one 'controls' the other or if both are controlled by a third person. One company is deemed to control another if it is that other's holding company within the meaning of CA 1985, or following its amendment, CA 1989. The principal effects of a group of companies having a single VAT registration are: first, that supplies of goods or services made to or by a member of the group are treated as supplied to or by the representative member of the group, and, secondly, supplies of goods or services between group members are disregarded for VAT purposes. Accordingly, where a preponderance of goods or services is supplied between the joint venture company and one of its participants, then it may be advantageous, depending upon whether either company makes exempt or taxable supplies, to ensure that these two companies are brought within the same VAT group registration.

Stamp duty

If the participants transfer assets to the joint venture company then stamp duty on the transfer will need to be considered although some form of relief from duty may be available. In addition, unless at the time that the assets are transferred from the participant to the joint venture company the two companies are in the same group (as defined in the Income and Corporation Taxes Act 1970, s 272), the transfer may trigger a tax charge on capital gains.

11.3 Partnerships

In considering a joint venture partnership, it is assumed that all participants in the joint venture are UK resident companies and that the partnership is a trading partnership managed and controlled in the United Kingdom.

Corporation tax

As long as a partnership includes a corporate member, then under ICTA, s 114, the profit or loss of the trade of the partnership is computed in the same way and for the same accounting periods as for a company except that:

(a) losses incurred in other accounting periods cannot be deducted;

(b) capital allowances and charges and charges on income are not immediately deductible in arriving at the total profit or loss;

(c) references in the legislation to distribution are ignored;

(d) changes in the membership of the partnership are ignored provided that there remains at least one corporate partner who was a partner before the change.

In arriving at the profit or loss of the partnership, a deduction will be allowed for any trading expenses incurred by one partner. Thus, if a partner takes on employees who devote their time to the partnership then the costs of employing them may be deducted from partnership profits.

Once the trading profit or loss of the partnership has been calculated, each partner's share is calculated according to its profit-sharing entitlement for the accounting period of the partnership in question. The partner's share of capital allowances and charges not deducted in arriving at the trading profit or loss is similarly calculated and each partner's share of the adjusted profits is subject to corporation tax as if it were a separate Schedule D Case I source of income. If the accounting period of the partner company differs from that of the partnership, the company's share of the partnership profits is apportioned on a time basis to the company's accounting period.

The company's share of the profits or losses will be included in its total profits or losses, and all normal corporation tax principles will apply to that part of the total profits or losses.

Thus a company may set other losses and reliefs against its share of partnership profit and, subject to the exception of terminal loss relief, may set its share of partnership losses and reliefs against other income. The ability to set partnership losses and reliefs against other income can often be very attractive particularly where the partnership incurs substantial amounts of capital expenditure eligible for tax relief. In addition, if the company is also a member of a group, it may be able to use the group relief provisions. However, if it is intended to make use of the group relief provisions, regard should be had to the anti-avoidance provisions of ICTA, s 116 which apply where a corporate partner's share in the profits or losses of an accounting period are enjoyed by other members of the partnership or where the company receives any payment or other benefit (other than a payment for group relief) in respect of its share of the loss of the partnership.

If this provision applies then the company cannot:

(a) set off its share of any partnership loss or charges on income against other profits;

(b) set off non-partnership trading losses, surplus capital allowances or charges on income against partnership profits;

(c) set off advance corporation tax against its corporation tax liability on its share of partnership profits.

Value added tax

Partnerships fall within the general principles of VAT. However, a partnership is not in itself a 'person' for VAT purposes but is a group of taxable persons trading jointly. Where a partnership exists and it consists of a group of taxable persons, the registration is usually made in the name of the partnership. Accordingly, if supplies of the partnership are likely to exceed the VAT registration threshold, then the partnership may be required to be registered.

11.4 Unincorporated associations

As mentioned in Chapter 3, an unincorporated association consists of a contractual relationship between the intending parties to the joint venture which does not amount to a partnership. The taxation consequences of this vehicle (if it can be called a vehicle) depend to a very large extent on the subject matter of the contracts concerned and on their terms and the following comments offer only general guidance.

Corporation tax

Any income etc received by a corporate joint venturer under the contract will form a part of its total profits and accordingly will be subject to corporation tax under normal principles. Conversely, expenditure incurred under the contract should be deductible in accordance with the normal rules.

Value added tax

Any fee received, in whatever form, by a taxable (for VAT purposes) participant supplying goods or services under the contract will, unless the supply is an exempt supply, be subject to VAT either at the standard rate or at the zero rate depending upon the nature of the supply. For companies receiving the supplies whose own supplies are fully taxable this should not be a concern. However, where the recipient of the supplies is not taxable or partially exempt then the whole or part of the VAT paid on the supplies to it will be irrecoverable and will represent an extra cost. The cost could be significant, the standard rate of VAT currently standing at 15 per cent.

Chapter 12

Competition law

12.1 Introduction

It is impossible to keep the establishment of a joint venture separate from competition law considerations. Both the domestic and the EEC rules may apply and so may other national systems, particularly if American or German interests are involved.

Here, the main features of the UK and EEC systems are briefly set out, but the non-specialist is warned that this area is complex, somewhat grey and, particularly insofar as the EEC rules are concerned, changeable.

12.2 UK law

There are two principal piece of legislation in the United Kingdom which are relevant to joint ventures. These are the Fair Trading Act 1973 (FTA), as amended by the Companies Act 1989 (CA 1989), and the Restrictive Trade Practices Act 1976 (RTPA). It is worth noting, however, that a recent White Paper on restrictive trade practices has indicated that the RTPA is likely to be replaced with something modelled on Article 85 of the EEC Treaty which deals with competition law (see 12.3 below).

Fair Trading Act 1973

The first question for joint venturers is to look at the FTA and decide whether there is a merger situation qualifying for investigation under s 64. Such a situation exists where:

(a) there is a transaction between two or more businesses;

(b) at least one of the businesses is carried on in the United Kingdom or by, or under the control of, a body corporate incorporated in the United Kingdom;

143

(c) the activities of one or more of the businesses cease to be distinct, in whole or in part, from those of the other businesses involved because:

    (1) they are brought under common ownership or control, which may happen if one business acquires an interest as low as 15 per cent in the activities of another business; or

    (2) either one of them ceases to be carried on at all, as a consequence of an arrangement designed to prevent competition between them; and

(d) either:

    (1) the value of the *gross* assets taken over exceeds £30,000,000; or

    (2) two or more of the businesses supply or acquire goods or services of the same description and together they account for at least 25 per cent of the goods or services of the relevant kinds supplied or acquired in the United Kingdom or in a substantial part of the United Kingdom.

It can be seen that there is no merger situation if the venture is a completely new enterprise. However, if an existing enterprise is contributed by either party to a joint venture in which a UK party is interested, there will be a merger situation and the question will be whether it satisfies either of the tests set out in paragraph (d) above.

In connection with the assets test, it is important to note the provisions of s 67(2)(a), which provide that the value of the assets taken over is the cumulative value of the assets employed in the business activities which cease to be distinct, except any business which remains under the same control or ownership. If no business remains under the same control or ownership (ie there is total integration), the business having the assets of the highest value is disregarded.

Where a merger qualifies for investigation, the Secretary of State for Trade and Industry, who is advised in this connection by the Director General of Fair Trading, has a discretion to refer the case to the Monopolies and Mergers Commission (MMC) for investigation. That discretion is exercised primarily in the light of the venture's impact on competition. Similarly if a case is referred to the MMC, that body will pay greater attention to its impact on competition.

But the MMC will also assess the merger in the light of the public interest as a whole, which is a much wider context (defined in FTA, s 84).

If the MCC considers a merger to be against the public interest, the Secretary of State may (and ordinarily will) prevent the merger from proceeding or, if it is already in existence, require it to be unscrambled. In certain cases, it is possible for the merger to be allowed to proceed on the basis of undertakings given by the parties as to their future behaviour.

There is no system of compulsory pre-notification or prior approval except in certain cases concerning newspapers. However, the risk of investigation (and possible divestiture) after the fact means that parties commonly seek clearance from the Secretary of State (via the Director General) before implementing their transaction.

Certain procedural changes were introduced by CA 1989. Notably:

— there is now a system of voluntary pre-notification for transactions that have not been concluded and which have been publicised. In such cases, subject to compliance with the procedural requirements and subject to certain exceptions, a merger reference cannot be made more than 45 working days at most after notice of the merger is given to the Director General; and

— the Secretary of State now has formal powers to accept undertakings to cure public interest objections to a transaction (eg by disposal of parts of a business) as a substitute for referring the transaction to the MMC for investigation. Such undertakings are negotiated with the Director General of Fair Trading.

Restrictive Trade Practices Act 1976

The other piece of legislation which is relevant in the context of competition is the RTPA which regulates restrictive agreements.

An 'agreement' is defined in s 43 of RTPA to include agreements and arrangements whether or not intended to be legally enforceable. The meaning of these terms has been judicially amplified and it is clear that it is the whole of the arrangements between the parties which will be considered, whether or not wholly in writing and whether or not in the same document.

The RTPA applies to agreements to which there are at least two parties carrying on certain kinds of businesses (generally the manufacture or supply of goods or the supply of certain services) within the United Kingdom under which relevant restrictions are accepted by two or more parties. It is not possible to list here all possible relevant restrictions in the case of joint ventures, or to outline the complicated structure of exemptions for which RTPA provides. Suffice it to say that agreements, in the wide sense, between joint venturers not to compete with the joint venture or agreements between themselves and/or with the joint venture body containing terms of the supply or purchase of goods may contain relevant restrictions for the purposes of RTPA.

If an agreement satisfies those requirements (and irrespective of its effect on competition), it must be furnished to the Director General of Fair Trading before any relevant restrictions come into effect and, in any event, within three months after the agreement has been made. Failure to furnish particulars of an agreement in due time makes the restrictions void and unenforceable. It also exposes the parties to the risk of injunctive proceedings at the instance of the Director General and third party actions for damages. If an agreement is furnished in due time, the parties are free to implement it whilst it is investigated.

Once an agreement has been furnished to the Director General, it will be placed on a public register (unless stringent tests of confidentiality can be satisfied), following which it will be reviewed to determine whether any of the restrictions accepted are significant. In the context of a joint venture, the Director General has indicated that he is likely to find restrictions insignificant provided that the joint venture does not materially diminish competition and provided that the restrictions are not beyond what is required for proper operation of the joint venture. If the restrictions are found to be insignificant, then the file will be closed at that point.

If any of the restrictions are found to be significant, the Director General has a duty to refer the agreement to the Restrictive Practices Court which decides whether the restrictions are in the public interest. Restrictions are assumed to be against the public interest unless the parties establish specific public benefits. If they fail to do that in respect of any restriction, the court must declare the restriction contrary to the public interest and will enjoin its further implementation.

As a matter of practice, it is extremely rare for agreements to be investigated by the court. Ordinarily, parties who cannot persuade the Director General that their restrictions are insignificant will modify their agreements to accommodate the Director General's objections.

12.3 EEC law

Both the European Coal and Steel Community (ECSC) Treaty and the European Economic Community (EEC) Treaty contain provisions dealing with competition law.

The ECSC deals with a narrow sphere of economic activity and is not dealt with here, but it should be noted that joint ventures falling within its ambit may require prior authorisation from the European Commission.

The relevant provisions of the EEC Treaty are to be found in Articles 85 and 86. Article 85 declares that agreements between undertakings which may affect trade between member states and which have as their object or effect the prevention, restriction or distortion of competition within the common market are prohibited. Such agreements are pro tanto illegal and unenforceable, and expose the parties to the risk of fines imposed by the European Commission and third party actions for damages in national courts. Article 85(3) provides that the prohibition may in certain circumstances be declared inapplicable, either by block exemption or by an individual decision. There is no block exemption dealing with joint ventures as such. Block exemptions relevant to certain types of joint venture are discussed below.

Article 86 prohibits any abuse of a dominant position within the common market by any enterprise insofar as it may affect trade between member states. As with Article 85, breach of Article 86 carries the risk of fines and civil damages actions. In practice, most joint ventures are capable of review under Article 85 and separate issues are unlikely to arise under Article 86.

The recent Council Regulation on the Control of Concentrations between Undertakings (Regulation (EEC) 4064/89 OJ L395/1, 30 December 1989, known as the Merger Regulation) introduces a system of mandatory pre-notification for 'concentrations' which satisfy certain economic criteria. The Regulation will apply to certain types of joint venture. A concentration is caught by the Regulation if it has 'Community dimension'. A concentration has Community dimension if:

(a) the aggregate worldwide turnover of all the parties taken together exceeds 5 billion ECU; and

(b) the aggregate Community turnover of at least two of the parties, taken individually, exceeds 250 million ECU;

unless each of the merging parties has over two-thirds of its Community turnover in one and the same member state, in which case it will not have Community dimension even if both the minimum thresholds are satisfied.

If a concentration has Community dimension, then the parties must notify it to the Commission and may, in most instances, be required not to give effect to the transaction until the Commission has concluded its review.

So far as joint ventures are concerned, the Regulation makes a distinction between two types of joint venture. A joint venture which performs 'on a lasting basis all the functions of an autonomous economic entity' and which does not give rise to a co-ordination of competitive behaviour, constitutes a concentration and may, therefore, be subject to the requirements of the Regulation. By contrast, an operation 'which has as its object or effect the co-ordination of the competitive behaviour of undertakings which remain independent' is not a concentration—such joint ventures will continue to be regulated by Articles 85 and 86.

When assessing a joint venture's compatibility with the EEC Treaty, the European Commission concerns itself with broadly the same issues as the UK authorities (namely, the extent to which the joint venture itself eliminates competition and the impact of particular restrictions on competition). Similar considerations are likely to apply in the context of the Merger Regulation.

So far as those joint ventures which constitute concentrations are concerned, the criteria for application of the Regulation are turnover-related (as described above). So far as other joint ventures are concerned, a transaction may fall outside Article 85(1) altogether if:

(a) it does not have the requisite effect on inter-state trade, for example where the joint venture has effect only on the territory of one member state (without producing any ramifications for businesses established elsewhere in the Community) or on the territories of third countries; or

(b) the parties' combined market share is low, typically less than 5 per cent; or

(c) the parties are neither actual nor potential competitors and the joint venture arrangements do not appreciably affect the position of third parties in downstream or upstream markets.

Where a joint venture does fall within the ambit of Article 85(1), the Commission's concern is likely to be most acute where the joint venture covers the markets in which the parties compete. Less, but still significant, concern may be felt where the parties compete in upstream or downstream markets. The least worrying combination is where the parties compete in quite unrelated markets, although the Commission may still be concerned to ensure that co-operation does not spread to that market.

Several Article 85(3) exemptions have been granted for joint ventures, typically where:

(a) the joint venture introduced new competition in a structurally competitive market by means of rationalisation, introduction of new or improved products or processes for the opening up of new markets; or

(b) the joint venture led to the reduction of structural over-capacities and helped undertakings in crisis sectors to return to viability.

Even if the Commission is willing to exempt the joint venture in principle, it may well require modification of particular provisions (such as those providing for post-dissolution non-competition, or for exclusive supply relationships between parents and the joint venture) as a condition of granting the exemption. It should also be remembered that exemption can only be granted for a finite period (typically ranging between five and twenty years).

As mentioned above, no block exemption applies to joint ventures generally. So where a joint venture falls within Article 85(1), the parties will have to seek specific exemption under Article 85(3). However, if the only reason for the joint venture falling within Article 85(1) is because of provisions relating to intellectual property, it may be possible to benefit from a block exemption. Even if a block exemption is not available, the closer those provisions are to the acceptable provisions specified in the relevant block exemption Regulation, the more likely it is that the joint venture will succeed in obtaining specific exemption. The block exemptions particularly relevant to technology joint ventures (Chapter 6) and collaboration agreements (Chapter 5) are as follows.

Technology joint ventures

The most important block exemptions for a technology joint venture are contained in the Patent Licensing Regulation (2349/84), the Know-how Licensing Regulation (556/89) and the Research and Development Regulation (418/85). Each can apply only in certain situations. Notably, the patent and know-how licensing block exemptions do not apply to a licensing agreement between competing undertakings which hold interests in a joint venture, or between one of them and the joint venture, if the licensing agreement relates to the activities of the joint venture. A mixed patent and know-how licensing agreement can benefit from the provisions of only one (and not both) of the relevant Regulations. Together the Patent and Know-how Regulations outline a fairly comprehensive code for patent and know-how licensing agreements. The Research and Development Regulation is of limited use: one condition is that it applies only where the parties' combined production of the products capable of being improved or replaced by the products to which the relevant agreement relates does not exceed 20 per cent of the EEC market or a 'substantial part' thereof. Furthermore, it does not apply to the marketing of the products.

Each block exemption specifies a list of clauses (so-called 'grey' clauses) which, although potentially anti-competitive, may be included in a relevant agreement and nonetheless be exempted from the application of Article 85. Examples of grey-listed clauses are the granting of exclusive licences or obligations on the licensee not to exploit the know-how or patent in territories reserved to other licensees or the licensor. The inclusion of such grey-listed clauses in an otherwise anti-competitive agreement will not ensure, however, that the agreement is exempted. If a clause falls within the relevant 'black' list of clauses, the agreement is immediately taken outside the block exemption, so that Article 85(1) will apply to it and an individual exemption should be sought. Examples of black-listed clauses are obligations on the licensee to assign rights in its improvements to the licensor, obligations on the licensee not to challenge the validity of the licensed intellectual property rights and restrictions on the licensee as to the customers he may serve. The detailed provisions of the Regulations will need to be carefully considered before any reliance may be placed on them.

Collaboration agreements

The block exemptions which are potentially relevant are those concerning Specialisation (417/85) and Research and Development (418/85). The Specialisation block exemption regulation covers certain agreements under which undertakings accept reciprocal obligations not to manufacture certain products but to leave it to others to manufacture them, or to manufacture them only jointly. Such specialisation obligations can be coupled with obligations concerning research and development which may fall within the Research and Development Regulation.

As mentioned above, if an agreement contains a black-listed clause then it is automatically taken outside the relevant block exemption. If the conditions for application of Article 85(1) were satisfied, an obligation such as that contained in clause 6 of the specimen agreement in Appendix 4 would probably take the agreement outside the Research and Development block exemption which withdraws the benefit of block exemption when the parties 'are restricted in their freedom to carry out research and development independently or in co-operation with third parties in a field unconnected with that to which the programme relates, *or after its completion, in the field to which the programme relates or in a connected field* (Article 6(a)). Such a clause might nevertheless qualify in certain circumstances for individual exemption under Article 85(3).

In contrast clause 3.2 of the specimen agreement should be acceptable since the Regulation permits obligations 'not to enter into agreements with third parties on research and development in the fields in which the programme relates or in a closely connected field during the execution of the programme' (Article 4(1)(b)). Since an absolute restriction is allowed, a qualified restriction should not give rise to any problems.

As expressed at the beginning of the chapter, the law in this area is complex and, in some cases, uncertain. The general principle seems to be if in doubt seek exemption or negative clearance for it may not only be one of the venturers who seeks to invalidate the terms of a successful joint venture—it may be a jealous competitor.

Chapter 13

Disputes settlement

13.1 Introduction

This chapter deals with disputes between the joint venturers. As noted in Chapter 4, a distinction should be drawn between disputes as to the commercial policy to be followed by the joint venture and those relating to the legal rights of the parties as between themselves. The former will rarely be suitable for the sort of dispute settlement methods considered below, and are more appropriately dealt with by the less conventional mechanisms described in Chapter 4. However, in the last resort the disputes settlement clause may have to deal with both types of problem and the mechanism used deserves more consideration than it often receives.

13.2 Arbitration, litigation or an expert?

The first question is who is to do the resolving: an arbitrator, a court or an expert. Each method has its advantages and disadvantages.

Arbitration

Speed and flexibility
In theory, it should be possible to resolve a dispute by arbitration considerably more quickly than would be possible, at least by a full trial, in the courts. A procedure can be agreed which is adapted to the particular case, omitting many of the time-consuming procedural steps which are intrinsic to court proceedings. The lengthy wait for a hearing, caused by backlogs in the courts, is avoided. And, under English law, the parties may agree to exclude their right of appeal (which is anyway limited) from the arbitrator's decision, thus greatly reducing the time which the proceedings may last.

These are real advantages. There are, however, qualifications. First, one must pick the right arbitrator; a busy arbitrator can result in delays as long as those of the courts. Secondly, and more fundamentally, the advantages of speed and flexibility are wholly dependent on the parties being able to agree and co-operate. One party may lack the will or the imagination required and insist on the full sequence of pleadings, discovery, etc. Even worse, if he wishes to be obstructive, the arbitrator's powers (under English law) to take action, for example where a party fails to keep to a set timetable or procedural orders, are limited and clumsy. In such cases arbitration proceedings can take a very long time.

Cost

Cost is linked to speed. If arbitration proceedings can be kept short, if discovery can be limited, then the cost will be kept down. If normal court procedure is followed, the legal fees involved will be the same as in court proceedings, but the parties will have to pay in addition the arbitrator's fees and the cost of hiring the necessary facilities.

Technical/legal knowledge

Arbitration allows the parties to choose an arbitrator who has already the background knowledge necessary to understand a technical dispute. This should reduce the time necessary for explanation, and avoid the need for the parties to call expert witnesses. Again, in practice one needs co-operative parties, or a firm arbitrator, if this advantage is to be fully realised.

In technical cases, a suitably-qualified arbitrator should also be more likely than an unqualified judge to reach the right technical result. On the other hand a non-legally qualified arbitrator will often have difficulty in dealing with legal issues that arise and which might have a decisive effect on the result. Arbitrators have something of a reputation for splitting the difference, irrespective of the legal merits.

Confidentiality

In theory arbitration proceedings are confidential. There is no public hearing and there is an accepted (though not established) duty to keep the substance of the proceedings confidential. In practice it may be difficult to enforce this duty. A more real advantage is that there is no writ on a public register to be inspected by the newspapers' court correspondents.

Lack of acrimony

This is not an advantage. Arbitration proceedings are usually every bit as acrimonious as litigation.

Enforcement

Perhaps surprisingly, arbitration awards are more readily enforceable abroad than are court judgments. This is because there is a very wide-ranging multilateral treaty for the enforcement of arbitration awards, the New York Convention of 1958, which has no real equivalent in the field of recognition of judgments. The United States for example is a party to the New York Convention, but not to any treaty with the United Kingdom for reciprocal enforcement of judgments. In many cases this difference will be one of ease and speed of enforcement, rather than eventual practicability, but that difference may be substantial.

Neutral forum

The last advantage will in many cases be the most compelling. Where the joint venture partners are from different countries, each may be reluctant to submit to the jurisdiction of the court of the other's country. Normally it would not be attractive, and may not be possible, for the parties to commit themselves to litigation in the courts of a country with which neither has any connection. Arbitration in a neutral forum may be the only acceptable alternative.

Expert determination

Contracts frequently provide for disputes to be determined by an individual, acting as an expert rather than as an arbitrator, in circumstances where it is clear that the draftsman does not appreciate the consequences of such a provision. Under English law, an expert is appropriate to decide a technical question of fact, which he may decide on the basis of his own expert knowledge. He is not obliged (unless the contract provides for it) to allow the parties to present arguments or evidence to him. He is not obliged to weigh those arguments judicially and choose between them. He cannot order discovery, nor are any of the court's back-up powers available (eg to grant injunctions or subpoenas), as they are in an arbitration. He is not obliged (again, unless the contract provides for it) to give reasons for his decision. If he gets it wrong, there is no possibility of appeal. The dissatisifed party may only upset his decision by suing him and the other party in the courts; and will only succeed if the decision was (a) reasoned and (b) fundamentally wrong. And the decision is not directly enforceable. It can only be enforced by a fresh action on the contract.

Therefore an expert determination clause is appropriate in, for example, share valuation or rent review provisions. It is not suitable for contracts in which questions of law, or disputes as to factual events, are likely to have to be resolved.

Litigation

The advantages and disadvantages of litigation will be apparent from the discussion of arbitration above. Litigation is most appropriate for the two ends of the spectrum:

(1) where one party has an extremely strong case, such that he may obtain summary judgment in the courts within two or three months; and

(2) the very complex case, where a great deal of factual evidence will be required, discovery of documents will be important and complex issues of law will have to be decided. In such a case, there may be limited scope for procedural short-cuts which could save time in an arbitration, and a court will be cheaper and better able to marshal the arguments than an arbitrator.

In between, and subject to the caveats set out above as to the need for imagination or co-operation, arbitration should produce a quicker result. In suitable cases an expert will be even faster. Unfortunately, it is seldom possible to predict at the drafting stage into which category a dispute arising out of the contract is likely to fall.

13.3 Speed versus the correct result

In the above, there has been little mention of the quality of justice. Sadly, a trade-off has to be made. The court represents the Rolls Royce approach: every fact is explored, every argument put and, if the first judge gets it wrong, there are appeal courts above him to turn to for remedy. But it all takes time. Any arbitration represents the next step down, in that there are limited rights of appeal and often an arbitrator who is not qualified to assess the legal arguments, and there can be some saving in time. Further down is arbitration subject to an exclusion agreement (so that there is no prospect of an appeal) and with procedural short-cuts which limit the parties' opportunities to present their arguments and search for helpful evidence in each others' files, and there will be considerable savings in time. At the bottom is expert determination, which may amount to the parties entrusting themselves to the expert's unaided judgment, for better or worse, but with the dispute all over in a few weeks.

Some contracts, and some joint ventures, are clearly suitable for one approach or another. The amount of money involved will of course be important. In others the choice will be determined by the temperament and expectations of the parties, both of which will probably have changed by the time the disputes clause comes to be invoked.

13.4 Drafting the clause

Arbitration clause

There are a number of questions to be decided before a suitable clause can be drafted:

Place of arbitration

This is surprisingly important. The parties may choose whatever system of law they like to govern the joint venture agreement and disputes arising out of it, but the procedural law governing the arbitration will be that of the forum. Thus any arbitration conducted in London, whatever the substantive law applicable, will be subject to the English procedural rules: from practical matters, such as whether an arbitrator can administer an oath to witnesses, to more fundamental points, such as the availability of an appeal to the English courts. It is important to choose a forum in which the procedural background law strikes the right balance of assisting the progress of the arbitration without subjecting it to undesired interference. The court's role of assisting the arbitration is especially important in non-institutional arbitrations, that is where the arbitration is not subject to a detailed set of rules produced by an institution such as the ICC.

Equally important, of course, are the other attributes of a suitable arbitration forum: its convenience for the parties and their lawyers, the availability and cost of accommodation, the standard of cuisine, etc.

Institutional or ad hoc arbitration

There is a variety of institutions who provide an arbitration support service: the International Chamber of Commerce, the London Court of International Arbitration, and others. Each provides a set of procedural rules and a mechanism for the selection of arbitrators, in return for a fee. It may also review the arbitrator's award before it is published. The rules should provide a reasonably complete procedural code, useful where little is known of the procedural rules of the forum. Similarly the use of an institution which has a panel of available arbitrators in different countries is useful in appointing an arbitrator where no suitable appointing institution in the forum concerned can be identified. Institutional arbitration results in a reasonably safe certainty as to procedure and appointment, in particular a timetable which should set a maximum duration for the proceedings, while sacrificing the chance that an ad hoc arbitration *might* have resulted in a more flexible and quicker result.

Most of the further matters considered below will be covered in an institutional set of rules, but should be specified in a non-institutional clause.

The arbitrator

Normally the clause will not identify a particular arbitrator. Instead it will provide for one arbitrator, to be agreed between the parties or in default to be selected by a given individual, frequently the head of an institution such as the Law Society, RIBA, etc. Which institution is named will depend upon the location of the arbitration and the technical qualifications likely to be required by the arbitrator. Likewise it may be appropriate to specify the qualifications which any arbitrator selected must possess. It is important to provide a default procedure, so that the selection of the arbitrator can go ahead after a specified number of days where one of the parties adopts an obstructive attitude and refuses to co-operate.

Occasionally a clause will provide for arbitration by three arbitrators, one selected by each of the parties and an umpire selected by the two arbitrators. This should be adopted only where the sums at stake are likely to justify it, as the costs are much higher and the difficulty of organising meetings can lead to delays.

Procedure

The appropriate procedure for any given dispute will depend on its facts. Therefore there is usually limited scope for laying down in advance the procedure to be followed (which is the problem with institutional rules). However if the parties are determined in advance on a quick and cheap arbitration of any dispute that may arise, it is quite possible to provide, for example, that the arbitration should be conducted without an oral hearing or discovery, and with evidence limited to documents and witness statements annexed to the parties' written submissions. That should produce a result within a couple of months. It might even be the right result.

Exclusion agreements

In many countries it is possible to exclude any right to appeal from the arbitrator's award to the national courts. Whether to exclude such a right is an important decision which will depend once again on the desired balance between speed and obtaining the correct result.

For English arbitrations, an exclusion agreement included in the original contract is only effective if one of the parties is a non-UK national. Where both parties are UK nationals, the exclusion agreement is only valid if entered into after the start of the arbitration.

Expert determination clause

As has been noted, an expert determination is not subject to the background rules applicable to arbitrations. Therefore any important procedural rules must be included in the expert clause. Otherwise the parties must try to persuade the expert to adopt them after his appointment.

We have explained above why expert determination is not suitable for disputes which are likely to involve resolving differing accounts of factual events or issues of law. Nevertheless, if the parties wish the expert to be obliged to permit them to make submissions to him, they should so provide in the clause. The same goes for witness evidence.

One important point is reasons for the decision. On present authorities it is extremely difficult to upset a 'non-speaking' certificate by an expert, that is one without reasons. It is easier (though still not easy) to challenge a wrong decision where reasons have been given. There is a limit to the extent to which parties should favour speed at the expense of the right result, and this is probably it. Note however that an expert may be personally liable to the parties if he reaches the wrong decision. A requirement to give reasons often makes a potential expert unwilling to serve, at least unless the parties agree not to sue him.

Jurisdiction clauses

The forum
The most important question in drafting a jurisdiction clause is of course which country's or state's courts are to be chosen. To a far greater extent than is the case with arbitrations, the forum chosen governs the procedure that will be followed in resolving any dispute, the length of the proceedings and the remedies available. The difference between, for example, the adversarial system of proceedings used in most common law countries and the more inquisitorial system used in many civil law countries is marked. Since local lawyers will almost always have to be used to conduct the proceedings, this choice will also affect the choice of lawyers. The convenience of the forum for parties and witnesses will again be important. Finally, the forum chosen will affect the substantive law, whatever the choice of law clause may say: an English court will not award multiple damages, and a French court will hold invalid a restriction that breaches Article 85 of the Treaty of Rome, even though in each case US law may be the governing law.

In practice parties tend to choose the forum with which they are most familiar. However the effect of the choice of forum on any proceedings that result is so profound that some comparative analysis of the potential fora should really be carried out. See for example Park & Cromie, *International Commercial Litigation*, Butterworths, 1990.

Exclusive/non-exclusive jurisdiction

Generally a jurisdiction clause will specify the courts of one country or state. However a clause may instead specify several countries' courts, perhaps allowing one party a choice, or it may specify that the court is to have non-exclusive jurisdiction. The intention of the latter provision is that parties should be able to sue either in the court specified or in any other country's courts which will accept jurisdiction. In many countries, the choice of a particular court without specifying that it is to have exclusive jurisdiction will result in it having non-exclusive jurisdiction. This is not the case for countries which are parties to the Brussels Convention on Jurisdiction and Enforcement of Judgments, Article 17 of which results in any choice of the courts of a member state being regarded as conferring exclusive jurisdiction on that court.

Both a clause naming several courts and one providing for non-exclusive jurisdiction should be effective, although local legal advice should be taken as to whether the courts chosen will give effect to any given clause. However the limitations on any jurisdiction clause should be recognised. In most cases the court chosen will accept jurisdiction, but a court in a common law country will usually (though not in Brussels Convention cases) retain a discretion to decline jurisdiction in favour of a clearly more suitable forum. The weaker the choice (eg where the court is one of several courts specified) and the less connection the dispute has with the court concerned, the more likely it is that this may happen. Similarly, if proceedings are brought in a court other than that chosen, the first court will usually decline jurisdiction. But it may not (and in some cases under the Brussels Convention, where a non-member state is specified, it must not).

Submission

It is generally not necessary to specify that the parties submit to the jurisdiction of the particular court, as well as conferring jurisdiction on it. However such an express statement may help enforce any subsequent judgment abroad, so is often included.

13.5 Choice of law, service of process, etc

Whatever the form of dispute resolution clause chosen, a choice of law clause will also be required. This will govern the substantive rights of the parties, as opposed to the procedural law of the suit, which will be that of the forum. The two are of course frequently different.

A service of process clause should likewise be included in all cases. This is especially important for proceedings in common law countries, where due service of the originating process is generally necessary in order for the proceedings to be validly commenced. Where necessary, an agent for process should be appointed within the same country as the chosen forum.

Finally, in agreements involving governments, diplomats, etc, a clause waiving sovereign or diplomatic immunity and consenting to execution against assets will be required.

Joint Venture Checklist

Contents

PART I GENERAL

A   Choice of vehicle
B   Preliminary issues
C   Applicable law etc
D   Identity of parties
E   The business of the joint venture
F   Intellectual property and competition
G   Funding of the joint venture

PART II INCORPORATED JOINT VENTURES

A   Capital structure and construction of the joint venture company
B   Articles of association
C   Joint venture shareholders' agreement
D   Transfer of shares
E   Other standard provisions

PART III UNINCORPORATED JOINT VENTURES

A   General
B   Management
C   Restriction of authority
D   Termination

Note: This checklist deals with the matters which will require consideration in most joint ventures. It does not cover topics such as collaboration agreements, property joint ventures or specialist joint ventures such as those in the oil and gas industry.

PART I GENERAL

A Choice of vehicle

		Text reference	*Appendix reference*
1	Is the relationship appropriate for a joint venture agreement or better suited to an alternative arrangement?	1.2 1.3 1.4	
2	Should the venture be conducted through a company or an unincorporated association?	2.5 3 4.1, 7.6 8.5	
3	Is the vehicle, if a company, to be a subsidiary or subsidiary undertaking of any of the parties?	2.5 8.5	
4	Should the company be limited or unlimited?	2.5	

B Preliminary issues

1	Are there any licences or consents required by the joint venturers before trading as a condition precedent to the venture?	2.4 6.5 7.7 12.3	
2	Are any of the joint venturers listed companies which might need to seek approval from, or to send a circular to, their shareholders?	2.4 8.2	
3	If the companies want to incorporate, do they want to trade prior to incorporation? If so do they want to trade as a partnership?	4.2 3.2	App 2, Cl 12
4	Do the parties want to have heads of agreement on points of principle? Are they to be binding, in whole or part?	2.3	
5	Are the parties to transfer confidential information to each other prior to contract? If so is a secrecy agreement required?	2.2 6.2 8.3	App 5

		Text reference	*Appendix reference*
6	Have the parties clarified their commercial objectives?	1 2.3 7.7 8.1	
7	Have any conflict of interest issues been addressed?	8.2 8.3	

C   Applicable law etc

1	Is the governing law to be that of England?	13.5	App 2, Cl 12.12
2	Is arbitration desirable? If yes, settle details.	13	App 2, Cl 12.12
3	Should there be an exclusive jurisdiction clause?	13.4	App 2, Cl 12.12
4	Should a UK agent for service of process be appointed?	13.5	App 2, Cl 12.12
5	Are there any UK or EEC anti-trust considerations?	12	
6	Is the joint venture to operate in a regulated industry?	2.4	

D   Identity of parties

1	Have the names of the parties to the joint venture together with the full address of their registered or principal office been specified?		
2	Should the joint venture company itself be made a party?	4.4	App 2

E   The business of the joint venture

1	What are the objectives of the joint venture?	1, 2.3 7.2, 7.7	App 2, Recitals, Cl 4
2	Is the joint venture to be restricted to geographical limits?		

		Text reference	*Appendix reference*
3	Are any authorisations, consents or licences required as conditions precedent for the joint venture?	2.4 6.5, 7.7 12.3	App 2, Cl 2
4	What ancillary contracts between the joint ventures are required and should those contracts be annexed to the agreement?	10	App 2, Cl 3.3
5	Are any of the shareholders to supply:	10	App 2, Cl 3.3 App 6

    (a)   staff?
    (b)   training?
    (c)   premises?
    (d)   assets other than cash?
    (e)   other services?

6	Are any contracts to be novated to the joint venture?	2.4	

F   Intellectual property and competition

1	Are licences or other rights from any of the joint venture partners required (eg intellectual property licences or agreements)?	6 10.4	
2	If intellectual property rights are required, are the participants in the joint venture meant to have privileged access? What will be the situation if the joint venture terminates?	6.2 6.7	
3	If intellectual property licences are required, what is the territorial scope, degree of exclusivity, flow-back rights, rights to sub-licences, right to improvements etc and the duration of any licence agreement?	6	
4	Are there any restrictive practice implications in connection with the joint venture?	12	
5	Should a confidentiality clause be	6.8	App 2, Cl 11.2

	Text reference	*Appendix reference*

inserted in the agreement to protect the joint venture?

6 Should there be an obligation on members to refer business to the joint venture company?

7 Are there any restrictions on the name of the joint venture?   10.4

G Funding of the joint venture

1 How much cash will be required to see the project through? Can cash-flow and budget forecast be arranged?   9   App 2, Cl 4.6

2 Should the finance be raised by way of issue of shares or loans, and if by way of shares should payment in kind (eg know-how) be accepted?   9   App 2, Cll 3, 6

3 What relationship should the proportion of the shares divided between the parties bear to the proportion of cash invested in the joint venture company?   9   App 2, Cl 6

4 If investment is by way of loan should security be given or should the debt be subordinated?   9

5 Should there be any obligation to make additional finance available and if there is such obligation should there be any limit to that obligation?   9   App 2, Cl 6

6 Should there be any special arrangements in case a party fails to provide further finance when due?   9.3

7 Should the parties' different interests in the joint venture be reflected in different classes of shares, eg those giving the right to a preferential dividend?   9

8 Are there available to the joint venture company any grants or subsidised facili-   5.2

	Text reference	*Appendix reference*
ties (eg local development grants and EEC grants) which may facilitate the funding of the project?		
9 Are there available to any of the participating parties any tax reliefs which may affect the method of investment (eg consortium relief or business expansion scheme relief)?	11	
10 Who are to be bankers to the joint venture?		App 2, Cl 3.3
11 If a loan facility is requested from the joint venture bank how is this to be guaranteed and regulated?		App 2, Cl 4.8

PART II   INCORPORATED JOINT VENTURES

A   Capital structure and constitution of the joint venture company

1 To what extent do the corporate statutes obviate the need for matters to be set out in a shareholders' agreement?	4.2 4.4	
2 Memorandum of association		
(a) Does the main objects clause of the memorandum accord with the business purpose of the company as agreed between the parties?	4.2	
(b) Should any rights be irrevocably entrenched in the memorandum of the company?	4.3	
3 What is the authorised/issued share capital to be?		App 2, Cll 3.2, 3.3 App 3, Arts 2.1, 3
4 What other form of finance is available?	9 8.5 8.6 8.7	App 2, Cl 6.2

		Text reference	*Appendix reference*

B   Articles of association

		Text reference	*Appendix reference*
1	Should Table A apply or be excluded?	4.2	App 2, Cl 3.2 App 3, Art 1
2	Share capital	4.3	App 3, Arts 2, 3
	(a) How should the share capital of the company be structured eg		
	(i) the rights to income and profits;	9.3	
	(ii) the rights to a return of capital;	4.3	
	(iii) the voting rights of each class of shares;	4.3	
	(iv) should redeemable/convertible shares be issued?	9.3	
	(v) should the right to appoint directors be entrenched in share rights?	4.3 9.3	App 2, Cll 4.3 4.4
	(vi) any ratchet mechanism?	8.5 9.3	
	(b) Should the company have power to issue redeemable shares and purchase its own shares?	9.3	App 3, Art 5 6.4
	(c) What restrictions should there be, if any, upon the modification or variation of rights of any class of share?	4.3	App 2, Cl 4.8 App 3, Art 2.2
	(d) Who should have the power of issue or disposal of shares?		App 2, Cl 4.8 App 3, Art 4
3	Transfer of shares	4.5 4.6 4.8	App 2, Cl 7 App 3, Arts 6–9
4	Should there be any restriction upon the increase, issue and alteration of the share capital of the company?	4.4 4.5	App 2, Cl 4 App 3, Arts 3–5
5	Should there be any specific provisions relating to the conduct of general meetings of the company:	4.3 4.4	App 3, Arts 10–14
	(a) what should be the quorum of members at a general meeting?		App 3, Art 10.1

		Text reference	*Appendix reference*
(b)	what should happen if a meeting is not quorate?		App 3, Art 10.2
(c)	who should receive notice of meetings and be entitled to attend?		
(d)	who should be chairman and should he have a casting vote?		App 3, Art 11
(e)	should provisions allow for meetings to be held at short notice or for resolutions to be passed by memorandum of the members?		
(f)	should the members be given the right to appoint a proxy, or in the case of corporate members, appoint a representative and if so under what terms?		App 3, Arts 13, 14
6 (a)	What provisions should there be regarding appointment and removal of directors?	4.3 4.6	App 2, Cll 3, 4 App 3, Arts 13, 15–19
(b)	Should a *Bushell v Faith* clause be inserted?	4.3	
(c)	Should directors be entitled to vote upon a contract in which they are interested?		App 3, Art 25
(d)	What should be a quorum for the board?		App 3, Art 21
(e)	Should specific borrowing powers be granted to the directors?		App 2, Cll 4, 6
(f)	What restrictions should be placed upon the board's power of decision?	4.6	App 2, Cl 4
(g)	What procedures should apply to the appointment/removal of special directors appointed as representative of a party to the agreement?	4.6	App 3, Arts 15, 17–19
(h)	Should a managing director be appointed?	4.6	App 2, Cl 4.7, 4.8
(i)	Should a chairman of the board of directors be appointed and should he have a casting vote?		App 2, Cl 4.7 App 3, Arts 11, 24
(j)	What notice of board meetings should directors be entitled to		App 2, Cl 4.7 App 3, Art 21

		Text reference	*Appendix reference*
	receive and what should be a quorum?		
(k)	Should directors be given the opportunity of appointing alternative directors?		App 3, Art 16
(l)	Who should be company secretary and should there be provision for an assistant secretary?		App 2, Cl 3.3
(m)	In whose charge should the company seal be?		
7	What should be the dividend policy of the company and when dividends should be paid? Is there to be a minimum distribution? How can the policy be altered?	4.6	App 2, Cll 4, 5
8	Should the company be authorised to capitalise its profits and reserves?		App 3, Art 26
9	Should there be any specific provisions relating to the keeping of accounting records?		
10	Should there be any specific provisions relating to the appointment or removal of the auditors?		App 2, Cll 3.3, 4.8
11	Should there be any specific provisions relating to the service of notices upon members eg appointment of a UK agent for service?		App 2, Cl 12
12	Should the articles provide an indemnity for directors in connection with work done or expenses incurred in the course of the company's business?		App 3, Art 27
13	Should any of the other matters agreed between the joint venture partners be entrenched in the articles of association of the joint venture company?	4	

	Text reference	*Appendix reference*

C Joint venture shareholders' agreement

	Text reference	Appendix reference
The following are matters which may in addition to the articles have an appropriate place in the shareholders' agreement. (*Note*: consider carefully the best place for these matters):	4	
1 Is there to be a fixed or minimum term for the agreement?		App 2, Cl 9
2 Do new articles of association of the company need to be adopted?		App 2, Cl 3.2
3 Registered office and appointments: (a) where should the registered office of the company be located?		App 2, Cl 3.3
(b) which firm should act as auditor?		App 2, Cll 3.3, 4.8
(c) should the agreement nominate a firm of solicitors to act as the company's solicitors?		App 2, Cl 3.3
(d) should the agreement nominate a specific bank to act as bankers to the company?		App 2, Cl 3.3
(e) who is to act as secretary?		App 2, Cl 3.3
5 Arrangements for issue of share capital	9 8.5	App 2, Cl 3.3
6 What provisions should relate to the termination of the agreement upon insolvency, breach or otherwise?	4.6 4.8	App 2, Cll 7, 8, 9
7 Deadlock: (a) do the parties wish to cover dead-lock in advance?	4.6	
(b) if so, should they consider: (i) referring to independent third party?	4.6 13	
(ii) the casting vote?	4.6	
(iii) arbitration?	4.6	
(iv) buy/sell option?	4.8	
(v) Russian roulette?	4.8	App 2, Cl 8
(vi) 'shoot out' (auction) options	4.8	

	Text reference	*Appendix reference*
8 Should the joint venture company liquidate in the event of termination of the joint venture? If so, how should the assets be distributed and any continuing know-how/intellectual property rights be dealt with upon dissolution?	6.7	App 2, Cl 9
9 Management and operations of the company:	4.6	App 2, Cl 4
(a) what should be the make-up of the board?	4.6	App 2, Cll 3, 4
(b) what provisions should relate to the removal or replacement of one of the parties' designated directors?		App 3, Arts 17–19
(c) is it necessary to include in the agreement provisions for appointment/removal/remuneration of directors or should these be in the articles?	4.2	App 2, Cl 4.8 App 3, Arts 17–20
(d) are there to be any restrictions upon the powers of the board? Can these restrictions be relaxed by the board as a whole or by the shareholders, and if the latter, all or a majority?	4.3 4.6	App 2, Cl 4.8
10 Should the agreement regulate the proceedings of the members eg notice of general meetings?		
11 Should the agreement govern the provision of additional capital or further development of the joint venture project?		App 2, Cll 4.2, 6

D Transfer of shares

1 Should shares be freely transferable?	4.8	App 2, Cl 7 App 3, Arts 6–8
2 If freely transferable to outsiders should the articles/agreement contain preemption rights?	4.5	App 3, Arts 7–9

		Text reference	*Appendix reference*
3	Should shares be freely transferable between associated/parent/subsidiary companies?		App 3, Art 6.1
4	Should shares be offered to other shareholders on a pro-rata basis at a 'fair price'?		App 3, Art 7
5	Who is to determine what is a 'fair price'? Is the auditor's/arbitrator's decision to be final?		App 3, Art 7.2
6	Should guidelines be given to the valuer as to what constitutes a 'fair price' eg reference to a formula based on earnings or profit criteria or the taking into consideration of the value of the holding as a minority/majority?		
7	Should it be a condition of any transfer to an outsider that the transferee covenants to comply with the terms of the shareholders' agreement?		App 2, Cl 10
8	Should the joint venture company be constituted the agent of the transferor for the purpose of making the transfer?		App 3, Art 7.1
9	Will the departure of an existing participant have other consequences upon the joint venture eg require a change of name?	10.4	
10	Should the agreement contain options for parties to purchase in the event of breach/insolvency?		App 2, Cl 7.2

E Other standard provisions

1	Who is to bear the costs of the preparation of the joint venture agreement? Who will pay any stamp duty?	2.2 8.3 11.2	App 2, Cl 12.6
2	Are there to be any special provisions relating to notices?	8.4	App 2, Cll 8.2, 12.1 App 3, Art 7.1

		Text reference	Appendix reference
3	What powers are there to be for the parties to amend the joint venture agreement?		App 2, Cl 12.7
4	Are the rights/obligations granted under the agreement to be assignable eg to subsidiaries or associated companies?		App 2, Cl 12.8 App 3, Art 6.1 App 4, Cl 16.1
5	Is the agreement to contain an arbitration clause?	13.2 13.3	App 2, Cl 12.12
6	Should the agreement contain confidentiality clauses or provisions preventing one party from misusing information in possession?	2.2 6.2 6.8	App 2, Cl 11.2
7	Should there be a 'force majeure' clause?		App 4, Cl 14
8	Covenants between the parties to notify each other of matters which might affect the subject of the joint venture.		
9	Provision for the preparation of annual budgets/forecasts.		App 2, Cl 4.6
10	Covenant by the company to provide the shareholders with operating information, eg (a) the right to inspect books of account and records of the company and any subsidiary; (b) the right to management and financial information; (c) monthly/quarterly reports and progress meetings.		App 2, Cl 4.6
11	(a) Is there to be a minimum distribution if profits are available? (b) When are dividends to be paid? (c) Is there to be provision for an interim dividend? (d) How can the dividend policy be changed?		App 2, Cl 5 App 2, Cl 4.8
12	Is the joint venture to be affected by the		App 2, Cl 7.2

	Text reference	*Appendix reference*

change of management or control of either party?

13 Which party is to be responsible for project insurance and what is to happen in the event of a claim?

14 Are provisions to be inserted relating to product marketing/advertising?

PART III   UNINCORPORATED JOINT VENTURES

A   General

1 Will the venture constitute a partner-   3.2
ship for the purposes of PA?

2 Are there more than 20 partners?   2.5

3 If the venture constitutes a partnership   3.2
do the parties wish to amend: 3.3
(a) all terms implied by PA?
(b) joint and several liability inter se?
(c) equal sharing of profits/losses (s 4(1))?
(d) personal indemnity (s 24(2))?
(e) interest on capital loans (s 24(3), (4))?
(f) right to management (s 24(5))?

4 What is to be the duration of the agreement?

5 How are the parties to contribute capital   9.2
to the venture?

6 Are there to be special arrangements in   9.2
case a venturer fails to contribute his capital?

7 Are the parties to contribute non-cash   3.5
assets to the venture or are assets which remain the property of any party to be used in the venture?

8 What accounting arrangements are to be made?

		Text reference	Appendix reference
9	Do the parties wish to reserve the right to compete with each other or the venture?		
10	Is the contract for the supply of services pursuant to SOGASA?	1.4	
11	Is it necessary to exclude, where possible, the terms implied by SOGASA or express alternatives?		
12	Does the contract contain any exclusion clauses to be considered in the light of UCTA?		

B Management

1	How is the venture to be managed?	3.3 7.7	
2	Is a central management arrangement envisaged?		
3	Are any special committees required?		

C Restriction of authority

1	What restrictions are to be placed on the ability of the parties to bind each other?	3.5 7.7	
2	Who is to have authority to bind the venture?	3.5	
3	What procedure is to be adopted to authorise action taken on behalf of the parties?	3.5	

D Termination

1	How is termination to be triggered?	3.5, 7.7	
2	Are special provisions dealing with termination required?	3.3, 3.5 7.7	
3	How are the venture assets to be dealt with on termination?	3.5 6.7	

Specimen Shareholders' Agreement for Joint Venture Company

THIS AGREEMENT is made the _____ day of _____ One thousand nine hundred and _____ BETWEEN [_____], whose registered office is at [_____ _____] (hereinafter called 'A Co') of the first part; and [_____], whose registered office is at [_____ _____] (hereinafter called 'B Co') of the second part; and [_____], whose registered office is at [_____ _____] (hereinafter called 'the Company') of the third part.

WHEREAS:

(A)   A Co and B Co have agreed to establish a joint venture company in the [Territory] to [carry on the Business].

(B)   The Company was incorporated in England on [_____] 19[____] and at the date hereof has an authorised share capital of £[_____] divided into [_____] Ordinary Shares of [____] each of which [_____] have been issued at a subscription price of [_____] per share and are held by A Co and B Co in the numbers set against their names in Schedule 1.

(C)   The Shareholders have agreed, subject to the satisfaction of the conditions precedent in Clause 2, to subscribe for 'A' and 'B' Shares on the terms and subject to the conditions hereinafter contained.

(D)   [It is the intention of the shareholders that each of them shall share equally in the management and control of the Company and] the Shareholders have agreed that their respective rights as shareholders in the Company shall be regulated by the provisions of this Agreement and the Articles and the Company has agreed with the Shareholders to comply with such of the matters herein contained as relate to the Company.

NOW IT IS HEREBY AGREED as follows:

1 INTERPRETATION

In this Agreement (including the Recitals):

1.1   the following words and expressions shall have the following meanings:

'"*A*" *Director*' means a director holding office pursuant to a notice given by the holder(s) of [a majority of] the issued 'A' Shares in accordance with the Articles;

'"*B*" *Director*' means a director holding office pursuant to a notice given by the holder(s) of [a majority of] the issued 'B' Shares in accordance with the Articles;

'*Articles*' mean the Articles of Association of the Company set out in Schedule 2 and to be adopted pursuant to Clause 3;

'"*A*" *Shares*' mean the Ordinary Shares to be designated 'A' Ordinary Shares in the capital of the Company as contemplated by Clause 3;

'"*B*" *Shares*' mean the Ordinary Shares to be designated 'B' Ordinary Shares in the capital of the Company as contemplated by Clause 3;

'"*A*" *Shareholders*' mean the persons from time to time registered as the holder(s) of 'A' Shares;

'"*B*" *Shareholders*' mean the persons from time to time registered as holder(s) of 'B' Shares;

'*Associated Company*' means a subsidiary or holding company of a Shareholder, and a subsidiary of such holding company;

'*Audited Accounts*' mean the report and audited accounts or consolidated accounts of the Company or, as the case may be, the Group for the financial year ending on the relevant balance sheet date;

'*Auditors*' mean [_____] of [_____] or such other firm of Chartered Accountants as shall be appointed auditors of the Company in accordance with this Agreement;

'*Board*' means the board of directors of the Company;

'*Business*' means the business of [_____];

'*Business Plan*' means the business plan for the Company in the form approved by or on behalf of the Shareholders on or before the date hereof;

'*Completion Date*' means [_____], 19[_____] or such later date as the parties may agree;

'*Directors*' means the 'A' Directors and the 'B' Directors;

'*Group*' means the Company and its subsidiaries (if any) and 'Group Company' means any one of them;

'*Shares*' mean the 'A' Shares and the 'B' Shares and any shares issued in exchange therefor by way of conversion or reclassification and any shares representing or deriving from such shares as a result of any increase in or reorganisation or variation of the capital of the Company;

'*Shareholders*' mean (subject to Clause 9) the 'A' Shareholders and the 'B' Shareholders from time to time;

'*Territory*' means [_____];

Other expressions defined for the purposes of the Companies Acts 1985–1989 shall bear the same meanings herein;

1.2   unless the context otherwise requires, any reference to a statutory provision shall include such provision as from time to time modified or re-enacted or consolidated so far as such modification or re-enactment or consolidation applies or is capable of applying to any transactions entered into hereunder;

1.3   references to Recitals, Clauses, Paragraphs and Schedules are to recitals, clauses, paragraphs and schedules of this Agreement;

1.4   the headings are for convenience only and shall not affect the interpretation hereof; and

1.5   unless the context otherwise requires, words importing the singular only shall include the plural and vice versa and references to natural persons shall include bodies corporate.

2   CONDITIONS

This Agreement is conditional upon
[*Here set out any required conditions—see 2.4 of the text of this book*]

3   ESTABLISHMENT AND STRUCTURE OF THE COMPANY

3.1 Meeting of the Board of Directors

On the Completion Date the Shareholders shall procure the holding of a meeting of the Board and the passing thereat of a resolution convening an Extraordinary General Meeting of the Company immediately following the adjournment of the meeting of the Board for the purposes referred to in Clause 3.2.

3.2 Extraordinary General Meeting

Upon the calling of the Extraordinary General Meeting the Shareholders shall give consents to short notice in respect of such Extraordinary General Meeting and shall attend and vote thereat in favour of resolutions (in such form as shall have been previously approved by the Shareholders):

3.2.1 designating the issued Ordinary Shares in the name of A Co as 'A' Shares and designating the issued Ordinary Shares in the name of B Co as 'B' Shares;

3.2.2 designating the [_____] unissued Ordinary Shares as [_____] 'A' Shares and [_____] 'B' Shares;

3.2.3 authorising the Directors to issue and allot the [_____] 'A' and [_____] 'B' Shares to the Shareholders in accordance with this Agreement; and

3.2.4 adopting the Articles in substitution for the existing Articles of Association of the Company.

3.3 Subscription for Shares

Forthwith upon the passing of the resolutions of the Company pursuant to Clause 3.2:

3.3.1 the Shareholders shall each complete, sign and deliver to the Company applications for the allotment to them of the number of 'A' or 'B' Shares set against their names below to be subscribed for in cash at a price of [_____] per share, together with a bankers' draft for the appropriate sum:
A Co   [_____] 'A' Shares
B Co   [_____] 'B' Shares

3.3.2 the Shareholders shall procure that the meeting of the Board referred to in Clause 3.1 is reconvened and that there are passed thereat resolutions:
(i) approving the Shareholders' applications for the 'A' and 'B' Shares and allotting those Shares, authorising the Shareholders' names to be entered in the Register of Members of the Company as holders of the Shares so allotted and directing the sealing of certificates in respect thereof;
(ii) adopting [_____] as the Company's accounting reference date (the Company's first accounting reference period to end on [_____]);
(iii) appointing [_____] as the Company's

Auditors, [_____] as its Solicitors and
[_____] Bank Plc as its bankers;

(iv) accepting the resignation of [_____] and
appointing [_____] as Secretary of the Company and changing the registered office of the Company to
[_____];

(v) approving [other agreements to be entered into by the
Company].

3.3.3 The Company shall issue [_____] 'A' Shares to A Co and
[_____] 'B' Shares to B Co and shall register the
Shareholders as the holders of such Shares and shall prepare,
seal and deliver to the Shareholders share certificates in respect
thereof in their names.

3.3.4 A Co shall appoint its first representative 'A' Directors
pursuant to the Articles and Clause 4.3.

3.3.5 B Co shall appoint its first representative 'B' Directors
pursuant to the Articles and Clause 4.4.

3.3.6 The Company and [_____] shall enter into
[other proposed agreements].

4 THE BUSINESS OF THE COMPANY AND ITS MANAGEMENT

4.1 Conduct of the Business

Each of the Shareholders agrees to exercise his or its respective rights
hereunder and as a shareholder in the Company and (insofar as it lawfully
can) so as to ensure that:

4.1.1 the Company performs and complies with all obligations on its
part under this Agreement and complies with the restrictions
imposed upon it under the Articles; and

4.1.2 the Business is conducted in accordance with sound and good
business practice and the highest ethical standards.

4.2 Promotion of the Business

4.2.1 The Shareholders acknowledge and agree that unless and until
the parties agree otherwise the business of the Company shall
be confined to the Business and that it is their intention to
develop and expand the Business by [_____].

4.2.2 Subject to the provisions of this Agreement, the Shareholders understand and agree that the Company shall use all reasonable and proper means to maintain, improve and extend the Business in accordance with the Business Plan (as the same may be amended by agreement between the Shareholders from time to time).

4.2.3 The Company and the Shareholders agree to procure that the Company and any subsidiaries shall have complete independence in their operations and that any expansion, development or evolution of the Business (whether to be conducted as part of or in connection with the Company's main business or ancillary to it) will only be effected through the Company or a wholly-owned subsidiary unless the prior consent of the holders of a majority by nominal value of both the 'A' and the 'B' Shares in issue is obtained and, if such consent is obtained, all Shareholders shall be entitled to participate in any firm or company formed for the purpose of such expansion, development or evolution pro rata to their holdings of Ordinary Shares unless all the Shareholders shall otherwise agree.

[4.2.4 A Co and B Co acknowledge that they and their respective Associated Companies may engage directly or indirectly in activities which are or may be competitive with the Business or any other business of the Company or its subsidiaries].

4.3 'A' Directors of the Company

4.3.1 The holder(s) of [a majority of] the issued 'A' Shares shall be entitled in accordance with the Articles to appoint up to [_____] persons as 'A' Directors.

4.3.2 A Co shall appoint (or confirm the appointment of) the following persons as the first 'A' Directors:
[_____]
[_____]

4.4 'B' Directors of the Company

4.4.1 The holder(s) of [a majority of] the issued 'B' Shares shall be entitled in accordance with the Articles to appoint up to [_____] persons as 'B' Directors.

4.4.2 B Co shall appoint (or confirm the appointment of) the following persons as the first 'B' Directors:

[——————————]
[——————————]

4.5 Consultation

Notwithstanding the provisions of the Articles, neither Shareholder will appoint a Director without reasonable prior consultation with the other with a view to reaching agreement on the person to be appointed.

4.6 Budgets and Financial Information

4.6.1 The Company shall prepare and submit to the Directors and to the Shareholders:

(i) on or before [——————] in each year a detailed draft operating budget for the Company and its subsidiaries (including estimated major items of revenue and capital expenditure) for the following [calendar] year, broken down on a monthly basis, and an accompanying cash-flow forecast, together with a balance sheet showing the projected position of the Company (and its subsidiaries (if any)) as at the end of the following calendar year;

(ii) within [three weeks] after the end of each calendar month, unaudited management accounts, such accounts to include a detailed profit and loss account, balance sheet and cash-flow statement, an analysis of sales and other revenue, a review of the budget together with a reconciliation of results with revenue and capital budgets for the corresponding month, and (if so required by the Board) a statement of the source and application of funds for such month; and

(iii) such further information as the Shareholders may from time to time reasonably require as to any and all matters relating to the business or financial condition of the Company or of any of its subsidiaries.

4.7 Board Meetings

4.7.1 Board Meetings shall be held no less than [four] times in every year and at not more than [three monthly] intervals and unless otherwise agreed by a majority for the time being of the 'A' Directors and of the 'B' Directors [seven] days' notice shall be given to each of the Directors of all meetings of the Board, at the address notified from time to time by each Director to the

Secretary of the Company. Each such notice shall contain, inter alia, an agenda specifying in reasonable detail the matters to be discussed at the relevant meeting, shall be accompanied by any relevant papers for discussion at such meeting and, if sent to an address outside the United Kingdom, shall be sent by courier or by telefax.

4.7.2 The Chairman of the Board shall be appointed by [a majority of] the ['A'/'B'] Directors and the Managing Director shall be appointed by [a majority of] the ['A'/'B'] Directors. The first Chairman shall be [_____] and the first Managing Director shall be [_____]. If the Chairman is not present at any Board Meeting, the Directors present may appoint any one of their number to act as Chairman for the purpose of the meeting.

4.8 Limitations on the Board's Powers of Management

The Shareholders shall procure, so far as they are able, that no action shall be taken or resolution passed by the Company or its subsidiaries except with the consent of [the holders of [a majority of] each class of shares] [[a majority of] the 'A' Directors and [a majority of] the 'B' Directors] in respect of the following matters ('reserved matters'):

4.8.1 the appointment, removal and conditions of employment of the Secretary or any Director [or senior executive] of any Group Company (other than the appointment or removal of Directors of the Company);

4.8.2 the selection of and any change in the Auditors;

4.8.3 the acquisition by a Group Company of any assets or property (other than in the ordinary course of business) at a total cost to the Group Company (per transaction) of more than £[_____];

4.8.4 the sale or disposition of any fixed assets of a Group Company for a total price per transaction of more than £[_____];

4.8.5 the borrowing by any Group Company of amounts which when aggregated with all other borrowings (or indebtedness in the nature of borrowings) of Group Companies would exceed £[_____] [, or the creation of any charge or other security over any assets or property of a Group Company except for the purpose of securing borrowings from bankers in the ordinary course of business of amounts not exceeding in the aggregate £[_____]]];

4.8.6 the giving by any Group Company of any guarantee or indemnity other than in the normal course of its business;

4.8.7 the consolidation or amalgamation of the Company with any other company;

4.8.8 the disposal of or dilution of the Company's interests, directly or indirectly, in any of its subsidiaries;

4.8.9 the acquisition by any Group Company of any share capital or other securities of any body corporate;

4.8.10 the making of any loan or advance to any person, firm, body corporate or other business;

4.8.11 the creation, allotment or issue of any shares in the capital of a Group Company or of any other security or the grant of any option or rights to subscribe in respect thereof or convert any instrument into such shares;

[4.8.12 the payment or declaration by the Company of any dividend or other distribution on account of shares in its capital;]

4.8.13 the cessation of any business operation of a Group Company;

4.8.14 the making of any material change in the nature or geographical area of the business of a Group Company;

4.8.15 the making by any Group Company of any contract with a Shareholder or Associated Company or of any contract of a material nature outside the normal course of the business of such Group Company;

4.8.16 the reduction of its capital, variation of the rights attaching to any class of shares in the capital of the Company or any redemption, purchase or other acquisition by the Company of any shares or other securities of the Company;

4.8.17 the adoption of any bonus or profit-sharing scheme or any share option or share incentive scheme or employee share trust or share ownership plan;

4.8.18 the making of any change to the Company's Memorandum or Articles;

4.8.19 the presentation of any petition for the winding up of a Group Company;

4.8.20 the commencement or settlement of any litigation, arbitration or other proceedings which are material in the context of the relevant company's business and which do not involve a member or director (or former member or director);

4.8.21 the appointment of a managing director or the granting of any power of attorney or other delegation of directors' powers;

4.8.22 the adoption of the annual accounts or amendment of the accounting policies previously adopted by the Company;

4.8.23 [Others].

In determining whether any of the matters described above require the approval of the Directors as aforesaid a series of transactions which when aggregated exceed the figure specified in the relevant paragraph shall be construed as a single transaction requiring such approval.

5 DISTRIBUTION POLICY AND DETERMINATION OF NET PROFIT

The Shareholders shall take such action as may be necessary to procure that:

5.1   the Annual General Meeting of the Company at which audited accounts or consolidated audited accounts (as the case may be) in respect of the preceding financial year are laid before the Shareholders is held not later than [six] months after the end of the relevant financial year;

5.2   the Auditors shall at the expense of the Company be instructed to report as to the amount of the profits for each accounting reference period which are available for distribution by the Company at the same time as they sign their report on the Audited Accounts for the accounting reference period in question;

5.3   the Company distributes to and among its members [such percentage] [not less than [_____]%] of its profits lawfully available for distribution in each financial year as the Board shall from time to time resolve, subject to the appropriation of such reasonable and proper reserves for working capital or otherwise as the Board may think appropriate.

6 FINANCE FOR THE COMPANY

6.1   The Shareholders acknowledge that, in addition to the share capital to be subscribed pursuant to Clause 3, the Company will require a further [_____] in order to fund its projected cash requirements under the Business Plan. [It is the intention of the Shareholders that such further finance will be provided by loans from A Co and B Co in proportion to their respective holdings of shares in the Company and on such commercial terms as they may agree with the Company].

6.2   If the Company requires capital in addition to that provided by the Shareholders pursuant to Clauses 3 and 6.1, it shall endeavour to obtain such finance from a third party lender on the basis that there shall be no recourse to the Shareholders and otherwise on the best terms which could reasonably be expected to be obtained in the open market [PROVIDED ALWAYS THAT nothing shall oblige any Shareholder to provide any guarantee or security in respect thereof or to put up the finance concerned].

7   TRANSFER OF SHARES

7.1   Otherwise than in accordance with the following provisions of this Clause or Clause 8 no Shareholder shall:

7.1.1   pledge, mortgage (whether by way of fixed or floating charge) or otherwise encumber its legal or beneficial interest in its Shares; or

7.1.2   sell, transfer or otherwise dispose of any of such Shares (or any legal or beneficial interest therein); or

7.1.3   enter into any agreement in respect of the votes attached to Shares; or

7.1.4   agree, whether or not subject to any condition precedent or subsequent, to do any of the foregoing.

7.2   If in relation to any of the Shareholders ('the Defaulting Shareholder'):

7.2.1   the Defaulting Shareholder fails to remedy any material breach on its part of this Agreement within 21 days from the service of any written notice by the holders of a majority of the 'A' Shares or 'B' shares complaining of such breach;

7.2.2   the Defaulting Shareholder enters into any composition or arrangement with its creditors generally or is unable to pay its debts within the meaning of section 123 (1) of the Insolvency Act 1986;

7.2.3   an encumbrancer lawfully takes possession or an administrative receiver is validly appointed over the whole or any part of the undertaking, property or assets of the Defaulting Shareholder;

7.2.4   an order is made or resolution is passed or a notice is issued convening a meeting for the purpose of passing a resolution or any analogous proceedings are taken for the appointment of an

administrator of or the winding up of the Defaulting Shareholder, other than a members' voluntary liquidation solely for
the purpose of amalgamation or reconstruction;

7.2.5 the Defaulting Shareholder is the subject of any change in its
control or ownership;

7.2.6 any of the matters referred to in sub-clause 7.2.2, 7.2.3, 7.2.4
or 7.2.5 above occurs in relation to any holding company for
the time being of the Defaulting Shareholder;

then upon written notice to the Defaulting Shareholder by any other
Shareholder this Agreement shall automatically terminate with respect to
the Defaulting Shareholder, but without prejudice to its obligations
under Clause 11.2 below.

7.3   Within thirty days after termination of this Agreement pursuant
to sub-clause 7.2 above any other Shareholder shall be entitled to serve a
notice on the Defaulting Shareholder requiring the Defaulting Shareholder to sell to it all (but not some only) of the Shares held by the
Defaulting Shareholder. If more than one other Shareholder serves a
notice on the Defaulting Shareholder under this sub-clause then such
notices shall take effect as if they required the Defaulting Shareholder to
transfer his shares to all other Shareholders who served such notices in
proportion to the number of shares held by them respectively.

7.4   The Directors shall request the Auditors to determine and certify
the sum per share considered by them to be the fair value thereof as at the
last date of such thirty-day period and the sum so determined and
certified shall be the price at which the Shares held by the Defaulting
Shareholder shall be transferred, and the provisions of Article 7.2 of the
Company's Articles of Association shall apply in relation to the Auditors'
role and expenses and the finality of their determination hereunder.
Completion of the transfer of shares hereunder shall take place at the
Company's principal place of business at twelve noon on the fifth business
day after the Auditors shall have certified the fair value of the Shares.

8   DEADLOCK ('Russian roulette')

8.1   If the Board or a general meeting of the Company is unable to
make a decision on a reserved matter within [two months] of such
reserved matter first being considered by the Board or general meeting
then [the holder(s) of a majority of the issued Shares of either class] (the
'Seller(s)') may serve a written notice (a 'Deadlock Notice'), in the case of
the holders of a majority of the 'A' Shares, on each holder of 'B' Shares
and in the case of the holders of a majority of the 'B' Shares, on each

holder of 'A' Shares (the 'Buyers') offering to sell (or procure the sale of) all the issued Shares of that class held by the Seller(s) ('the Sale Shares') to the Buyers or, failing which, to purchase the Buyers' Shares in accordance with the following provisions of this sub-clause.

8.2   The Deadlock Notice shall specify the price at which the Seller(s) is or are prepared to sell the Sale Shares to the Buyers ('the Deadlock Price') but shall not include any other condition whatsoever.

8.3   The Deadlock Notice shall be deemed to:

8.3.1   constitute an offer by the Seller(s), open for acceptance by one or more of the Buyers for [one month] from the date of service of the Deadlock Notice (the 'Buyer Purchase Period'), to sell all (but not some only) of the Sale Shares to one or more of the Buyers on the Transfer Terms at the Deadlock Price; and

8.3.2   constitute an alternative offer by the Seller(s) to purchase all (but not some only) of the Buyers' Shares within [seven] days after the end of the Buyer Purchase Period on the Transfer Terms at the Deadlock Price if the Buyers do not elect to purchase all the Sale Shares before the expiry of the Buyer Purchase Period;

and shall be irrevocable without the written consent of the Shareholders (other than the Seller(s)). For the purposes of this Clause the 'Transfer Terms' means free from all claims, equities, liens and encumbrances together with all rights attaching thereto at the date of service of the Transfer Notice.

8.4   One or more of the Buyers may at any time before the expiry of the Buyer Purchase Period serve notice in writing upon the Seller(s) of its or their desire to purchase all (but not some only) of the Sale Shares on the terms set out in this clause (a 'Buyer Purchase Notice') which may not be expressed to be subject to the fulfilment of any condition whatsoever. [In case of competition the Shares shall be sold to Buyers who have served a Buyer Purchase Notice in proportion (as nearly as may be without involving fractions or increasing the number sold to any member beyond that applied for by him) to their existing holdings of Shares.] Upon service of a Buyer Purchase Notice on the Seller(s) the latter shall be bound to sell (upon payment of the Deadlock Price), and the Buyer(s) who have served a Buyer Purchase Notice shall be bound to purchase (at the Deadlock Price), all the Sale Shares, which the Sellers shall transfer on the Transfer Terms.

8.5   If none of the Buyers serves a Buyer Purchase Notice before the expiry of the Buyer Purchase Period, the Buyers shall be deemed to have declined the offer by the Seller(s) referred to in sub-clause 8.3.1 and the

Buyers shall be bound to sell (upon payment of the Deadlock Price), and the Seller(s) shall be bound to purchase (at the Deadlock Price), all the Buyers' Shares, which the Buyers shall transfer on the Transfer Terms.

8.6   In the following sub-clauses, 'the Seller(s)' means the holder(s) of the Sale Shares and 'the Buyers' means the person(s) who, in accordance with the foregoing provisions of this Clause, have become bound to purchase them.

8.7   Completion of the sale and purchase of the Sale Shares shall be completed on the day which is [three] business days after the end of the Buyer Purchase Period and at such reasonable time and place as the Buyers may specify by not less than thirty-six hours' written notice to the Seller(s) whereupon:

8.7.1 the Seller(s) shall deliver to the Buyer(s) a duly executed transfer or transfers in favour of the Buyer(s) or as it or they may direct together with the relative share certificates in respect of the Sale Shares and a power of attorney in such form and in favour of such person as the Buyer(s) may nominate so as to enable the Buyer(s) to exercise all rights of ownership in respect of the Sale Shares including, without limitation, the voting rights thereto;

8.7.2 against such delivery, the Buyers shall pay the Deadlock Price to the Sellers by bankers' draft for value on the date of completion;

8.7.3 the Shareholders shall procure (insofar as they are able) that the said transfer or transfers shall be registered;

8.7.4 the Sellers shall do all such other things and execute all such other documents as the Buyer(s) may require to give effect to the sale and purchase of the Sale Shares; and

8.7.5 if requested by [a majority of] the Buyer(s) the Sellers shall procure the resignation of all the Directors appointed by them (and their predecessors in title to the Sale Shares) and such resignation shall take effect without any liability on the Company for compensation for loss of office or otherwise.

8.8   If the Seller(s) shall fail or refuse to transfer any Shares in accordance with its or their obligations hereunder the Company may authorise some person to execute and deliver on its or their behalf the necessary transfer and the Company may receive the purchase money in trust for the Seller(s) and cause the Buyers to be registered as the holder(s) of such Shares. The receipt of the Company for the purchase money shall be a good discharge to the Buyers (who shall not be bound to see to the

188

application thereof) and after the Buyer(s) has or have been registered in purported exercise of the aforesaid powers the validity of the proceedings shall not be questioned by any person.

8.9 If each Shareholder shall receive an effective and properly delivered Deadlock Notice, the first such notice to be properly delivered shall prevail.

[8.10 Upon a transfer of all the Shares held by a Shareholder in accordance with this Clause:

8.10.1 the Shareholder shall repay all loans, loan capital, borrowings and indebtedness in the nature of borrowings outstanding to the Company from that Shareholder (together with any accrued interest);

8.10.2 the Company shall repay all loans, loan capital, borrowings and indebtedness in the nature of borrowings outstanding to that Shareholder (together with any accrued interest); and

8.10.3 the continuing Shareholders shall use all reasonable endeavours (but without involving any financial obligation on their part) to procure the release of any guarantees or indemnities given by such Shareholder to or in respect of the Company and, pending such release, shall indemnify such Shareholder in respect thereof.]

9 DURATION AND TERMINATION

9.1 Except as otherwise provided herein, this Agreement shall continue in full force and effect without limit in point of time until the earlier of the following events:

9.1.1 the holders of [a majority by nominal value of] the 'A' Shares and of [a majority by nominal value of] the 'B' Shares in issue agree in writing to terminate this Agreement; and

9.1.2 an effective resolution is passed or a binding order is made for the winding up of the Company;

provided, however, that this Agreement shall cease to have effect as regards any Shareholder who ceases to hold any Shares save for any provisions hereof which are expressed to continue in force thereafter.

10 NEW SHAREHOLDERS

The parties shall procure that no person other than a Shareholder acquires shares in the Company (whether by transfer or allotment) unless he covenants with the other parties to this Agreement (in a form reasonably acceptable to each of them) to observe this Agreement and, in the case of a transferee, to perform all the obligations of the transferor under this Agreement and thereupon each such transferee or allottee shall be treated as a Shareholder for the purposes of this Agreement.

11 RIGHTS TO INFORMATION; CONFIDENTIALITY

11.1 Rights of inspection and information

The Company shall permit any Director designated by a Shareholder in writing, at the requesting Shareholder's expense, to discuss the affairs, finances and accounts of the Company and its subsidiaries with their officers and other principal executives all at such time as may reasonably be requested, and all books, records, accounts, documents and vouchers relating to the business and the affairs of the Company and its subsidiaries shall at such time be open to the inspection of any such person, who may make such copies thereof or extracts therefrom as such person may deem appropriate. Any information secured as a consequence of such discussions and examinations shall be kept strictly confidential by the requesting Shareholder.

11.2 Confidentiality

11.2.1 All communications between the parties, the Company and/ or any of them and all information and other materials supplied to or received by any of them from the others which is either marked 'confidential' or is by its nature intended to be for the knowledge of the recipient alone, and all information concerning the business transactions and the financial arrangements of the parties or the Company with any person with whom any of them is in a confidential relationship with regard to the matter in question coming to the knowledge of the recipient shall be kept confidential by the recipient unless or until the recipient party can reasonably demonstrate that any such communication, information and material is, or part of it is, in the public domain through no fault of its own, whereupon to the extent that it is in the public domain or is required to be disclosed by law or in pursuance of employment duties, this obligation shall cease.

11.2.2 The Shareholders shall use all reasonable endeavours to procure the observance of the above-mentioned restrictions by the Company and shall take all reasonable steps to minimise the risk of disclosure of confidential information, by ensuring that only they themselves and such of their employees and directors whose duties will require them to possess any of such information shall have access thereto, and will be instructed to treat the same as confidential.

11.2.3 The obligation contained in this Clause 11 shall endure, even after the termination of this Agreement, without limit in point of time except and until such confidential information enters the public domain as set out above.

[11.2.4 A Shareholder on ceasing to be a Shareholder will hand over to the Company all correspondence, budgets, schedules, documents and records belonging to or relating to the business of the Company and will not keep any copies thereof.]

12 NOTICES AND GENERAL

12.1 Notices

Notices, demands or other communications required or permitted to be given or made hereunder shall be in writing and delivered personally or sent by prepaid first class post with recorded delivery, or by telex, or legible telefax addressed to the intended recipient at its address set out in this Agreement or to such other address or telex or telefax number as any party may from time to time duly notify to the others. Any such notice, demand or communication shall, unless the contrary is proved, be deemed to have been duly served (if given or made by telefax or telex) on the next following business day in the place of receipt or (if given or made by first class letter) forty-eight hours after posting and in proving the same it shall be sufficient to show, in the case of a letter, that the envelope containing the same was duly addressed, correctly stamped and posted and, in the case of a telex or telefax, that such telex or telefax was duly despatched to a current telex or telefax number of the addressee.

12.2 Remedies

No remedy conferred by any of the provisions of this Agreement is intended to be exclusive of any other remedy which is otherwise available at law, in equity, by statute or otherwise, and each and every other remedy shall be cumulative and shall be in addition to every other remedy given hereunder or now or hereafter existing at law, in equity, by statute or otherwise. The election of any one or more of such remedies by any of the parties hereto shall not constitute a waiver by such party of the right to pursue any other available remedy.

[12.3 Time

Time shall be of the essence as regards the provisions of this Agreement, both as regards the times and periods mentioned herein and as regards any times or periods which may, by agreement between the parties, be substituted for them.]

12.4 Severance

If any provision of this Agreement or part thereof is rendered void, illegal or unenforceable in any respect under any law, the validity, legality and enforceability of the remaining provisions shall not in any way be affected or impaired thereby.

12.5 Survival of Rights, Duties and Obligations

Termination of this Agreement for any cause shall not release a party from any liability which at the time of termination has already accrued to another party or which thereafter may accrue in respect of any act or omission prior to such termination.

12.6 Costs

Each party shall bear its own costs and expenses incurred by it in connection with this Agreement.

12.7 Entire Agreement

This Agreement (together with the Schedules hereto) constitutes the entire agreement between the parties and save as otherwise expressly provided no modification, amendment or waiver of any of the provisions of this Agreement shall be effective unless made in writing specifically referring to this Agreement and duly signed by the parties hereto.

12.8 Assignment

12.8.1 This Agreement shall be binding on the parties hereto and their respective successors and assigns.

12.8.2 None of the parties hereto shall be entitled to assign this Agreement or any of its rights and obligations hereunder except to a permitted transferee of that party's Shares which has complied with Clause 10.

12.9   Conflict with the Articles

In the event of any ambiguity or discrepancy between the provisions of this Agreement and the Articles, then it is the intention that the provisions of this Agreement shall prevail and accordingly the parties shall exercise all voting and other rights and powers available to them so as to give effect to the provisions of this Agreement and shall further if necessary procure any required amendment to the Articles.

12.10   No Partnership

Nothing in this Agreement shall be deemed to constitute a partnership between the parties hereto nor constitute any party the agent of any other party for any purpose.

12.11   Further Assurance

Each Shareholder shall co-operate with the others and execute and deliver to the others such other instruments and documents and take such other actions as may be reasonably requested from time to time in order to carry out, evidence and confirm their rights and the intended purpose of this Agreement.

12.12   Governing Law etc

12.12.1 This Agreement shall be governed by and construed in accordance with the laws of England.

12.12.2 [All disputes between the parties as to any matter arising out of or in connection with this Agreement shall be referred to the arbitration in [London] of a single arbitrator to be appointed by agreement between the parties or, if such agreement is not reached within [twenty-one] days of the earlier date on which the name of a proposed arbitrator shall have been submitted by either party to the other for the purpose of the reference, to be appointed by [the President or Vice-President for the time being of The Law Society].] [The parties irrevocably agree that the courts of [England] shall have [exclusive] jurisdiction to settle any disputes

which may arise out of or in connection with this
agreement.]

12.12.3 [_____] hereby appoints [_____
_____] as its agent for service in relation to any matter
arising out of this Agreement.

IN WITNESS whereof this Agreement has been entered into the day and
year first before written.

SCHEDULE 1

THE SHAREHOLDERS

Name   *Address*   *No of shares*

SCHEDULE 2

[Form of Articles of Association to be adopted]

Specimen Articles of Association

ARTICLES OF ASSOCIATION

THE COMPANIES ACTS 1985–1989

COMPANY LIMITED BY SHARES

ARTICLES OF ASSOCIATION

OF

[_____] LIMITED

(adopted by Special Resolution passed on [_____] 19____)

PRELIMINARY

1   The regulations contained in Table A in The Companies (Tables A to F) Regulations 1985 (as amended so as to affect companies first registered on the date of the adoption of these Articles) shall, except as hereinafter provided and so far as not excluded by or inconsistent with the provisions of these Articles, apply to the Company to the exclusion of all other regulations or Articles of Association. References herein to regulations are to regulations in the said Table A unless otherwise stated.

SHARE CAPITAL

2.1   The share capital of the Company [at the date of the adoption of these Articles] is £[_____] divided into [_____] 'A' Shares of

[_____] each and [_____] 'B' Shares of [_____] each. The said shares shall carry the respective voting rights and rights to appoint and remove Directors and be subject to the restrictions on transfer hereinafter provided, but in all other respects shall be identical and rank pari passu.

[2.2 Any amendment to these Articles or to the Memorandum of Association shall be deemed to be a variation of the rights attached to the 'A' Shares and the 'B' Shares.]

ISSUE AND PURCHASE OF SHARES

3   The authorised share capital of the Company shall consist only of 'A' Shares of [_____] each and 'B' Shares of [_____] each in [equal proportions/the proportions [____] to [____]]. The issued share capital of the Company shall always consist of 'A' Shares and 'B' Shares in such proportions.

4   Subject to section 80 of the Companies Act 1985, all unissued shares shall be at the disposal of the Directors and section 89(1) of the Companies Act 1985 shall not apply. Unissued shares in the capital of the Company for the time being may however be issued only in such a manner as to maintain the proportions specified in Article 3 above and so that on each occasion 'A' Shares and 'B' Shares are issued at the same price and on the same terms as to payment and otherwise. After the first issue of shares made by the Directors, no share of either class shall be issued otherwise than to members holding shares of the same class except with the consent in writing of all the members.

5   Except with the consent in writing of all the members, the powers conferred by Regulations 3 and 35 shall be exercised only in such a manner as to maintain the proportions specified in Article 3 above. Regulations 3 and 35 shall be modified accordingly.

TRANSFER OF SHARES

6.1   Subject to the provisions of Regulation 24 any share may at any time be transferred:

6.1.1   to a member holding shares of the same class; or

6.1.2   by any corporate member to a company which has acquired in connection with a scheme of amalgamation or reconstruction the whole or the main part of the undertaking and assets of such member or to a Member of the Same Group; or

6.1.3 to any person with the consent in writing of all other members of the Company; or

6.1.4 to any person in accordance with the provisions of any agreement for the time being binding on all the members and the Company.

6.2 If, while it holds shares in the Company, a Transferee ceases to be a Member of the Same Group as the Transferor from which (whether directly or by a series of transfers under paragraph 6.1.1 and/or paragraph 6.1.2 above) the Relevant Shares were derived, it shall be the duty of the Transferee to notify all the other members in writing that such event has occurred and the Transferee shall be bound (except as all the other members may in writing otherwise determine) to transfer the Relevant Shares to the Transferor or a Member of the Same Group as the Transferor, any such transfer being deemed to be authorised under the foregoing provisions of this Article, but subject to the provisions of Regulation 24.

6.3 For the purposes of this Article:

6.3.1 'company' includes any body corporate;

6.3.2 'a Member of the Same Group' means, in relation to any company, a company which is for the time being a holding company of that company or a subsidiary of that company or a subsidiary of any such holding company (as such terms are defined in the Companies Acts 1985–1989);

6.3.3 'Transferor' means a member which has transferred or proposes to transfer shares to a Member of the Same Group;

6.3.4 'Transferee' means a company for the time being holding shares in consequence (directly or indirectly) of a transfer or series of transfers of shares between Members of the Same Group (the relevant Transferor in the case of a series of such transfers being the first Transferor in such series);

6.3.5 'the Relevant Shares' means and includes (so far as the same remain for the time being held by any person(s) being the holder(s) thereof on the adoption of these Articles or by any person(s) in consequence of a transfer or series of transfers of shares to such person(s) pursuant to paragraph 6.1 above) the shares originally held by or transferred to such person(s) and any additional shares issued to such person(s) by way of capitalisation or acquired by such person(s) in exercise of any right or option granted or arising by virtue of the holding of the

Relevant Shares or any of them or the membership thereby conferred.

6.4 Except in the case of a transfer expressly authorised by the preceding sub-clause or made in accordance with the procedure set out in Article 7 below, no transfer of a share shall be registered without the sanction of an effective resolution of the Directors and if such sanction is not given or refused within eight weeks after the transfer is lodged for registration the sanction shall be deemed to have been refused at the expiration of such period and the transferee shall be notified accordingly.

7 Except in the case of a transfer of shares expressly authorised by the last preceding Article (a 'Permitted Transfer'), the right to transfer shares or to dispose of any shares or any interest in shares in the Company shall be subject to the following restrictions and provisions, namely:

7.1 Before transferring or disposing of any shares or any interest in any shares the person proposing to transfer or dispose of the same ('the Proposing Transferor') shall give a notice in writing (a 'Transfer Notice') to the Company that he desires to transfer the same. The Transfer Notice shall constitute the Company his agent for the sale of the shares therein mentioned (together with all rights then attached thereto) at the Prescribed Price during the Prescribed Period to any member in the same capacity and subject to the same restrictions as his existing membership [or to any other person selected or approved by the Directors] and shall not be revocable except with the consent of the Directors.

7.2 If not more than one month before the date on which the Transfer Notice was given the Proposing Transferor and the Directors shall have agreed a price per share as representing the fair value thereof or as being acceptable to the Proposing Transferor then such price shall be the Prescribed Price (subject to the deduction therefrom of any dividend or other distribution declared or made after such agreement and prior to the said date). Otherwise upon the giving of the Transfer Notice the Directors shall request the Auditors to determine and certify the sum per share considered by them to be the fair value thereof as at the said date and the sum per share so determined and certified shall be the Prescribed Price. The Auditors shall act hereunder at the cost and expense of the Company as experts and not as arbitrators and their determination shall be final and binding on all persons concerned and in the absence of fraud the Auditors shall be under no liability to any such person by reason of their determination or certificate or by anything done or omitted to be done by the Auditors for the purposes thereof or in connection therewith.

7.3 If the Prescribed Price was agreed as aforesaid prior to the said date the Prescribed Period shall commence on such date and expire [three months] thereafter. If the Prescribed Price was not so agreed the Prescribed Period shall commence on such date and expire [three months] after the date on which the Auditors shall have notified the Directors of their determination of the Prescribed Price pending which the Directors shall defer the making of the offer hereinafter mentioned.

7.4   All shares included in any Transfer Notice shall first by notice in writing be offered by the Company to all members holding shares of the same class (other than the member to whose shares the Transfer Notice relates or any member who has given a Transfer Notice in respect of any shares or who is bound to give a Transfer Notice in respect of his shares or any of them) for purchase at the Prescribed Price on terms that in case of competition the shares so offered shall (in accordance with but subject to the provisions of the next following paragraph) be sold to the acceptors in proportion (as nearly as may be without involving fractions or increasing the number sold to any member beyond that applied for by him) to their existing holdings of shares of the same class. Such offer shall limit a time (not being less than twenty-one days) within which it must be accepted or in default will lapse.

7.5   Any shares not so accepted shall be offered by the Directors (in the case of 'A' Shares) to each holder of 'B' Shares (other than, if relevant, the member to whose shares the Transfer Notice relates or any member who has given a Transfer Notice in respect of any shares or who is bound to give a Transfer Notice in respect of his shares or any of them) and (in the case of 'B' Shares) to each holder of 'A' Shares (other than, if relevant, the member to whose shares the Transfer Notice relates or any member who has given a Transfer Notice in respect of any shares or who is bound to give a Transfer Notice in respect of his shares or any of them) for purchase at the Prescribed Price in the same manner (mutatis mutandis) as set out in paragraph 7.4 above. [Any shares not so accepted may be offered by the Directors to such persons as they may think fit for purchase at the Prescribed Price.]

7.6   If the Company shall within the Prescribed Period find members [or other such persons as aforesaid] ('Purchasers') to purchase the shares concerned or any of them and give notice in writing thereof to the Proposing Transferor he shall be bound, upon payment of the Prescribed Price, to transfer such shares to the respective Purchasers. Every such notice shall state the name and address of the Purchaser and the number of shares agreed to be purchased by him and the purchase shall be completed at a place and time to be appointed by the Directors not being less than three days nor more than ten days after the date of such notice. [Provided that if the Transfer Notice shall state that the Proposing Transferor is not willing to transfer part only of the shares concerned this paragraph shall not apply unless the Company shall have found Purchasers for the whole of such shares.]

7.7   If a proposing Transferor shall fail or refuse to transfer any shares to a Purchaser hereunder the Directors may authorise some person to execute and deliver on his behalf the necessary transfer and the Company may receive the purchase money in trust for the Proposing Transferor and cause the Purchaser to be registered as the holder of such shares. The receipt of the Company for the purchase money shall be a good discharge to the Purchaser (who shall not be bound to see to the application thereof) and after the Purchaser has been registered in purported exercise of the aforesaid powers the validity of the proceedings shall not be questioned by any person.

7.8   If the Company shall not within the Prescribed Period find Purchasers willing to purchase all the shares and gives notice in writing thereof to the Proposing Transferor, or if the Company shall within the Prescribed Period give to the Proposing Transferor notice in writing that the Company has no prospect of finding Purchasers of shares, or any of them, the Proposing Transferor at any time thereafter up to the expiration of [two months] after the end of the Prescribed Period shall be at liberty (subject to the provisions of Regulation 24) to transfer those shares for which the Company has not within the Prescribed Period given notice that it has found (or has given notice that it has no prospect of finding) Purchasers to any person on a bona fide sale at any price not being less than the Prescribed Price (after deducting, where appropriate, any dividend or other distribution declared or made after the date of the Transfer Notice and to be retained by the Proposing Transferor). Provided that:

7.8.1   if the Transfer Notice shall state that the Proposing Transferor is not willing to transfer part only of the shares concerned he shall not be entitled hereunder to transfer any of such shares unless in aggregate the whole of such shares are so transferred; and

7.8.2   the Directors may require to be satisfied that such shares are being transferred in pursuance of a bona fide sale for the consideration stated in the transfer without any deduction, rebate or allowance whatsoever to the Purchaser and if not so satisfied may refuse to register the instrument of transfer.

8   No share and no interest in any share shall be held by any member as a bare nominee for or sold or disposed of to any person unless a transfer of such share to such person would rank as a Permitted Transfer. If the foregoing provision shall be infringed [or if the holder of any share shall

die or, being an employee of the Company or of its subsidiary, ceases to be so employed then] the holder of such share shall be bound to give a Transfer Notice in respect thereof.

9.1   For the purpose of ensuring that a transfer of shares is a Permitted Transfer or that no circumstances have arisen whereby a Transfer Notice is required to be given hereunder the Directors may from time to time require any member or any person named as transferee in any transfer lodged for registration to furnish to the Company such information and evidence as the Directors may think fit regarding any matter which they may deem relevant to such purpose.

·9.2   In any case where the Directors have duly required a Transfer Notice to be given in respect of any shares and such Transfer Notice is not duly given within a period of one month, or such longer period as the Directors may allow for the purpose, such Transfer Notice shall (except and to the extent that a Permitted Transfer of any of such shares shall have been lodged) be deemed to have been given on such date after the expiration of the said period as the Directors may by resolution determine and the provisions of the Article relating to Transfer Notices shall take effect accordingly.

PROCEEDINGS AT GENERAL MEETINGS

10.1   Save as herein otherwise provided, the quorum at any General Meeting shall be two or more members present in person or by proxy including one person being or representing a holder of any of the 'A' Shares and one person being or representing a holder of any of the 'B' Shares. Regulation 40 shall be modified accordingly.

10.2   If at any adjourned meeting such a quorum is not present within ten minutes from the time appointed for the adjourned meeting (or such longer interval as the chairman of the meeting may think fit to allow) the meeting shall be dissolved except that if a meeting to consider a resolution or resolutions for the winding up of the Company and the appointment of a Liquidator be adjourned for want of a quorum and if at such adjourned meeting such a quorum is not present within five minutes from the time appointed for the adjourned meeting, any one or more members present in person or by proxy shall constitute a quorum for the purposes of considering and if thought fit passing such resolution or resolutions but no other business may be transacted. Regulation 41 shall be extended accordingly.

11   The chairman at any General Meeting shall not be entitled to a second or casting vote. Regulation 50 shall not apply.

12 In the case of a corporation a resolution in writing may be signed on its behalf by a Director or the Secretary thereof or by its duly appointed attorney or duly authorised representative. Regulation 53 shall be extended accordingly.

VOTES OF MEMBERS

13 On a show of hands every member who is present in person shall have one vote, and on a poll every member who is present in person or by proxy shall have one vote for every share of which he is the holder; Provided that (i) no shares of either class shall confer any right to vote upon a resolution for the removal from office of a Director appointed or deemed to have been appointed by holders of shares of the other class, and (ii) if at any meeting any holder of shares is not present in person or by proxy the votes exercisable on a poll in respect of the shares of the same class held by members present in person or by proxy shall be pro tanto increased (fractions of a vote by any member being permitted) so that such shares shall together entitle such members to the same aggregate number of votes as could be cast in respect of all the shares of that class if all the holders thereof were present. Regulation 54 shall not apply.

14 An instrument appointing a proxy (and, where it is signed on behalf of the appointor by an attorney, the letter or power of attorney or a duly certified copy thereof) must either be delivered at such place or one of such places (if any) as may be specified for that purpose in or by way of note to the notice convening the meeting (or, if no place is so specified, at the registered office) at least [one] hour before the time appointed for holding the meeting or adjourned meeting or (in the case of a poll taken otherwise than at or on the same day as the meeting or adjourned meeting) for the taking of the poll at which it is to be used or be delivered to the Secretary (or the chairman of the meeting) on the day and at the place of, but in any event before the time appointed for holding, the meeting or adjourned meeting or poll. An instrument of proxy shall not be treated as valid until such delivery shall have been effected. Regulation 62 shall not apply.

NUMBER OF DIRECTORS

15 The maximum number of Directors shall be [_____] or such other number as the Company may from time to time by Ordinary Resolution determine. The first Directors shall consist of [_____] persons who shall be designated as 'A' Directors (and shall be deemed to have been appointed under Article 17 by the holders of the 'A' Shares) and [_____] persons who shall be designated as 'B' Directors (and

shall be deemed to have been appointed under Article 17 by the holders of
the 'B' Shares). Regulation 64 shall not apply.

ALTERNATE DIRECTORS

16.1   The holders of [a majority of] any one class of shares may at any
time appoint any person (including another Director) to be the alternate
Director of any Director of the relevant class and may at any time
terminate such appointment. Any such appointment or termination of
appointment shall be effected in like manner as provided in Article 17
hereof. The same person may be appointed as the alternate Director of
more than one Director. Regulations 65 to 68 shall not apply.

16.2   The appointment of an alternate Director shall determine on the
happening of any event which if he were a Director would cause him to
vacate such office or if the Director of whom he is the alternate ceases to be
a Director.

16.3   An alternate Director shall be entitled to receive notices of all
meetings of the Directors and of all committees of Directors of which the
Director of whom he is the alternate is a member to attend and vote and be
counted in the quorum at any such meeting at which the Director of
whom he is the alternate is not personally present and generally to
perform all the functions of the Director of whom he is the alternate in his
absence and the provisions of these Articles shall apply as if he were a
Director of the relevant class. If he shall be himself a Director or shall
attend any such meeting as an alternate for more than one Director his
voting rights shall be cumulative.

APPOINTMENT AND REMOVAL OF DIRECTORS

17   The holders of [a majority of] the 'A' Shares may from time to time
appoint [_____] persons to be Directors, and the holders of [a
majority of] the 'B' Shares may from time to time appoint [_____]
persons to be Directors, but so that not more than [_____
Directors] [one-half of the maximum number of Directors for the time
being authorised] shall at any one time hold office by virtue of
appointment by holders of 'A' Shares nor shall more than [_____
Directors] [one-half of such maximum number] at any one time hold
office by virtue of appointment by holders of 'B' Shares. In these Articles
the expressions 'A' Director and 'B' Director respectively designate
Directors according to the class of shares holders of [a majority of] which
have appointed or are deemed to have appointed them. The Directors

shall not be subject to retirement by rotation. Regulations 73 to 80 shall not apply.

18   The office of a Director shall be vacated in any of the events specified in Regulation 81 and also if he shall be removed from office by the holders of [a majority of] the relevant class of shares or shall in writing offer to resign and the Directors shall resolve to accept such offer.

19   Any such appointment or removal by the holders of [a majority of] the relevant class of shares shall be in writing served on the Company and signed by the holders of [a majority of] the issued 'A' Shares or 'B' Shares (as the case may be). In the case of a corporation such document may be signed on its behalf by a Director or the Secretary thereof or by its duly appointed attorney or duly authorised representative.

REMUNERATION OF DIRECTORS

20   Any Director who serves on any committee, or who otherwise performs services which in the opinion of the Directors are outside the scope of the ordinary duties of a Director, may be paid such extra remuneration by way of salary, commission or otherwise as the Directors may determine. Regulation 82 shall be extended accordingly.

PROCEEDINGS OF DIRECTORS

21   The quorum at a meeting of Directors shall be two of which one shall be an 'A' Director and one a 'B' Director, provided that if within half an hour of the time appointed for the holding of any meeting of the Directors either an 'A' Director or a 'B' Director shall not be present the Directors present shall resolve to adjourn that meeting to a specified place and time (which shall not be earlier than three nor later than seven days after the date originally fixed for the meeting). At such adjourned meeting the quorum necessary for the transaction of the business of the Directors shall be any two Directors. An alternate Director shall be counted in the quorum in the same capacity as his appointor but so that not less than two individuals will constitute the quorum. Regulation 89 shall not apply.

22   No Director shall be appointed otherwise than as provided in these Articles. Regulation 90 shall be modified accordingly.

23   A committee of the Directors shall include at least one 'A' Director and one 'B' Director and the quorum for a meeting of any such committee

shall throughout the meeting be at least one 'A' Director and one 'B' Director.

24 All business arising at any meeting of the Directors or of any committee of the Directors shall be determined only by resolution. [The Chairman shall not be entitled to a second or casting vote. Regulation 88 shall be modified accordingly.]

25 On any matter in which a Director is in any way interested he may nevertheless vote and be taken into account for the purposes of a quorum and (save as otherwise agreed) may retain for his own absolute use and benefit all profits and advantages directly or indirectly accruing to him thereunder or in consequence thereof. Regulations 94 to 98 shall be modified accordingly.

CAPITALISATION OF PROFITS AND RESERVES

26 The Directors may, with the sanction of a Special Resolution of the Company, capitalise any sum standing to the credit of any of the Company's reserve accounts (including Share Premium Account and Capital Redemption Reserve) or any sum standing to the credit of profit and loss account by appropriating such sum to the holders of 'A' Shares and 'B' Shares in the proportions in which such sum would have been divisible amongst them had the same been a distribution of profits by way of dividend and:

26.1 on behalf of the holders of 'A' Shares applying that part of such sum distributable amongst them in paying up in full unissued 'A' Shares for allotment and distribution credited as fully paid up to and amongst them; and

26.2 on behalf of the holders of 'B' Shares applying that part of such sum distributable amongst them in paying up in full unissued 'B' Shares for allotment and distribution credited as fully paid up to and amongst them;

in the proportion aforesaid. The Directors may do all acts and things considered necessary or expedient to give effect to any such capitalisation, with full power to the Directors to make such provisions as they think fit for the case of shares becoming distributable in fractions (including provisions whereby the benefit of fractional entitlements accrues to the Company rather than to the members concerned). The Directors may authorise any person to enter on behalf of all the members interested into an agreement with the Company providing for any such capitalisation and matters incidental thereto and any agreement made under such authority shall be effective and binding on all concerned. Regulation 110 shall not apply.

INDEMNITY

27 Subject to the provisions of and so far as may be permitted by law, every Director, Auditor, Secretary or other officer of the Company shall be entitled to be indemnified by the Company against all costs, charges, losses, expenses and liabilities incurred by him in the execution and discharge of his duties or in relation thereto including any liability incurred by him in defending any proceedings, civil or criminal, which relate to anything done or omitted or alleged to have been done or omitted by him as an officer or employee of the Company and in which judgment is given in his favour (or the proceedings are otherwise disposed of without any finding or admission of any material breach of duty on his part) or in which he is acquitted or in connection with any application under any statute for relief from liability in respect of any such act or omission in which relief is granted to him by the Court. Regulation 118 shall not apply.

Specimen Collaboration Agreement and Associated Project Contract

THIS AGREEMENT is made the [_____] day of [_____] One thousand nine hundred and [_____] BETWEEN
[_____] (hereinafter called 'the Company') of the one part; and
[_____] (hereinafter called 'the Contractor') of the other part.

WHEREAS:

(A)   The Company [wishes] [has been formed] to undertake, organise and promote the research and development of new products and processes and has now decided to [fund] [promote] the research and development of [_____] [full details of which are set out in Schedule [_____]] (hereinafter called 'the Field').

(B)   The Company is desirous of acquiring intellectual property rights and in consideration thereof is willing to fund research projects, pay for the purchase of the relevant equipment and the costs of employing research workers upon acceptable terms [and grant royalty free licences for research purposes to persons undertaking the relevant projects].

(C)   The Company and the Contractor have agreed to collaborate in the Field in accordance with the terms and conditions herein contained.

NOW IT IS HEREBY AGREED as follows:

Part I: Collaboration and project contracts in the field

1   DEFINITIONS

In this Agreement (including the Recitals):

1.1   the following words and expressions shall have the following meanings:

'*Confidential Information*' means the confidential information defined in Clause 10;

'*the Field*' means the Field referred to in Recital (A);

'*Project*' means a project for research and/or development in the Field sought to be undertaken by the Contractor;

'*Project Contract*' means a contract drawn up by the Company pursuant to Clause 5 authorising a Project and executed by or on behalf of the parties hereto;

'*Proposal*' means a proposal submitted by or on behalf of the Contractor to the Company pursuant to Clause 3.2;

'*Protocol*' means a protocol as defined in Clause 5;

'*the Work*' means research and/or development arising from the performance of a Project and any other work identified in a Project Contract;

1.2   References to Recitals and Clauses are to Recitals and Clauses of this Agreement.

1.3   The headings are for convenience only and shall not affect the interpretation hereof.

1.4   Unless the context otherwise requires, words importing the singular only shall include the plural and vice versa and references to natural persons shall include bodies corporate.

2   DURATION OF AGREEMENT

This Agreement shall, subject as hereinafter provided, remain in force until the [fifth] anniversary of the date of this Agreement and thereafter shall continue automatically unless terminated by not less than [six] months' prior notice by either party, such notice to expire on or after the said anniversary.

3   COLLABORATION

3.1   The Contractor will, if during the term of this Agreement it seeks to undertake a Project, offer each such Project to the Company for support and exploitation upon the terms set out in this Agreement.

3.2   An offer falling within the terms of Clause 3.1 shall be made by way of the presentation of a proposal to the Company in the form prescribed in Clause 4 (or such other form as the Company and the

Contractor may agree) and shall remain open for acceptance for [ninety] days and if the Company shall not have accepted such offer within that period the Contractor may thereafter (but not before) offer such opportunity to any third party provided that such latter offer is not made on terms more favourable to the third party than the terms offered to the Company.

4 PRESENTATION OF PROPOSALS

Each Project shall be presented by or on behalf of the Contractor to the Company by way of a proposal in writing detailing the following matters:

4.1 the subject matter and the objectives of the research and/or development and of the programme or plan which it is proposed to carry out including details of any intellectual property rights subsisting or applied for in respect of the subject matter of the research and/or development, and copies of any patent application and/or specification or the like prepared or filed in respect thereof;

4.2 the facilities required in order to carry out the research and/or development;

4.3 the personnel of the Contractor proposed to carry out the Project; and

4.4 the estimated time and cost of accomplishing each stage of the research and/or development.

5 PROJECT CONTRACTS AND PROTOCOLS

If the Company has, pursuant to receipt of an offer from the Contractor (whether made for or on behalf of another person) falling within the terms of Clause 3 written to the Contractor confirming that it will support the relevant Project then (i) the Contractor shall, within [thirty] days of such confirmation, in consultation with the Company procure the preparation of a protocol (any such protocol is hereinafter called a 'Protocol') comprising a comprehensive description of the work to be undertaken in furtherance of the Project; (ii) the Company shall, at the Company's option, within [thirty] days of receipt of such protocol draw up a draft Project Contract authorising the Contractor to undertake the subject matter of the Protocol and, unless otherwise agreed, the terms and conditions set out in Part II and Part III of this Agreement shall be deemed to be incorporated into the Project Contract; and (iii) the Contractor shall, at the Company's option, either execute such Project Contract or seek to agree another Project Contract with the Company on as similar terms as possible.

6 COMPETITION

[Insert appropriate provisions for the mutual restriction of the parties from collaborating with third parties in respect of any project covering the same subject matter as the Project. Consider also including provisions obliging the Company to exploit the Project once developed.]

Part II: The terms and conditions of each project contract

7 DEFINITIONS

In each Project Contract (a) the provisions of Clause 1 shall be incorporated into such Contract and (b) the term 'Project' in the provisions contained in Part II and Part III of this Agreement and incorporated into the Contract shall mean the subject matter of the Project Contract.

8 THE WORK

8.1 All the Work is undertaken for the benefit of the Company. The Contractor will procure the disclosure of the results of the Work to the Company.

8.2 Where the Company has specified the necessity for any stage authorisation, the Project will not proceed until the Company has signed a stage authorisation. The Company may so sign or not sign at its entire discretion.

8.3 The Contractor shall procure the following:

8.3.1 Reports

The Company shall generally be provided with reports at [three] monthly intervals on all the Work. On completion of the Project, the Company shall receive, within [thirty] days, a final report detailing the Work;

8.3.2 Standards

All the Work will be conducted in accordance with generally accepted standards of good practice at the time as applicable to such work and the Contractor will be responsible for the implementation of and compliance with all safety and other legislative requirements which apply to the Project;

8.3.3 Personnel, Facilities and Equipment

The Contractor shall procure that such personnel, facilities, materials and equipment as are required for the proper execution of the Project are made available for the Project;

8.3.4 *Products and Processes*

8.3.4.1 Where any Project requires the production for the Company of an experimental or prototype model the Contractor will use all reasonable endeavours to ensure that any such experimental or prototype product will be generally suitable for the purpose for which it is produced and will perform generally in accordance with the product specification defined in the relevant Project Contract. Further, the Contractor will deliver to the Company or its nominee the said experimental or prototype product together with a report on its performance and [two] copies of user documentation and technical and support documentation for use with the said product; and

8.3.4.2 where any Project involves the development of a process the Contractor shall use all reasonable endeavours to ensure that the process meets the specification defined in the relevant Project Contract. Further the Contractor will deliver to the Company or its nominee such information as would enable the Company to perform the process in the manner envisaged by the relevant Project Contract.

9 PAYMENT

Subject as provided below, payment shall be made by the Company as provided in the payment schedule appearing in the relevant Project Contract. The Contractor shall be responsible for all costs and expenses incurred in carrying out the Work unless otherwise agreed. Invoices issued by the Contractor pursuant to such schedule are payable within [thirty] days of presentation unless the Company gives written notice to the Contractor within such period disputing any amount and at the same time pays any undisputed amount.

10 RIGHTS IN THE WORK

All rights in any discovery, invention, design, copyright or other work made in the course of the Work shall belong to the Company. Accordingly:-

10.1 Assignment

The Contractor hereby agrees to assign [and procure that its employees shall take all such steps as are necessary to assign] all rights (including intellectual property rights) that subsist in products, processes and documentation produced as a result of the Work in all countries in the world to the Company. The Contractor shall, at the Company's request and cost, take all such steps as the Company may consider necessary or desirable to register any of such rights and to record the assignment of any of such rights.

10.2 Patents and other intellectual property rights

As soon as any discovery or invention is made in the course of the Work which the Contractor considers may be capable of patent protection or other form of protection, the Contractor shall forthwith inform and provide full details to the Company (and no other person). The Contractor shall [and shall procure that its employees shall] execute all such documents and do all such things as the Company shall reasonably require to vest in the Company all the Contractor's [or its employees'] rights in and to any such discovery or invention.

10.3 Confidentiality

The Contractor acknowledges that the Company may wish to preserve confidentiality in the Work as well as, or instead of, relying on patent or other protection. The Contractor will not disclose to any third party the results of the Work or any discoveries, inventions, designs, copyright or other works made in the course of the Work including any reports or other relevant documentation ('Confidential Information'). The Contractor will use its best endeavours to procure that no person working on the Project shall disclose to any third party any Confidential Information including submitting for publication any report, article or paper relating directly or indirectly to the Work (unless such report, article or paper deals entirely with information in the public domain and/or matters not relating directly or indirectly to the Work). The Contractor will ensure that all persons who have access to Confidential Information are aware of these restrictions, and the Contractor will procure that all such persons are contractually bound to observe appropriate restrictions and/or are aware of their obligations under common law.

11 LICENCE TO USE THE RESULTS OF THE WORK

The Company may agree to grant to the Contractor a licence to use the results of the Work. This will be specified in the relevant Project Contract. The following terms will apply to that licence:

11.1 such licence shall be non-exclusive, royalty free, for research purposes only at the Contractor and may not be assigned, sub-licensed or otherwise transferred to any other person, firm, or other entity;

11.2 the Company gives no warranty as to the performance of such results or suitability of the results for any purposes;

11.3 the Company disclaims all liability (other than in respect of any liability for negligence causing death or personal injury) and any conditions, warranties or terms (whether express or implied, statutory or otherwise) in, under and with respect to the licence; and

11.4 the Contractor shall hold the Company harmless from all liability arising out of any use of the results of the Work by the Contractor during the period of the licence.

12 SHARING ARRANGEMENTS

If any invention or discovery made in the course of the Work is commercially exploited by the Company, the Company will, after consultation with the Contractor, procure that there is paid to the Contractor an appropriate royalty, having due regard to the effort made and the expenditure incurred by the Company in bringing the invention or discovery to commercial exploitation.

13 WARRANTIES AND UNDERTAKINGS

13.1 The Contractor warrants that it is free to enter into Project Contracts, and that [to the best of its knowledge, information and belief] there are no adverse third party patents, copyrights or other intellectual property rights which might affect the Work or its exploitation.

13.2 The Contractor shall indemnify the Company and hold the Company harmless with respect to any liability, loss, damage, expense or claim in connection with any Project that arises or results from any wilful default, fraud, negligent act or omission on the part of the Contractor or any person allowed by it to work on or participate in the Project.

Part III: Common terms of this agreement and each project contract

14 FORCE MAJEURE

If due performance of this Agreement or any Project Contract by any party thereto is affected in whole or in part by reason of any event, omission, accident or other matter beyond the reasonable control of such party, such party shall give prompt notice thereof to the other party or parties and shall be under no liability for any loss, damage, injury or expense (whether direct or consequential) suffered by the other party or parties due to the affected performance. Such party shall use all reasonable efforts to avoid or overcome the causes affecting its performance and shall fulfil all outstanding performance as soon as it becomes practicable to do so. In the event of any such delay or disruption of any Project, the parties will use their reasonable endeavours, if appropriate, to modify the work programme to overcome such difficulties.

15 TERMINATION

15.1 If a party to this Agreement or any Project Contract:

15.1.1 enters into liquidation other than for the purposes of reconstruction or amalgamation, ceases or threatens to cease to carry on business or has a receiver (including an administrator) appointed or execution or other process levied against any of its undertaking, property or assets which is reasonably considered to have a materially adverse effect on its ability to perform its obligations under this Agreement or (in the case of termination of a Project Contract) under the Project Contract; or

15.1.2 fails to remedy any material breach of this Agreement or (in the case of termination of a Project Contract) any material breach of the Project Contract within 30 days of the other party giving notice in writing to that effect;

the other party may terminate this Agreement or the relevant Project Contract (as the case may be) forthwith by notice in writing.

15.2 On termination of this Agreement by the Contractor by notice pursuant to Clause 15.1 the Contractor will (subject to the Company satisfying the Contractor that it is able to and does make all payments thereunder as the same fall due) be obliged to complete all Project Contracts executed prior to such termination, and this Agreement shall remain in force for such purpose accordingly.

15.3 Termination of this Agreement or any Project Contract shall be without prejudice to the rights of the parties immediately prior to such termination.

16 GENERAL

16.1 The Company may assign this Agreement and any Project Contract or sub-contract any of its rights or obligations thereunder. The Contractor may not assign this Agreement or any Project Contract nor sub-contract its obligations under any of them without the consent in writing of the Company which consent will not be unreasonably withheld.

16.2 Nothing in this Agreement shall render any party hereto a partner or agent of the other party and no party hereto shall hold itself out as such.

16.3 This Agreement and all Project Contracts will be interpreted and governed in accordance with the laws of England.

IN WITNESS whereof this Agreement has been entered into the day and year first above mentioned.

Specimen Project Contract

THIS CONTRACT is made the [_____] day of [_____] One thousand nine hundred and [_____] BETWEEN
[_____] whose registered office is at [_____] (hereinafter called 'the Company') of the one part; and
[_____] of [_____] (hereinafter called 'the Contractor') of the other part.

WHEREAS

(A) The Contractor has pursuant to a Collaboration Agreement dated [_____] and made between the Company and the Contractor (hereinafter called 'the Collaboration Agreement') proposed to the Company that a project (hereinafter called 'the Project') be undertaken involving [DESCRIBE PROJECT] as more particularly set out in the protocol attached to this Contract (hereinafter called 'the Project Protocol').

(B) It is the intention of the parties hereto that this Contract shall be a Project Contract for the purposes of the Collaboration Agreement and accordingly the terms of the Collaboration Agreement applying to Projects shall apply to this Contract.

NOW IT IS HEREBY AGREED as follows:

1 This Contract shall be deemed to have commenced on [_____] (hereinafter called 'the Commencement Date').

2 The terms of the Collaboration Agreement shall (save as set out below) apply mutatis mutandis to this Contract to the extent that this Contract shall be deemed to be a 'Project Contract' as defined in the Collaboration Agreement and accordingly the terms and conditions referred to in Part II and Part III of that Agreement shall be deemed to be incorporated into this Contract except to the extent that such terms and conditions are inconsistent with the provisions hereinafter appearing.

3   The Contractor shall carry out the work described in the Project Protocol.

4   The Company shall pay to the Contractor upon completion, to the satisfaction of the Company, of each stage of the Project (the first such stage commencing with the Commencement Date) and delivery of any report required to be furnished in connection with such stage, a sum calculated as set out in the Schedule hereto.

[5   The Company agrees to grant to the Contractor in relation to any product or process arising from performance by the Contractor of its obligations under this Contract, a licence upon the terms of Clause 11 of the Collaboration Agreement.]

[6   The provisions of Clause 8.2 of the Collaboration Agreement shall apply to this Contract on the basis that all but the first of the stages referred to in the Project Protocol shall require authorisation by the Company before commencement.]

[7   Further terms, if appropriate, relating to performance of the Contractor's services, insurance, assignment, etc.]

IN WITNESS whereof this Agreement has been entered into the day and year first above written.

THE SCHEDULE above referred to

[Payment arrangements]

THE PROJECT PROTOCOL

Note: The Project Protocol should
   (a) describe the project work in detail; and
   (b) list any break points and stages; and
   (c) specify the reports and stages of the project to which payments will be linked—see Clause 4 of the Project Contract.

Specimen Secrecy Agreement

THIS AGREEMENT is made the [_____] day of [_____] One thousand nine hundred and [_____] BETWEEN
[_____] whose registered office is at [_____ _____] ('[_____]'); and
[_____] whose registered office is at [_____ _____] ('[_____]').

WHEREAS:

(A)   Each party wishes to receive from the other certain confidential information about the other, its Subsidiaries and their businesses for the purpose of considering the formation of a joint venture between the parties in the field of [_____] ('the joint venture').

(B)   Each party is willing, in consideration of being supplied with confidential information about the other, to give the undertakings contained in this Agreement and, in consideration of such undertakings, the other party is willing to supply such confidential information, subject to the provisions of this Agreement.

NOW IT IS HEREBY AGREED as follows:

1   DEFINITIONS

In this Agreement:
   '*Associate*', in relation to either party, means any company within the same Group as such party;

   '*Confidential Information*' means, in relation to either party, information relating to it, its Associates and their businesses made available by it to the other party (or its Representatives), whether before or after this Agreement is entered into, for the purpose of considering, advising in relation to or furthering the joint venture (and any information or analysis derived from such information) but shall not include information which is or becomes generally available to the public (other than as a result of disclosure by the party to whom it is furnished hereunder or its Associates or Representatives contrary to their respective obligations of confidentiality);

'*Group*' means, in relation to any person, all corporations which are Holding Companies or Subsidiaries of it or of any such Holding Company;

'*Holding Company*' and '*Subsidiaries*' shall bear the meaning given to them in section 736 of the Companies Act 1985, as amended from time to time;

'*Representatives*', in relation to either party, means its directors, officers, employees and consultants or those of other companies within its Group and its professional advisers advising in relation to the joint venture; and

'*writing*' includes telex, cable, fax and other forms of written material transmitted electronically.

2 CONFIDENTIAL INFORMATION

2.1 Each party shall, and shall procure that the members of its Group and [(so far as it is [reasonably] able to do so)] its Representatives and Associates shall, subject to Clause 3, whether or not the joint venture commences business, except to the extent the other party has given its prior consent in writing:

2.1.1 not make any announcement or otherwise publicise the proposals for the joint venture or any other arrangement with the other party;

2.1.2 keep the joint venture confidential and at all times keep confidential all Confidential Information relating to the other party and not disclose them to anyone other than to Representatives of the first party [who have been previously approved in writing by the other party and] who need [in the reasonable opinion of the first party] to know such information for the purposes of considering, advising in relation to or furthering the joint venture and who are aware of the obligations of confidentiality and agree to keep the joint venture and such Confidential Information confidential [and to be subject to the same restrictions to which the first party is subject pursuant to this Clause 2.1];

2.1.3 use the Confidential Information relating to the other party only for the purpose of considering, advising in relation to or furthering the joint venture and not use it for any other purpose whatsoever and shall not permit the Confidential Information to go out of its possession or custody and control (other than as aforesaid);

2.1.4 not with a view to obtaining information about the other party or its Group or their businesses contact any Representatives of the other party in circumstances that are likely [in its reasonable opinion] to give rise to suspicions that the joint venture is being planned or contemplated; and

2.1.5 immediately, on receipt by the first party of a request in writing by the other party to do so, deliver up to the other party or its order all written Confidential Information (including any copies, analyses, memoranda or other notes made by the first party or its Representatives or Associates in relation thereto) in its or their possession or under its or their custody and control and [so far as it is practicable to do so (but, in any event, without prejudice to the obligations of confidentiality contained herein)] expunge any Confidential Information from any computer, word processor or other device in its or their possession or under its custody and control containing such information Provided that, instead of delivering up to the other party any such analyses, memoranda or other notes, the first party may immediately destroy the same;

2.1.6 if the joint venture does not proceed, return to the other party all Confidential Information in its possession including all copies made of documents comprised in the Confidential Information;

2.1.7 if so requested, furnish to the other party a certificate of a [director] of the first party confirming that [to the best of his knowledge, information and belief, having made all proper enquiries,] the provisions of this Clause have been fully complied with.

2.2 Either party, if so requested prior to procuring or permitting any of its Representatives or Associates to receive Confidential Information or information about the joint venture shall (and, if so requested subsequently, shall so far as it is [reasonably] able to do so) procure that such Representatives or Associates execute an undertaking in favour of the other party (in terms reasonably required by the other party) to be bound by the obligations of confidentiality set out in Clause 2.1.

3 DISCLOSURE

If either party, by reason of any legal requirement [or any regulation or rule of any stock exchange on which its shares are listed] or any governmental or quasi-governmental authority [or the Panel on Take-overs and Mergers or its equivalent], is required to make any announcement concerning the joint venture or other arrangements with the other party or to disclose Confidential Information, it will be entitled to do so Provided that, so far as it is practicable to do so, prior to such announcement or disclosure it consults with the other party as to such requirement and with a view to agreeing the timing and content of such announcement or disclosure.

4 GOVERNING LAW ETC

[*See Specimen Shareholders' Agreement, clause 12.12 at p 193*]

IN WITNESS whereof this Agreement has been entered into the day and year first above written.

APPENDIX 6

Part I: Specimen Secondment Agreement

THIS AGREEMENT is made the [_____] day of [_____] One thousand nine hundred and [_____] BETWEEN [_____] whose registered office is at [_____] (hereinafter called 'the Employing Company') of the one part; and [_____] whose registered office is at [_____] (hereinafter called 'the Secondee Company') of the other part.

WHEREAS:

(A) The Employing Company holds [_____] per cent of the issued share capital of the Secondee Company.

(B) On [_____] 19[_____] the Employing Company and [_____] [and the Secondee Company] entered into a Shareholders' Agreement to regulate the conduct of the business of the Secondee Company.

(C) To assist the Secondee Company in the conduct of its business the Employing Company is prepared to provide the services of some of its employees to the Secondee Company on the terms set out below.

NOW IT IS HEREBY AGREED as follows:

1 INTERPRETATION

In this Agreement (including the Schedule hereto):

1.1 the following words shall have the following meanings:

'*Employees*' mean the employees to be seconded at the date of this Agreement to the Secondee Company and whose names are set out in the Schedule hereto;

'*Shareholders' Agreement*' means the agreement referred to in Recital B;

'*Secondment*' means the secondment established by this Agreement.

1.2   The headings are for convenience only and shall not affect the interpretation hereof.

1.3   Unless the context otherwise requires, words importing the singular only shall include the plural and vice versa.

2   DURATION

Subject as hereinafter provided the Employing Company will second the Employees to the Secondee Company for a period being the shorter of:

2.1 [_____] years/months from [_____] 19[____], or,

2.2   the period from [_____] 19[____] to the date of termination of this Agreement pursuant to Clause 9.

3   REPLACEMENT EMPLOYEES

3.1   If at any time during the continuance of this Agreement any one or all of the Employees shall cease to be employed by the Employing Company for whatever reason the Employing Company's obligation to second such Employee or Employees shall cease forthwith but the Employing Company's obligation to second all the remaining Employees (if any) shall continue and the Company shall [not] be required to second a suitably qualified and experienced replacement employee or employees to the Secondee Company.

3.2   Notwithstanding any other provisions of this Agreement, the Secondee Company agrees that the Employing Company shall not be obliged to second any Employee [or provide a replacement Employee] during any such time as any Employee may be absent due to [sickness or to] holiday properly taken in accordance with their entitlement under their contract of employment with the Employing Company [provided that, in the case of holiday, the Secondee Company shall first agree with the Employing Company such period of absence].

4   SERVICES

4.1   The Employing Company shall [use its reasonable endeavours to] procure that:

  4.1.1 The Employees shall perform the services and act in the capacity stated alongside their names in the Schedule hereto together with any further services [whether in the United Kingdom or elsewhere] which the board of directors of the

Secondee Company shall reasonably request or direct, although the appointment of the Employees in such capacity as aforesaid shall be non-exclusive.

4.1.2 The Employees shall devote [the whole of their time, attention and skill to the duties of their Secondment] [such of their time, attention and skill as may be required by the Secondee Company from time to time for the proper performance of their duties of the Secondment. The amount of time to be devoted to the Secondment duties and the time at which such duties are to be performed will be notified by the Secondee Company to the Employing Company in advance and shall be subject to the agreement of the Employing Company].

4.1.3 Each of the Employees shall report to and act in accordance with the requests and directions of [the person set alongside his name in the Schedule hereto] [the board of directors of the Secondee Company].

4.1.4 Each of the Employees to be seconded hereunder shall have the necessary competence, experience and qualifications to perform the services and act in the capacity for which they are seconded and shall comply with all applicable laws [rules or regulations of lawfully constituted regulatory authorities] and observe the terms of the Shareholders' Agreement;

4.1.5 All services to be provided by the Employees hereunder shall be carried out with all reasonable skill and care;

4.1.6 The Employees shall:
(a) submit reports to the board of directors of the Secondee Company in such format and at such frequency as the said board may reasonably require giving details of all aspects of the duties carried out by them; and
(b) promptly notify the said board of directors of the Secondee Company of any matter coming to their attention which could have a material effect on the business or affairs of the Secondee Company.

4.2 The Employing Company acknowledges and shall procure that the Employees shall acknowledge that during the term of their Secondment the Employees may be required to act or serve as officers, authorised signatories, nominees or in any other personal capacity on behalf of the Secondee Company and/or any of its subsidiaries, as may be [reasonably] required by the board of directors of the Secondee Company, and the Employing Company hereby undertakes and shall procure that each of the Employees shall undertake to resign all or any such appointments upon the termination of their secondment.

4.3 Save as may otherwise be agreed the Employing Company will second the Employees to the Secondee Company on the terms under which they are from time to time employed by the Employing Company, copies of which have been provided to the Secondee Company. The Employing Company will notify the Secondee Company of any changes which are made to the same during the continuance of this Agreement.

5 DUTIES OF THE SECONDEE COMPANY

5.1 The Secondee Company agrees that it will observe the terms under which the Employees are employed by the Employing Company as if it were the actual employer of the Employees and that it will not do or omit to do anything which would cause the Employing Company to breach any of its obligations to the Employees.

5.2 The Secondee Company shall report to the Employing Company [bi-annually] [in writing] on the conduct and progress of the Employees.

6 RESTRICTIONS ON AUTHORITY

The Employing Company will take such steps as·the Secondee Company may reasonably require (including the obtaining of undertakings from each Employee to observe the following restrictions) to procure that no Employee shall without express written approval of the board of directors of the Secondee Company [do any act or thing outside the ordinary course of business of the Secondee Company or] commit the Secondee Company to any obligation or commitment for a value in excess of £[_____], or act in contravention of or inconsistent with [the Shareholders' Agreement [and the Articles of Association of the Secondee Company] or] any internal regulations adopted from time to time by the Secondee Company and notified in writing to the Employing Company.

7 INDEMNITY

[The parties hereto agree that [whilst performing duties for the Secondee Company] during the Secondment the Employees shall be deemed to be the agents of the Secondee Company and that the Secondee Company shall be liable to the Employing Company for any act, omission, error or judgment (whether or not negligent or otherwise actionable) which may be committed [by the Employee whilst performing duties for the

Secondee Company] [during the Secondment]. [The Secondee Company shall indemnify and keep indemnified the Employing Company from and against all and any claims, rights, remedies, costs, expenses or proceedings of whatever nature whether but not by way of limitation arising at common law or under statute against the Employing Company arising out of acts or omissions of any of the Employees during the Secondment.]

8 PAYMENT FOR SERVICES

8.1 The Secondee Company shall pay to the Employing Company a fee [of £_____] [calculated on the basis and payable at the times set out in [_____].

8.2 The Employing Company shall submit invoices to the Secondee Company in respect of the amount due each [month] and shall show any VAT payable on the said monthly amount separately.

8.3 On expiry or termination of the Secondment of one of the Employees [for any reason] any sum paid in advance in respect of that Employee and not earned by the said Employee on termination of his Secondment or on termination of this Agreement shall be repaid to the Secondee Company.

8.4 In addition to the fees payable to the Employing Company pursuant to clause 8.1 above, the Secondee Company shall pay, discharge, indemnify and keep the Employing Company indemnified against all expenses and disbursements reasonably and properly incurred by the Employees in connection with the performance and discharge of their duties on behalf of the Secondee Company, upon presentation to the Secondee Company of the supporting invoices and receipts in respect of such expenses and disbursements.

9 EARLY TERMINATION

9.1 If at any time during the continuance of this Agreement and the Secondment:

9.1.1 an Employee commits any act or makes any omission (whether or not in connection with the Secondment) which would entitle the Secondee Company to dismiss him summarily if he were employed by the Secondee Company on the terms and conditions under which he is employed by the Employing Company; or

9.1.2 an Employee's employment with the Employing Company shall have been terminated, including but without limiting the generality of the foregoing, by the voluntary resignation by an Employee from his employment with the Employing Company; or

9.1.3 an Employee conducts himself in a manner prejudicial to the business of the Secondee Company (whether or not in connection with the Secondment); or

9.1.4 an Employee is guilty of dishonesty or is convicted of an offence (whether or not in connection with the Secondment);

then either party hereto shall notwithstanding any other provision of this Agreement be entitled to terminate this Agreement in respect of that Employee by giving summary notice in writing to the other.

[9.2 If either party hereto commits any material breach of their obligations under this Agreement then the other shall be entitled to terminate this Agreement forthwith by written notice to the other.]

9.3 If at any time during the continuance of this Agreement and the Secondment the Shareholders' Agreement shall terminate, [or if the Employing Company shall cease to hold any shares in the Secondee Company] then this Agreement shall thereupon automatically cease and determine.

10 CONFIDENTIALITY

10.1 The Employing Company shall not and·shall [use its reasonable endeavours to] procure that none of the Employees shall use, divulge or communicate to any person (other than those whose province it is to know the same or with authority from the Secondee Company) any trade secrets or information which are for the time being confidential to the Secondee Company and/or any of its subsidiaries and are not in the public domain ('Confidential Information') which any Employee may have received or obtained during the term of this Agreement. This restriction shall continue to apply after the termination of this Agreement for whatever cause without limit in point of time, but shall cease to apply to information or knowledge which may come into the public domain otherwise than through the unauthorised disclosure by or the fault of the Employing Company, or any Employee. The Employing Company undertakes and shall procure that the Employees shall undertake to return to the Secondee Company or any of its subsidiaries upon request from any or all of them and upon termination of this Agreement all materials, whether documentary or otherwise, together with copies thereof containing Confidential Information and not to take further copies of any of the above mentioned documents or materials after termination of this Agreement.

10.2   Where the Secondee Company shall have obtained any Confidential Information from any third party under an Agreement which includes any restriction on disclosure known to the Employing Company or any of the Employees, the Employing Company shall not and shall procure that no Employee shall without the prior consent in writing of the Secondee Company at any time (whether during the term of this Agreement or after its termination or for whatever cause) infringe such restrictions.

11   NON-COMPETITION

[*Consider inserting clauses obliging the Employing Company to obtain from the Employees covenants and undertakings restricting them from competing with the Secondee Company or soliciting its customers and staff.*]

12   DISCIPLINARY MATTERS

If any difficulty of a disciplinary or other nature arises in respect of any of the Employees during the Secondment, the Secondee Company will notify the Employing Company which shall then deal with such problems as it thinks appropriate.

13   HEALTH AND SAFETY

The Secondee Company shall comply with the provisions of the Health and Safety at Work Act 1974 ('HSWA') and any statutory re-enactment or modification thereof or any rules or regulations made thereunder in so far as the same concern the Employees [and any other relevant legislation]. The Secondee Company shall also co-operate with the Employing Company in respect of any action which it wishes to take in respect of the Employees in order to fulfil its duties under the HSWA in so far as the same concern the Employees whilst on Secondment.

14   INTELLECTUAL PROPERTY

[For the avoidance of doubt] the parties hereto agree that during the Secondment any invention, design, copyright or other intellectual property made by any of the Employees whether alone or with anybody else shall be owned by [the Employing Company].

15   NO PARTNERSHIP

This Agreement shall constitute a contract for services between the parties and nothing in this Agreement shall constitute a partnership between the Employing Company and the Secondee Company nor create the relationship of employer and employee between the Secondee Company and any of the Employees.

16 NOTICES

Notices by either of the parties hereto must be given in writing addressed to the other party at its registered office or principal place of business for the time being and any such notice given by letter shall be deemed to have been given at the date on which the letter would have been delivered in the ordinary course of postal transmission as the case may be.

17 GOVERNING LAW

This Agreement shall be governed by and construed in accordance with the laws of England and each of the parties hereto submits to the jurisdiction of the English Courts as regards any claim or matter arising under this Agreement.

IN WITNESS whereof this Agreement was entered into the day and year first above written.

THE SCHEDULE
Employees on Secondment

Name   *Job title*   *Reporting to*

Part II: Letter from Employing Company to Employee Being Seconded

[Date]

Dear [_____]

Further to our recent discussions we are writing to invite you to accept Secondment to [_____] ('the Secondee Company') on the terms set out below.

For the avoidance of doubt you will remain an Employee of [_____] ('the Employing Company') throughout the period of the Secondment and the period of your Secondment shall count as part of the period of your continuous employment with the Employing Company.

Except as provided below your terms and conditions of employment as set out in your contract of employment with the Employing Company remain unchanged. In the event of any inconsistency between the terms of this letter and your contract of employment the terms of this letter shall prevail. If any changes are made to your contract of employment during the term of the Secondment then the Secondment shall be on the terms of your revised contract of employment and this letter.

1   The Secondment will commence on [_____] and will continue subject as provided in this letter until [_____].

2   At the end of the Secondment your employment with the Employing Company will (except as mentioned below) continue, but the job which you will be given will not necessarily be that which you are performing presently although it will be suitable alternative employment.

3   During the Secondment you will devote [the whole of your time, attention and skill to the duties of the Secondment] [such of your time, attention and skill as may be required by the Secondee Company from time to time for the proper performance of the duties of your Secondment and you will be required to perform the duties at such time or times and at

such notice as the Secondee Company may reasonably require subject to the Employing Company's prior agreement].

4 (A) During the Secondment you will act as [insert job title] of the Secondee Company, reporting to [_____].

    (B) You shall at all times during the Secondment use all reasonable skill and care in the performance of your duties and act at all times in the best interests of the Secondee Company.

  [(C) You are required to report [monthly] in writing to the Employing Company on the Secondment duties which you have performed for that month and to the board of directors of the Secondee Company in such format and at such intervals as they may reasonably require].

    (D) You will promptly notify the board of directors of the Secondee Company of any matter coming to your attention which could have a material effect on the business or affairs of the Secondee Company.

5 During the Secondment your salary will continue to be paid by and reviewed by the Employing Company and all other contractual benefits will continue in accordance with the terms of your employment with the Employing Company.

6 The Secondment will terminate forthwith if (a) you cease to be employed by the Employing Company for whatever reason (including but without limiting the generality of the foregoing your own voluntary resignation); or (b) the Shareholders' Agreement (regulating the affairs of the Secondee Company) terminates; or (c) the Employing Company ceases to hold any shares in the Secondee Company; or [(d) arrangements between the Employing Company and the Secondee Company for the Secondment terminate].

7 (A) The Employing Company shall notwithstanding any other provision in this letter have the right to terminate the Secondment forthwith at any time if:

     (i) you commit any act or make any omission (whether or not in connection with the Secondment) which would entitle the Secondee Company to dismiss you summarily if you were employed by the Secondee Company on the terms and conditions under which you are employed by the Employing Company; or

     (ii) you conduct yourself in a manner prejudicial to the business of the Secondee Company (whether or not in connection with the Secondment); or

     (iii) you are guilty of dishonesty or are convicted of an offence (whether or not in connection with the Secondment).

(B) If the Secondment is terminated under (A) above then the Employing Company shall treat your conduct giving rise to a termination under (A) above as a breach of the terms and conditions of your employment with the Employing Company and the Employing Company shall have the right to terminate your employment with the Employing Company forthwith by notice in writing to you.

8 Any difficulty of a disciplinary or grievance nature which arises during the Secondment shall be dealt with by the Employing Company [in accordance with its Disciplinary and Grievance Procedure].

9 For the purposes of this letter 'Secondment' means the terms under which you are to be seconded to the Secondee Company as established by the terms of this letter.

10 For the avoidance of doubt you shall not be an employee of the Secondee Company during the Secondment.

11 Without prejudice to any other duty owed to the Employing Company or any other company which is a subsidiary, associated or holding company of the Employing Company you agree that:

(a) you shall during the Secondment as may be [reasonably] required by the board of directors of the Secondee Company act or serve as an officer, authorised signatory, nominee or in any other personal capacity on behalf of the Secondee Company and/or any of its subsidiaries and you undertake that you shall resign all or any such appointments upon the termination of the Secondment [and should you fail to do so the Employing Company is hereby irrevocably authorised to appoint some person in your name and on your behalf to sign and do any documents or things necessary to give effect to your resignation[s]]. [*Note:* if these words are included, the letter should be executed as a deed];

(b) you shall not during the Secondment without the express written approval of the board of directors of the Secondee Company [do any act or thing outside the ordinary course of business of the Secondee Company or] commit the Secondee Company to any obligation or commitment for a value in excess of £[_____], or act in contravention of or inconsistent with [the Shareholders' Agreement [and the Articles of Association of the Secondee Company or] any internal regulations adopted from time to time by the Secondee Company which are notified in writing to you by the Employing Company;

(c) you shall not use, divulge or communicate to any person (other than those whose province it is to know the same or with authority from the Secondee Company) any information or trade secrets which are confidential to the Secondee Company and/or any of its subsidiaries and which are not in the public domain ('Confidential Information') which you may have received or obtained during the Secondment. This restriction shall continue to apply after the termination of the Secondment (however occasioned) without limit in time, but shall cease to apply to information or knowledge which may come into the public domain otherwise than through your unauthorised disclosure or fault;

(d) on the termination of the Secondment you shall upon request from the Secondee Company or any of its subsidiaries return to any or all of them all materials, whether documentary or otherwise, together with copies thereof containing Confidential Information (as defined in sub-paragraph (c) of this paragraph 11 above) and you shall not take further copies of any of the above mentioned documents or materials after termination of the Secondment; and

(e) where the Secondee Company shall have obtained Confidential Information (as defined in sub-paragraph (c) of this paragraph 11 above) from any third party under an Agreement which includes any restriction on disclosure made known to you you shall not without the prior consent of the Secondee Company (whether during the term of the Secondment or after its termination or for whatever cause) infringe such restrictions.

[Add here any non-competition restrictions to be imposed.]
[If requested by the Secondee Company you will enter into a direct agreement or direct agreements with it in the same terms mutatis mutandis as any or all of the above undertakings.]

Please sign, date and return to [_____] by [_____] 19[_____] the attached copy of this letter to indicate your acceptance of the Secondment and your agreement to the terms and conditions of this letter.

Yours sincerely

For and on behalf of
[_____]

I hereby accept the Secondment to the Secondee Company on the terms and conditions set out in the above letter. I acknowledge and accept that the above letter is a variation of the terms and conditions of my employment with the Employing Company.

Signed _____   Dated _____

Index